THE PROPHETIC LITERATURE
AN INTRODUCTION

THE PROPHETIC LITERATURE
AN INTRODUCTION

David L. Petersen

WJK WESTMINSTER
JOHN KNOX PRESS
LOUISVILLE · KENTUCKY

Book design by Sharon Adams
Cover design by Mark Abrams

First edition
Published by Westminster John Knox Press
Louisville, Kentucky

This book is printed on acid-free paper that meets the American National Standards Institute Z39.48 standard. ∞

PRINTED IN THE UNITED STATES OF AMERICA

04 05 06 07 08 09 10 11—10 9 8 7 6 5 4 3

Library of Congress Cataloging-in-Publication Data is on file at the Library of Congress, Washington, D.C.

ISBN 0-664-25453-5

*This book is dedicated to my parents,
Kermit and Charlotte Petersen.*

Contents

Abbreviations

AB	Anchor Bible
ABRL	Anchor Bible Reference Library
ATANT	Abhandlungen zur Theologie des Alten und Neuen Testaments
ATD	Das Alte Testament Deutsch
BETL	Bibliotheca ephemeridum theologicarum lovaniensium
BLS	Bible and Literature Series
BS	Biblical Seminar
BThSt	Biblisch-Theologische Studien
BZAW	Beihefte zur Zeitschrift für die alttestamentliche Wissenschaft
CBQMS	Catholic Biblical Quarterly Monograph Series
EdF	Erträge der Forschung
ETL	*Ephemerides theologicae lovanienses*
EvT	*Evangelische Theologie*
FAT	Forschungen zum Alten Testament
FOTL	Forms of the Old Testament Literature
FRLANT	Forschungen zur Religion und Literatur des Alten und Neuen Testaments
HSM	Harvard Semitic Monographs
IBC	Interpretation: A Bible Commentary for Teaching and Preaching
ICC	International Critical Commentary
IRT	Issues in Religion and Theology
JBL	*Journal of Biblical Literature*
JSOT	Journal for the Study of the Old Testament
JSOTSup	Journal for the Study of the Old Testament: Supplement Series
OBO	Orbis biblicus et orientalis

OTG	Old Testament Guides
OTL	Old Testament Library
SAA	State Archives of Assyria
SAAS	State Archives of Assyria Studies
SBLDS	Society of Biblical Literature Dissertation Series
SBLMS	Society of Biblical Literature Monograph Series
SBT	Studies in Biblical Theology
SBTS	Sources for Biblical and Theological Study
SHCANE	Studies in the History and Culture of the Ancient Near East
VT	*Vetus Testamentum*
VTSup	Vetus Testamentum Supplements
WBC	Word Biblical Commentary
ZAW	*Zeitschrift für die alttestamentliche Wissenschaft*

Preface

This volume is intended to introduce biblical prophetic literature. Unlike many other studies, it does not proceed in chronological fashion. It offers no explicit history of prophecy or prophetic literature as such. Rather, both the introduction and the subsequent chapters are devoted to the salient features of prophetic literature.

The first chapter presents a programmatic statement about the nature of prophetic literature, both inside and outside the canon. I seek to establish working definitions for two inherently problematic concepts: prophet and prophetic literature. Only after the ambiguity of these terms has been addressed and only after refined definitions have been created can consistent analysis of biblical, prophetic literature proceed. As we will see, ancient Israelite prophecy as a whole is characterized by diversity. Hence, the introduction paints, in broad strokes, the world of prophecy as a diverse phenomenon. In similar fashion, biblical prophetic literature is multifaceted, appearing in various literary manifestations including both prose and poetry. Here too the introduction offers an overview of prophetic literature in order to set the stage for analysis of each prophetic book as well as prophetic literature that stands outside those books.

Ensuing chapters treat the four major biblical books: Isaiah, Jeremiah, Ezekiel, and the Book of the Twelve. Primary attention for each book is given to (1) setting the historical and social context of the prophet and the book, (2) exploring the structure and characteristic literary features present in the book, and (3) identifying and discussing theological issues that are of special significance in the book. The chapter devoted to the Book of the Twelve offers capsule analyses of the individual biblical books that make up this larger mosaic. The final chapter of the book attends to two different tasks: discussing prophetic literature (e.g., the oracles of Balaam, the legends about Elisha) that lies outside the boundaries of biblical books and analyzing various traditions about prophets (e.g., the notion of a prophet like Moses).

I appreciate having received permission from Abingdon Press to include in the first chapter material that was originally published as "Introduction to Prophetic Literature" in *The New Interpreter's Bible*.

As with most scholarly endeavors, this book is not the result of one individual's work. I am grateful to Robert Buller, Gregory Glover, and Gene Tucker for reading and commenting on various portions of this manuscript. Carey C. Newman read the entire manuscript and offered valuable suggestions that have helped improve the volume. I also would like to thank Davis Perkins for his interest in this project during its seminal stages.

1

Introduction

Prophetic literature entails far more than words that prophets spoke. That much is clear. But how much more? That is not easy to say. Indeed, that question prompts an even more fundamental one: What finally counts as prophetic literature? There have been two basic answers to this question: the canonical answer (i.e., the canon labels certain portions of the Hebrew Bible as prophetic literature), and the authorial answer (i.e., what a prophet says or writes is deemed to be prophetic). But, as we shall see, each answer presents problems.

PROPHETIC LITERATURE: DEFINITIONS AND ORIGINS

Definitions

One important definition of prophetic literature derives from the traditional divisions of the Hebrew Bible canon.[1] This is the "canonical" answer. Both early Jewish and Christian traditions attest a tripartite understanding of the Hebrew Bible: Torah (*torah*), Prophets (*nebi'im*), and Writings (*ketubim*). The second of these divisions is made up of Joshua, Judges, 1–2 Samuel, 1–2 Kings, as well as the Major Prophets (Isaiah, Jeremiah, Ezekiel) and Minor (Hosea–Malachi) Prophets. This list might appear odd. Though one would expect to find the books attributed to prophets here, it is surprising to discover that narrative, historical literature—the "former prophets"—have also been classified as prophetic literature.

Scholars have offered several explanations for this classification, but their answers remain suggestive rather than definitive. First, the

1

Deuteronomistic History (Deuteronomy–2 Kings) attests that God spoke to Israel through prophets during the course of its existence. The first book of that history, Deuteronomy, views Moses as a prophet (Deut. 18:15–18), and the last book, 2 Kings, affirms that God had "warned Israel and Judah by every prophet and every seer" (2 Kgs. 17:13). These historical books attest to an understanding of history in which the prophets as those who admonished, indicted, and judged were of critical importance. Though kings are important (hence the title), prophets are even more so, especially since they were present— as personified by Moses, Deborah, and Samuel to name just three— even before kingship commenced in Israel.

A second reason for classifying these historical books as prophetic literature derives from a different understanding of prophets. The books of Chronicles provide an important key. There prophets are presented as historians. For example, 1 Chr. 29:29 states, "Now the acts of King David, from first to last, are written in the records of the seer Samuel, and in the records of the prophet Nathan, and in the records of the seer Gad." To be sure, the books of Kings refer to sources that were used by the historian: for example, "Now the rest of the acts of Manasseh, all that he did, and the sin that he committed, are they not written in the Book of the Annals of the Kings of Judah?" (2 Kgs. 21:17). However, no author for these sources is ever identified in Kings. In contrast, Chronicles attributes such sources to prophets, whom the Chronicler apparently understood as historians. Hence, historical works such as "Kings" (though not apparently Chronicles) may be understood as "the prophets," since prophets were viewed as Israel's early historians.

Both of these explanations share an important underlying and often unstated assumption, namely, that Israel's prophets were of fundamental importance for understanding Israel's history. Their presence testifies to God's concern for the people Israel. Still, valuable as this understanding might be, it presents problems. Few readers today naturally think of Joshua or 2 Samuel as prophetic literature.

We may identify a second kind of answer to the question about what finally counts as prophetic literature: the "authorial" response. Some would suggest that prophetic literature is what prophets wrote or spoke. One could count the words of Micah, Amos, or Haggai as prophetic literature. Here prophets are not so much historians as authors, those who created literature—whether oral or written—that has been preserved in the Old Testament.

An important component of the authorial definition for prophetic literature is a high evaluation of that which prophets are understood to have said. That is, such speeches are often understood to be God's own speech. Many utterances in the books attributed to prophets commence with the phrase, "Thus says the LORD" (e.g., Amos 1:3). To hear these words is, as it were, to hear God's words. Moreover, some interpreters view poetry as "inspired" language, and in the case of the Old Testament, inspired not simply by one of the muses but rather by Israel's God. Finally, if wisdom literature is written or spoken by Israel's sages, then by analogy prophetic literature must have been written or spoken by Israel's prophets.

Regrettably, the matter is not so simple. There is considerable literature *about* prophets, but not all of it was written by them. The Bible presents two clear examples. The first involves the prophet Elisha and the literature associated with him. The book of 2 Kings includes a number of stories about this prophet. These stories are routinely included in assessments of Israel's prophets even though someone other than Elisha must have been the author. As we shall see, these stories most probably originated in an oral storytelling environment. In fact, the Bible attests to such a setting: "Now the king was talking with Gehazi the servant of the man of God, saying, 'Tell me all the great things that Elisha has done.' While he was telling the king how Elisha had restored a dead person to life . . ." (2 Kgs. 8:4–5). One can read the story about Elisha, the Shunammite woman, and her son (2 Kgs. 4:8–37) and well imagine Gehazi, or another of Elisha's supporters, the "sons of the prophets" (2 Kgs. 6:1), as its author. Someone like Gehazi, not Elisha, is the author of these stories.

The same could be said about Baruch, Jeremiah's scribe. The book of Jeremiah includes a number of stories told about the turbulent character whose name heads the book. These stories are clearly biography, not autobiography. Someone other than the prophet wrote about important episodes (e.g., Jeremiah 28) or major periods in his life (Jeremiah 37–44). A good candidate for the author is Baruch, the scribe who wrote down words that Jeremiah had spoken (see Jer. 45:1). Unless we want to exclude such chapters from the corpus of prophetic literature, we will need to think about scribes such as Baruch, and not just people like Jeremiah, as authors of prophetic literature.

In short, some of the literature attributed to a prophet was clearly written by someone other than the prophet. The previous cases involved literature in which the prophet was described. However, one may also refer to instances in which the prophet ostensibly speaks or writes, but the content of the text makes it difficult to think that the prophet in question actually wrote or spoke such words.

We enter here a range of biblical scholarship that some may find troubling, namely, the attempt to discern the difference between "authentic" and "secondary" prophetic literature. For example, for over a century scholars have pored over the book of Isaiah, in part attempting to determine what portions of that book might be attributed to Isaiah ben Amoz, who lived in the late eighth and early seventh centuries B.C.E. There is now a consensus that much in that book (particularly in chaps. 40–66) dates to the sixth and fifth centuries. Put another way, Isaiah ben Amoz could not have written major portions of the book attributed to him. (See the commentaries on Isaiah 1–39 and 40–66 for discussion of these issues.) If one wants to construe most of the book of Isaiah as prophetic literature, one must accept someone other than the historical Isaiah as the author of some of the literature attributed to him. This same situation also holds for sections of many other prophetic books (e.g., Zechariah 9–14). Unless one is willing to deny that such material in prophetic books is prophetic literature, the authorial answer will not suffice.

What then is prophetic literature? Prophetic literature is literature that attests to or grows out of (i.e., is generated by) the activity of Israel's prophets. This is the generative answer. One can, of course, view the words of a prophet as prophetic literature. However, one must also deem a story about a prophet to be prophetic literature. Prophets can produce prophetic literature, but so can someone who is not known as a prophet. Moreover, as the above examples suggest, prophetic literature can be composed as poetry but also as prose.

Origins

Such considerations push us in the direction of asking about the origins of prophetic literature. Obviously, one essential element is the presence and activity of a prophet or intermediary.[2] That individual could either write or speak prophetic literature—such was the case with Isaiah and Habakkuk, who are attested as both speakers and writers (Isaiah 7–8; Habakkuk 1–2). However, as we have already seen, other individuals contemporaneous with "prophets" (e.g., Gehazi and Baruch) could also speak or pen prophetic literature.

The two sorts of prophetic literature (prose accounts and poetic speeches), dating to roughly the period in which a prophet was active, possessed remarkable generative abilities. For example, the images of Zion present in the accounts and speeches of and about Isaiah ben Amoz offered later Israelites profound and productive ways for thinking about Zion—Jerusalem as God's chosen abode. In times long after that of the eighth-century prophet Isaiah, such as the Persian period (fifth century), authors composed literature that made its way into the book of Isaiah (material that can be found in chaps. 56–66). Other such anonymous individuals (whether or not we understand them to be prophets is an interesting question) produced a significant percentage of that which appears in prophetic books. We need to look to these anonymous individuals and their times for the origins of prophetic literature, as well as to the times of the originating prophets.

In sum, prophetic literature can be understood from multiple perspectives. Moreover, a search for the origins of prophetic literature may end at various places—with the prophet, with a contemporary of the prophet, or with prophetic traditionists, the anonymous authors and editors who preserved and added to the emerging corpus of prophetic literature. The words of a prophet or the prophet's contemporaries generated remarkable literary activity. The prophet's sayings and accounts, or those of the prophet's contemporaries, remained alive and elicited new words and accounts, a process that resulted in extensive books such as Isaiah or Jeremiah. Israelite prophetic literature seems to have had an almost inherent capacity to elicit elucidation at a later time.

ISRAEL'S PROPHETS

Though prophetic literature is the primary focus of this volume, we also need to place the prophets themselves in our field of vision. The word *prophet* derives from the Greek noun *prophetes*, which means, primarily, "to foresee." To understand prophets in the Old Testament in this sense is unfortunate and misleading for at least two reasons. First, the notion of seeing into the future, of predicting what will happen, is only one small facet of what Israel's prophets were about. To be sure, Israel's prophets could and did speak about the future, but they also addressed the present and referred to the past. They were not essentially in the business of providing horoscopes for those in Judah and Israel.

Diverse Roles

The use of one title, "prophet," belies the diversity among Israel's prophets. We possess considerable evidence of this diversity. Perhaps most indicative are the various titles or labels used to describe those individuals. There are four such titles in the Hebrew Bible: *ḥōzeh* ("seer"), *rō'eh* ("diviner"), *'îš hā'ĕlōhîm* ("man of God"), and *nābî'* ("prophet"). As the typical English equivalents suggest, two of the four nouns derive from words meaning "to see." The first noun, *ḥōzeh*, apparently means quite simply an individual who receives and reports visions (e.g., Amos 7:12), but also appears to function interchangeably with the noun *nābî'* (e.g., Isa. 29:10; 30:10). The second noun, *rō'eh*, is associated primarily with the figure of Samuel. In the pivotal scene in which this noun appears, Samuel functions rather like a diviner, namely, someone who is able to communicate with the world of the sacred in order to discover information that will be useful to those who consult him: "perhaps he [i.e., Samuel] will tell us about the journey on which we have set out" (1 Sam. 9:6). After Saul and his companion reach the town, they must go with Samuel to a shrine and then eat with him. Divinatory activity may have taken place in either context.

The third title, *'îš hā'ĕlōhîm*, is especially prominent in the stories about Elijah and Elisha, particularly the latter. The literary character of these stories corroborates a judgment that the "man of God" can best be understood as a "holy man," a type of individual attested in numerous religious traditions. Such people possess the power of the holy and hence are dangerous, powerful, and due appropriate respect. Unlike visionaries, who occasionally engage in trance or possession behavior, the holy man personifies the deity in the midst of the profane world. A classic example is provided by 2 Kgs. 6:1–7. Elisha, here characterized as "the man of God," makes an iron ax head float to the surface of the Jordan River, into which it had accidentally fallen. Such powers belong to the world of the sacred. Elisha does not need to pray; he can simply act, since he possesses those powers.

The most frequent term for prophet is *nābî'*. Scholars have not reached a consensus about its root meaning, but the term probably signifies someone called to a certain task. Hence, it is no accident that call or commissioning narratives appear in several prophetic books (e.g., Isaiah 6; Jeremiah 1; Ezekiel 1–2). Over time, this term became the standard one by means of which prophets were known, as 1 Sam. 9:9 reflects: "for the one who is now called a prophet [*nābî'*] was formerly called a seer."

One suspects that the use of these four role labels for a prophet reflected linguistic usage in different times and places. For example, the term *nābî'* may have been particularly prominent in Israel, while the label *ḥōzeh* appears to have been of special import in Judah. Moreover, these labels surely emphasized different things a prophet did, for example, report visions or utter oracles. However, as a roster of contemporary role labels such as clergyperson, priest, pastor, or minister suggests, there was probably considerable overlap in what various prophets were about. Israel's prophets were writers and/or speakers. They could receive communications from the deity in various ways (e.g., auditions and visions). Still, it is possible to identify one element common to all prophets. They functioned as intermediaries between the human and the divine worlds. They could represent humans to God (Amos 7:2) or God to humans (Amos 5:4). They could act with the power of God within the mundane world (e.g., Elisha). They could envision the cosmic world (Amos 7:4; Zech. 1:7–17), they could participate in the divine council (Isaiah 6; 1 Kings 22), and they could analyze the machinations of humans (Micah 3). Prophets were truly boundary figures, standing between the world of the sacred and secular.

If prophets are to be understood as intermediaries, some comment is necessary about the relationship between the two major classes of what might be called religious professionals: priests and prophets. An absolute distinction between prophets and priests did not exist in ancient Israel. Some prophets were also priests. Jeremiah was born into a priestly family that resided in Anathoth, a small town not far from Jerusalem. This priestly house probably traced its roots to Abiathar, who was exiled to Anathoth, the ancestral dwelling, for having supported Adonijah rather than Solomon (1 Kgs. 2:26–27). Ezekiel too is accorded priestly status (Ezek. 1:3), again as a function of his birth. Unlike Jeremiah, Ezekiel was probably a member of the priestly line, the Zadokites, which had primary responsibility for the temple in Jerusalem. Zechariah was another prophet born into a priestly family. His genealogy, "Zechariah son of Berechiah son of Iddo" (Zech. 1:1), is also attested in the book of Nehemiah (12:16), where the genealogy is part of the listing for priestly ancestral houses. At least three prophets—Jeremiah, Ezekiel, and Zechariah—belonged to priestly families.

The priestly-prophet connection is even stronger than matters of lineage. The book of Joel offers a remarkable scenario in which the prophet appears to *function* as a priest. In a time of national crisis, Joel calls for Israelites to engage in ritual lamentation at the temple (1:13–14). He then utters the words that the priest would have spoken to the deity (1:19). In response to their calls for help, the deity then speaks through the prophet, affirming that the concerns of the people have been heard (2:18–20). The prophet Joel undertakes just such work as one might expect from an intercessory priest. Another prophetic book, Zephaniah, depicts the prophet (Zeph. 3:14–15) calling Israelites to the service of song. They are to praise the deity for having moved from a time of judgment to a time of restoration.

In sum, we do well to remember that prophets could not only exercise various roles but could even act as priests. Such behavior should prevent us from thinking about prophets in a simple and/or monolithic fashion. One way to avoid such an approach is to set the prophets within the specific contexts in which they were active.

Historical Setting

Prophets, as a class of religious specialists, are not present in all times or in all societies. Similarly, prophets were not present in all periods of Israel's existence. It is difficult to speak about Israelite society in any strong historical sense much before the time of David (ca. 1000 B.C.E.). In literature that depicts Israel's understanding of itself prior to that time (the Pentateuch or the books of Joshua and Judges), references to prophets are rare or unusual. (Moses is a significant exception.) Abraham (Gen. 20:7), Miriam (Exod. 15:20), and Deborah (Judg. 4:4) are labeled as prophets, but they seem odd when viewed as such. Deborah is better understood as a judge, Abraham as a patriarch. Certain notions of the prophetic role (i.e., the prophet as intercessor) have affected the ways in which Israelite authors viewed these individuals. An ancient Israelite writer may view Abraham as a prophet when he prays on someone else's behalf, even though intercession may be neither characteristic of much prophetic activity nor of Abraham's own behavior.

Individuals who function as intermediaries and who are known as prophets began to appear at the time that Israel adopted statehood as its form of government—in biblical terms, when Israel gained a king. Moreover, within seventy-five years from the time that Judah was destroyed (as an independent state with a king), individually named prophets seem to have become a thing of the past. Thus, there is a strong correlation between Israel's existence as a monarchic state and the presence of prophets in its midst.

This correlation may reflect several different features of prophetic behavior. Prophecy requires certain conditions in order to exist.[3] Among them are an "audience" that will recognize someone as a prophet. Kings were one such audience. Moreover, there may be a need for protection of a prophet when they proclaim something unpopular, for example, the powerful individuals who helped Jeremiah (Ahikam son of Shaphan [Jer. 26:24] or Ebed-melech the Cushite [Jer. 38:7–13]). Finally, certain historical moments may produce greater needs for prophecy than do other times. Israel, from roughly 1000 B.C.E. to 500 B.C.E.—though not uniformly during this half-millennium—met these conditions.

During these five hundred years, Israel lived through a number of major changes or crises: the inception of statehood, national schism, Neo-Assyrian threats and the destruction of the northern kingdom, the Neo-Babylonian threat and the destruction of Judah, life in exile, and attempts at restoration in the land. Prophets addressed these pivotal moments, each of which we must examine briefly.

For example, Nathan and Gad appeared during the lifetime of David, Israel's first true king. Both of these prophets interact directly with the king; they do not speak to a larger public.[4] Nathan confronts David after he has impregnated Bathsheba and had her husband killed (2 Samuel 11–12) and is able to trick David into indicting himself for this blatant misuse of royal power. Gad, too, critiques the king after he has undertaken a census designed to assay the number of men available for battle (2 Samuel 24). In both cases, the prophet challenges the holder of a new political office by calling him to account based on Israel's prior religious and ethical traditions. In the midst of this new political configuration, Israelites must have been asking the question: What does it mean for a king to function in an Israelite/Yahwistic setting? In some measure, then, these prophets are a voice from the past, attempting to relate Israel's defining norms to a new political situation. Moreover, the prophets interpret Israel's current life and how what Israelites do now will affect their future. Prophets are concerned with past, present, and future.

David's grandson faced the next critical challenge. The united monarchy, made up of tribes with regional loyalties, was a fragile nation. The Deuteronomistic History reports that even before Rehoboam had angered representatives from northern tribes, a prophet, Ahijah the Shilonite, had informed Jeroboam that he would be king of the new northern kingdom (1 Kings 11). These events (ca. 922 B.C.E.) spelled the end of the united monarchy and the creation of two nations, both of which claimed Yahweh as their state god. Israelite history writers affirm that a prophet played a critical role in the creation of the divided monarchy.

The next major development on the political landscape was the threat posed by the reconsolidated Neo-Assyrian Empire in the eighth century. Although his predecessors should be credited with major initiatives, it was Tiglath-pileser III (745–727) who began military campaigns in Syria-Palestine. These attacks (ca. 740–730) are attested both in biblical texts (2 Kings 15) and Assyrian annals. Moreover, they provide the context for two prophetic books: Amos and Hosea.

During this period, two prophets, Amos, a Judahite who came to Israel, and Hosea, a native Israelite, addressed those in the northern kingdom, which was subject to greater pressure from the Neo-Assyrians than was its southern neighbor, Judah. Both Amos and Hosea understood the dire straits facing Israel. One can comb the books and discover various images of military attack and destruction. Amos speaks of people being taken into exile (e.g., 6:7), forcibly removed from their homes and resettled elsewhere, a practice used by the Neo-Assyrians when assuming control of a new area. Hosea likewise refers to the decimation of warfare: "[T]herefore the tumult of war shall rise against your people, and all your fortresses shall be destroyed" (10:14).

However, Hosea and Amos do more than simply see the signs of the times and state them in a poetic way. Instead, these individuals, as did those who came after them, interpreted these events from the perspective of Israelite religious and ethical traditions. These prophets understand Yahweh's hand to be at work behind whatever the Neo-Assyrians are doing. It is for this reason that Hosea continually describes the deity's work in the first person: "I will cast my net over them; I will bring them down like birds in the air; I will discipline them" (Hos. 7:12). Although Neo-Assyrian chariotry may set out against Israelite troops, Hosea understands that it is really Yahweh who is disciplining the Israelites.

In addition, Amos and Hosea try to explain to those in Israel why they are to suffer such a dire fate. Interestingly, the reasons they offer are diverse. Amos inveighs against social and economic practices in the northern kingdom, whereas Hosea focuses on religious and political misdeeds. Still, although they offer different kinds of critiques, the prophets share two basic assumptions: (1) that the destruction is a punishment and (2) that Israel had violated what it had earlier agreed to do. The prophets do not indict Israel for violating some new norm. If anything is new, it is the freedom with which the prophets talk about the deity. One might say that their theologies are more creative than their ethics.

The next pivotal moment involves the same empire, but now as it confronts Judah. New prophets are involved: Micah and Isaiah. Though it would be a mistake to read all prophetic texts as direct reflections of historical circumstance, some texts do attest to particular moments in a stark way. Micah 1:10–16 is such a text. These verses contain a number of city names. Those that have been identified with actual sites all sit to the south and west of Jerusalem. The Neo-Assyrian annals report that Sennacherib destroyed a number of Judahite cities. One of these, Lachish (v. 13), has been excavated. There is one layer attesting to destruction brought by military means and that almost certainly reflects Sennacherib's campaign in 701. Micah sets such Neo-Assyrian action within the context of a Judah and especially a Jerusalem that is filled with rampant violence. Micah 3:1–4 indicts those who rule from Jerusalem. They are responsible for both the suffering they inflict in the capital and the suffering that the Neo-Assyrians are inflicting throughout the land.

Isaiah, too, knows of this same set of events, which were of such significance that they are narrated in both Isaiah and Kings (Isaiah 36–37; cf. 2 Kings 18–19). Moreover, what transpires provides a key for understanding much in the book of Isaiah. These chapters address a question that must have vexed those who heard Micah's words: Whom does the Lord support? One could hear Micah (and Amos and Hosea) and think that Yahweh supported the efforts of those who were attacking Judah. The Assyrians were the means by which God was punishing his people. According to Isa. 36:10, the Assyrians themselves were making this very point. Isaiah, through a divine oracle, responds that God will protect Jerusalem, "for my own sake and for the sake of my servant David" (37:35). Isaiah, finally, knows more about what God will do—and why—than do the Assyrians. Through him and other prophets, Israelites can understand such moments as more than an attack by an imperial enemy.

Almost a century passed before prophets appeared prominently again, which they did as the Neo-Assyrian Empire was ousted from the ancient Near Eastern stage by the Neo-Babylonians. The book of Nahum might be read as a treatise on the necessity for such destruction. However, this is a minor chapter when compared with the role that the Neo-Babylonians will play within Syria-Palestine. The Babylonians defeated Nineveh, the Neo-Assyrian capital, in 612. Then in 597, and again in 587, they attacked Judah, destroying Jerusalem in the second campaign. It is, therefore, no accident that two of the three so-called Major Prophets date to this time. If Judahites had been asking questions in 701, they must have been shouting them in 587. How could Yahweh let Judah and the temple in Jerusalem be destroyed? Before 587, Jeremiah and Ezekiel affirmed the necessity of such punishment. And both before and after that date, they explained why such radical action had become necessary. Ezekiel focuses on the ways in which Judah had insulted God's holiness, whereas Jeremiah continues a line of attack begun by Hosea but now directed against Judah: The Judahites have acted in a promiscuous fashion by worshiping other gods. Moreover, their political policies stand at odds with what Yahweh desires them to do. Here again, times of radical change elicit the need for radical explanations.

Both Jeremiah and Ezekiel stand astride the decisive date of 587. After the time of destruction, they and other prophets (e.g., Haggai and Zechariah) wrestle with questions about what comes next. Will God be with his people? Will there still be a covenant? Will the new chapter be written with those in exile or those who return to the land? Prophets, not priests or sages, were the ones responding to such questions. Ezekiel addresses these questions by using visionary language about a field of bones: Could they live again (Ezekiel 37)? Second Isaiah (the prophet responsible for Isaiah 40–55) thinks about a Jerusalem that would have its streets paved with gold (Isa. 54:11–12). Jeremiah speaks in terms of a new covenant (Jer. 31:31). Haggai anticipates a restoration of the prior monarchic order (Hag. 2:20–23). Zechariah envisions a new order, with both priest and king in leading roles (Zechariah 4). Different though these perspectives are, they share one essential affirmation, namely, that God will continue to be with the people.

With the rebuilding of the temple and its rededication in 515, such individually named intermediaries begin to pass from the scene. Prophetic literature continues to be written, but it now occurs in the form of notes, additions, and supplements to earlier words. As a province in the Persian Empire, Judah may no longer have required prophets or possessed the prerequisites for prophetic activity. Moreover, the very character of Yahwism had changed, from the religion of a nation-state roughly coextensive with the boundaries of Judah and Israel to a religion that could be practiced in the land but also elsewhere, such as Egypt and Mesopotamia. This new form of religion, oriented around divine instruction, did not so much need new "words," new oracles from the deity, but instead interpreters of words that already existed, particularly those of the Torah. Judaism, this new religion, did not need prophets as had its predecessor religion, Yahwism.

Social Setting

Historical circumstance provides only one way in which to contextualize Israel's prophets. Social setting offers another fruitful angle of vision. A number of popular understandings of Israelite prophecy picture prophets as something akin to desert mystics, walking into Israelite cities and raving at the residential population.[5] Earlier comments about prophets as priests suggested problems with such a view. However, the question of the social setting for prophecy deserves even more attention.

The social location of Israel's prophets can be compared with the location of intermediaries in other cultures.[6] Such anthropological research has resulted in understandings of prophets quite different from earlier models. For example, most prophets appear to undertake their activities within an urban setting. In fact, most appear to have lived in cities or, at a minimum, to have been associated with specific towns (e.g., Amos of Tekoa, Jeremiah of Anathoth).

The anthropologist Ioan Lewis theorizes that intermediaries could appear either in a central or peripheral setting.[7] By that, he means that prophets could function at different places in the society. An intermediary might be located in or near the circles of power. Alternatively, a prophet might be part of a disenfranchised group. Many popular understandings of Israel's prophets have placed them in the latter setting. Rarely, however, was that the case, either in Israel or throughout the ancient Near East. One of the first prophets, Nathan, is embedded in the structure of the royal court. He has the direct ear of the king; he can judge the king and name the son who will succeed David. Likewise, over four hundred years later, one of the last prophets, Haggai, in the oracle with which the book concludes, speaks to an heir of the Davidic house. Such proximity to the king or prince symbolizes the prophet's close connection to political power during many periods of ancient Israelite history.

To be sure, Israel's prophets spoke on behalf of those without power and on behalf of those oppressed by the powerful. Amos challenges those "who oppress the poor, who crush the needy" (4:1). However, Amos himself was apparently a well-off farmer who engaged in both animal husbandry and the production of crops. Micah indicts those who "covet fields, and seize them; houses, and take them away; they oppress householder and house, people and their inheritance" (2:2). Yet Micah may well have belonged to the group of elders who were responsible for the governance of Moresheth, his village. In sum, there is considerable evidence for thinking that the prophets were not impoverished or members of a lower class. Instead, they articulate values that involve concern for those who might be oppressed by powerful groups or structures in Israelite and Judahite society.

Problems with Prophecy

A final comment needs to be made about prophecy as a form of intermediation in ancient Israel. Prophecy, as such, may have a fatal flaw. Prophecy can work well if there is one prophet speaking to somebody who will take that prophet seriously. The situation becomes problematic when two prophets appear and say things that contradict each other, especially if both prophets use the standard language of an Israelite prophet. This problem has often been termed the conflict between true and false prophecy.

Classic exemplars appear in 1 Kings 22 and Jeremiah 28. In the latter case, Jeremiah confronts another prophet, Hananiah, who has presented a divine oracle (vv. 2–4) from Yahweh. However, Hananiah's words of hope stand in stark contrast with the words of judgment that Jeremiah has been proclaiming. Though Jeremiah responds with his own comments, Hananiah uses a symbolic action, removing an ox yoke that Jeremiah had been wearing. Jeremiah, without any other prophetic alternative, leaves the scene. Later, after Jeremiah receives a divine oracle, he can challenge Hananiah in public.

One can imagine the difficulties felt by those who had witnessed the initial confrontation. They had no easy way of knowing which prophet was telling the truth. In fact, the Deuteronomic rules that govern such a case (Deut. 18:15–22) stipulate that one should wait and see which individual's words would turn out to be true. But when prophets' words require action, such inactivity would not be possible. Moreover, prophets could disagree about assessments of the present and past, not just about pronouncements concerning the future. This potential for conflict between prophets may have provoked such difficulty that other forms of seeking information from the deity developed, such as priestly admonition or scribal intermediation, neither of which allowed for a direct public challenge.

Prophets, then, appeared primarily in times of crisis during the period when Israel and Judah existed as monarchic states, and shortly thereafter. They addressed both the nation's leaders and the overall population based on their understanding of Israel's religious traditions. They were embedded in rather than distinct from the structures of Israelite society.

PROPHETIC LITERATURE
IN THE ANCIENT NEAR EAST

Since intermediation is a well-attested form of religious behavior in many societies, it should come as no surprise that prophets appeared in ancient Near Eastern societies other than Israel. In fact, the Old Testament reports both explicitly and implicitly—often polemically—that prophets of other religions existed. Deuteronomy 13:1–2 alerts us to the existence of such prophets: "If prophets or those who divine by dreams appear among you and promise you omens or portents, and the omens or the portents declared by them take place, and they say, 'Let us follow other gods' (whom you have not known) 'and let us serve them' . . ." The authors of Deuteronomy not only knew about the existence of such prophets, they understood something about their power. A story such as Elijah's confrontation with the prophets of Baal on Mount Carmel (1 Kgs. 18:20–40) only makes sense if Israelites had experience with these prophets and understood them to be effective intermediaries between Baal and those who venerated him.

For obvious reasons, most references to prophets for gods other than Yahweh are couched in a polemical tone, just as are references to the veneration of those gods. As a result, the case of Balaam son of Beor (Numbers 22–24) is particularly interesting. Balaam was a non-Israelite, but also, according to Israelite tradition, was able to function as an intermediary between Israel's God and a Moabite and Midianite audience. He utters an "oracle of one who hears the words of God, who sees the vision of the Almighty" (Num. 24:4). Though not an Israelite prophet, Balaam does the same sorts of things that one would expect from an Israelite prophet.

Our knowledge about this non-Israelite prophet has been significantly enhanced due to an important discovery in 1967. Archaeological work at Tell Deir 'Alla, which would have been part of ancient Ammon, revealed a fragmentary plaster inscription dating to the eighth century B.C.E. That inscription attests to the activities of an individual named Balaam, son of Beor, almost certainly the same individual whose work is described in Numbers 22–24. There could be no more graphic confirmation of Israelite prophecy as a phenomenon typical of the larger ancient Near Eastern environ. The inscription begins with the following introduction: "The account of [Balaam, son of Beo]r, who was a seer of the gods. The gods came to him in the night, and he saw a vision like an oracle of El."[8] Thereafter the inscription recounts the lamentation he undertakes after apprehending the vision, which he then recounts: The gods assembled in a council (cf. 1 Kings 22; Jer. 23:18) in order to plan a devastating destruction. Darkness and the reversal of the social order will ensue (elements attested prominently in Old Testament prophetic texts as well; see, e.g., Isa. 3:4; Amos 8:9). Though much of the remainder of the inscription is so fractured that it is difficult to read, the part that is legible presents a picture of prophetic behavior essentially similar to that in other Old Testament texts. Visions in the night (i.e., dreams; cf. the Greek notion of "sleeping vision") were a typical form of communication between the prophet and the world of the deity. The divine council, in which Yahweh is surrounded by minor deities (in the Old Testament, "all the host of heaven" [1 Kgs. 22:19]; "heavenly beings" [literally "sons of God," Job 1:6]), is important in many prophetic texts. For example,

Isaiah is commissioned to work as a herald on behalf of such a council (Isaiah 6). Balaam, like Israelite prophets, responded in a public way to the "private" communication at night. In so doing, that which he knew became public knowledge: "Sit Down! I will tell you what the Saddayin have done. Now, come, see the works of the gods!" Finally, inside and outside Israel, such behavior was memorialized in written form in order to testify to the powerful revelation of what the gods were doing.

Perhaps the most important trove of ancient literature that illumines Israelite prophetic activity dates to a far earlier epoch than do Balaam or any Israelite prophets. On the upper Euphrates River, at the city of Mari, archaeologists have discovered an archive that dates to the eighteenth century B.C.E., just before Hammurabi, of law code fame, ruled in Babylon. This archive contains not only economic and political records but also a series of clay tablets recording the work of various prophets. These Mari prophets were known by various titles, as were the Israelite prophets.

The Mari texts are all relatively brief. One such text (ARM X 7) is here quoted in its entirety. Zimri-Lim is the king, Sibtu is his wife, and Selebum is a prophet situated at the temple of the deity Annunitum.

> Speak to my lord: Thus Sibtu your maid-servant. The palace is safe and sound. In the temple of Annunitu, on the third day of the month, Selebum went into a trance. Thus spoke Annunitum: "O Zimri-Lim, with a revolt they would put you to the test. Guard yourself. Put at your side servants, your controllers whom you love. Station them so they can guard you. Do not go about by yourself. And as for the men who would put you to the test, I shall deliver these men into your hand." I have now hereby dispatched to my lord the hair and fringe of the cult-player.[9]

This is a highly formulaic text—the phrase "Thus spoke Annunitum" is parallel to a phrase in numerous Old Testament texts: "Thus says the LORD." The prophetic messages are routinely addressed to the king. Some individual offers a message, which is then reported to the king by a confidant, whereas in ancient Israel the prophet often conveys his or her own message directly to the king (the case with Baruch presenting Jeremiah's message is a notable exception). The text above is typical of many Mari texts that focus on the safety and security of the king. Such focus on the monarch is present in Israel as well, though not always in preserving his safety (cf. Isaiah 7; 38). Mari texts do on occasion challenge the king, especially if the prophet thinks that the monarch has not been providing properly for the maintenance of a temple.

This same Mari text includes two other elements that require mention. First, the text refers to the means by which the prophet received information: a trance. Anthropologists describe this as possession behavior, for which there is some evidence in the Hebrew Bible (e.g., 1 Sam. 19:20). More to the point, prophetic literature often identifies the means by which a prophet receives information about the world of the divine—through audition, vision, or possession. Second, the final sentence of the text refers to the hem of the garment and the hair from the head of Selebum. Such items were collected in order to identify and verify the source of a particular prophetic message. Some scholars have suggested similar origins for superscriptions to or within prophetic collections (e.g., Isa. 8:1, 16). The prophets' messages were powerful; they could influence military behavior and matters of state. Kings, especially, could not afford to put up with irresponsible prophetic speech. Hence, those who exercised the role of prophet were held accountable in this way.

The Mari texts, though in an archive, betray no attempt to create a collection associated with an individual. Also, there is no evidence of later additions or reflections as one finds in Israelite prophetic literature.

A final set of texts reflects prophetic activity in the Neo-Assyrian period (ca. eighth–seventh centuries B.C.E.). Though less well known than the Mari texts, these tablets chronicle prophets contemporaneous with Isaiah and Micah. These texts apparently present the oracles of nine women and four men known as prophets, a striking divergence from the gender of Israelite prophets. One well preserved text reads:

> Fear not, Esarhaddon!
> I am Bel. (Even as) I speak to you,
>   I watch over the beams of your heart.
> When your mother gave birth to you,
>   sixty great gods stood with me and protected you.
> Sin was at your right side, Samas at your left;
>   sixty great gods were standing around you
>   and girded your loins.
> Do not trust in man.
>   Lift up your eyes, look to me!
> I am Ishtar of Arbela; I reconciled Assur with you.
> When you were small, I took you to me.
>   Do not fear; praise me!
> What enemy has attacked you while I remained silent?
> The future shall be like the past.
> I am Nabu, lord of the stylus. Praise me!
> By the mouth of the woman Baya, "son" of Arbela.[10]

One feature of the Neo-Assyrian texts is particularly striking: More than one oracle is present on a tablet. One tablet from Nineveh includes five oracles, all apparently attributed to the same prophet. Moreover, the middle oracle seems to have been placed there because of its central importance for the overall sequence, namely, the basis for a covenant between the god Assur and the royal house of Assyria.[11] The third collection commences with a prologue or introduction prior to the citation of the oracles, and the oracles themselves have been arranged in a temporal sequence. One might view this text as a primal form of a prophetic book. The other collections include the utterances of different prophets. Still, the translator of these texts writes, "It appears that the oracles collected in these tablets were arranged chronologically and, it seems, thematically, as well."[12]

In sum, we know that prophets were active both inside Israel and throughout the larger ancient Near East. These prophets engaged in similar forms of activity, including reporting visions and uttering oracles. As a result, prophetic literature appears both in Israelite and other cultures. What is distinctive about the prophetic activity in ancient Israel is the monumental literary creations that derived from the work of these prophets. There is simply no prophetic text from ancient Mesopotamia, Syria-Palestine, or Egypt that can compare with the books of Isaiah or Hosea, for example, whether viewed from the perspectives of size, breadth of vision, or literary complexity.

LITERARY PERSPECTIVES

The nonbiblical prophetic literature from the ancient Near East that has survived occurs in the form of single clay tablets or plaster inscriptions, each typically attesting to one prophetic performance. In contrast, the biblical prophetic books are, for the most part, collections of numerous speeches from or incidents in a prophet's life. Most of these biblical books are more than a piling up of oracles, as if a series of clay tablets were simply lined up on a shelf and then copied. Some books represent a meaningful ordering and carefully structured presentation of speeches and reports. For example, Ezekiel moves from indictment and judgment on Israel (chaps. 1–24) to judgment on foreign nations (chaps. 25–32) to hope for Israel (chaps. 33–48). Other books (e.g., Hosea) appear minimally ordered and without the aforementioned formulae. Some books include preexisting collections (e.g., the oracles against the nations in Amos 1–2 or the series of oracles about kings in Jer. 21:11–23:8). Others appear simply as one collection, without readily discernible subunits (e.g., Micah). Hence, the astute reader may recognize different levels of prophetic literature: the individual saying or report, intermediate collections of such units, and the prophetic book itself.

In this regard, prophetic literature presents great challenges to readers. For example, a reader encountering Hosea 13, Amos 4, or Micah 4 sees chapters written entirely in poetry. But these chapters do not present single poems. Instead, they are made up of smaller oracles and sayings. The key to comprehending these chapters is discerning the constituent elements of which they are made up. Only after these individual entities have been identified is it then possible to approach a larger collection or even a book in its entirety.

Prose and poetry might seem to offer a convenient way of categorizing prophetic literature, if one assumed that poetry equals speech and prose equals story, as some scholars have suggested. Unfortunately, the matter is not so simple for at least three reasons. First, the boundary between prose and poetry is not always easy to discern. For example, if one compares the RSV and NRSV translations of Ezek. 17:2–10, one discovers that the earlier group of translators deemed those verses to be prose, whereas the later group of translators deemed them to be poetry. Indeed, the distinction between formal prose and loosely structured poetry is often difficult to discern. Second, some speeches, whether of the deity or a prophet, are conveyed in prose (e.g., Ezekiel 25). Third, not all prose texts (apart from speeches) constitute stories. These difficulties notwithstanding, I propose two basic categories with which to understand prophetic literature: prose accounts and poetic speech.

Prose Accounts

Most exemplars of prophetic literature that report the activity of prophets are conveyed in prose. But they are not all stories if by that we mean a prose narrative that includes what literary critics have described as an arc of tension or plot, namely, a beginning point, followed by a complication that is then resolved. Put simply, a story may report, but not all chronicles or reports are stories in this strict sense.

Careful reading of accounts, most of which are composed in prose, should attend in the first instance to their literary features. For example, the accounts about Elisha present a peculiar figure, on occasion a troublesome miracle worker and at other times a benevolent intercessor. One does well to ask questions such as: What sort of character has the writer depicted in an account? At what point does an account of that character's activity become a story?

It is helpful to identify at least seven basic types of prose accounts in Israelite prophetic literature:

Symbolic Action Report

The symbolic action report describes prophetic behavior that is designed to convey a message. Isaiah 20:1–6 provides a classic example of the straightforward form. God commands Isaiah to walk naked for three years "as a sign and a portent against Egypt and Ethiopia." We are not told that Isaiah was to proclaim anything. Action, rather than words, provides the key element. As we work through this report, we discover that the message was directed not to these foreign nations but instead to "the inhabitants of this coastland," Judah's near neighbors. The text does not exhibit interest in any qualms Isaiah might have had about undertaking this task, and we do not hear how those in Judah responded to this naked man in their midst. One can readily conceive an imaginative or entertaining story about Isaiah having comported himself in this way. But the author was interested in using the form of the symbolic action report, not in exploring the narrative potential of such prophetic behavior. The book of Ezekiel includes a number of comparable examples of symbolic action reports (e.g., Ezek. 4:1–3; 5:1–4). Reporting human behavior and its significance for an audience constitute the key elements in such accounts.

Commissioning Report

These accounts, sometimes termed call narratives, do not occur in all prophetic books. But they are so interesting, and regular in general form, that they have elicited much attention.[13] Jeremiah 1:4–10, Isaiah 6, and Ezekiel 1–3 are the clearest examples. (On formal grounds, Isa. 40:1–11 may belong here as well.) All three texts identify a "conversation" between the deity and the prophet that appears to depict the prophet's initiation into that role. However, these texts are not biography but instead highly theologized accounts, each one influenced by imagery and ideas important to the prophetic book of which it is a part (e.g., the prominence of word in Jeremiah 1 versus the imagery of holiness in Ezekiel 1–3).

Commissioning reports are typically made up of six elements— divine confrontation, introductory word, commission, objection, reassurance, and sign—all of which are present in another nonprophetic commissioning report, the commissioning of Abraham's servant, which may be found in Gen. 24:2–9. The regularity of the commissioning report in prophetic books is due to the use of such discourse in the commissioning of messengers throughout ancient Israel.

Like the symbolic action report, the commissioning report does not comprise a formally plotted story. One could easily imagine Isaiah 6 being told as a story—for example, to explore whether or not Isaiah's "uncleanness" (v. 5) would prevent him from becoming a prophet—but the basic elements of narrative are absent. Instead, the ancient authors attest to the fact of commissioning, not why (or how) it happened. Moreover, these accounts focus on an essential element of an individual prophet's message or role (i.e., Jeremiah as a prophet to the nations who announces both destroying/overthrowing and building/planting). They do not explore the prophet's personality or human capacities.

Vision Report

Two of the four role labels used to describe prophets may be translated "seer." Hence, it is not surprising that references to visionary behavior— "this is what the Lord GOD showed me" (Amos 7:1) or "I looked up and saw . . ." (Zech. 2:1)—figure prominently in prophetic books. Such behavior is also attested in formulae that introduce prophetic books, such as "the book of the vision of Nahum" (Nah. 1:1), "the vision of Obadiah" (Obadiah 1), or "the oracle that the prophet Habakkuk saw" (Hab. 1:1).

Several prophetic books contain reports of that which a prophet "saw." Two of these visions occur in the commission reports (Isaiah 6; Ezekiel 1–3). However, elsewhere, prophets offer vision reports not simply as inaugural moments but as reports that are part of their prophetic vocation. Interestingly, these vision reports regularly occur in a series. Amos reports five visionary experiences (Amos 7:1–9; 8:1–3; 9:1–4). Ezekiel offers four vision reports, which begin in 1:1; 8:1; 37:1; and 40:1, respectively. Zechariah 1–6 contains eight vision reports. Jeremiah offers two very brief reports (Jer. 1:11–13). Each book presents its vision reports in a regular, one might even say stereotypical, manner.

In the earliest vision reports, those of Amos, the seer understands immediately what he has experienced. For example, Amos perceives the deity "calling for a shower of fire, and it devoured the great [watery] deep and was eating up the land" (Amos 7:4). Immediately thereafter, the prophet intercedes on behalf of Israel, an act that implies Amos understood all too well what he had seen. The same is true for the visions of Ezekiel, though this prophet is now accompanied on his visionary journey by the deity, who explains to Ezekiel the implications of what he sees (e.g., Ezek. 8:17–18). With the book of Zechariah, the prophet is not so easily able to comprehend what he sees: "And I looked up and saw four horns. I asked the angel who talked with me, 'What are these?'" (Zech. 1:18). By this time, there has been a major change in the vision reports. Earlier the prophet had a vision and understood what it meant; now the prophet sees something but needs some other agent to explain the vision's significance. This tradition of vision as separate from the interpretation continues in the apocalyptic visions of the book of Daniel: "As for me, Daniel, my spirit was troubled within me, and the visions of my head terrified me. I approached one of the attendants to ask him the truth concerning all this" (Dan. 7:15–16).

Legend

The legend is another major exemplar of the prose account. It offers a report about something holy, whether object (e.g., the ark of God, see 2 Sam. 6:6–7) or person. As we saw earlier, one of the role labels for a prophet was "man of God." From the perspective of the history of religions, such an individual can be understood as a holy person, someone who possesses supernatural power. As with the previous two types of literature, a legend need not be written as a story (though there is a strong tendency in this direction). For example, 2 Kgs. 2:23–24—just two verses—make up one such account. Elisha encounters some boys who taunt him, whereupon he curses them and they are killed. This is an account, not a story. There is no tension to be resolved, simply a report that when someone bothers a holy man, that person is likely to end up dead. However, most biblical prophetic legends are written as narratives. A good example is found in 2 Kgs. 4:1–7 (cf. 1 Kgs. 17:8–16). Here the widow of one of Elisha's band of prophetic disciples lives in dire straits due to her poverty. Her children are about to be taken into debt slavery. Elisha saves the day by having olive oil appear in superabundant quantities behind the closed doors of her dwelling. The creditors are kept miraculously at bay. Moreover, there is a subtle subplot, namely, the widow could have had even more oil than she did since the oil "stopped flowing" when she ran out of vessels that she had collected. Her notions of what might be possible limited the amount that she would receive. The legend has become a story, one with a didactic aside.

Prophetic Historiography[14]

Prophetic historiography is a prose literature that recounts events in the world of public affairs and the ways in which prophets are related to them. For example, both the books of Isaiah and Jeremiah include chapters that overlap material found in Kings. Isaiah 36–39 is essentially the same as 2 Kgs. 18:13–19:37, and Jeremiah 52 is coextensive with 2 Kgs. 24:18–25:30. Isaiah the prophet appears in Isaiah 36–39, whereas Jeremiah is not mentioned in Jeremiah 52. However, what Jeremiah said and did help set the context for this later overview of Jerusalem's defeat. What appears in the historical books can appear in a prophetic book as well. This fact has a bearing on how we think about prophetic literature, namely, as literature that can attest to the interplay between prophetic activity and the events that prophets address.

Isaiah 36–39 provides an account of Sennacherib's attack on Jerusalem during the reign of Hezekiah. The first chapter focuses on an Assyrian official's (the Rabshakeh) challenge to all those in Jerusalem. After Hezekiah laments this situation at the temple, Isaiah offers an oracle (Isa. 37:6–7) in which God promises to save Israel from this military threat: "I myself will put a spirit in him [Sennacherib], so that he shall hear a rumor, and return to his own land." Then, after another plea from Hezekiah, Isaiah again offers an oracle (Isa. 37:21–35). After this speech, the Neo-Assyrian threat is lifted. For this historian, to narrate the events of Sennacherib's campaign is also to recount the prophetic oracles that this challenge elicited.

These chapters attest to the role of the prophet in major national affairs, especially those involving the monarch and military challenges to the nation. Moreover, such prophetic historiography presupposes that the prophet has a critically important role in times of national crisis. Hezekiah prays to God, and God offers a response through the prophet so that the king and others know what will be happening. Not all Israelite history writing presumed such a role for the prophets, but even apart from such so-called prophetic historiography there is evidence that ancient Israelites understood the prophetic word to have a major place in the historical process (e.g., "as he had foretold through all his servants the prophets" [2 Kgs. 17:23; cf. 24:2]).

Biography

Biography in the ancient world was not the same enterprise as the volumes we might purchase today. Along with an interest in an individual's life—a feature common to all biography—ancient biographies included attention to a primary thesis or theme that could be elucidated by attention to that life. Not all accounts about a prophet are typical of ancient biographies. Some, however, are, such as Jeremiah 37–44. These chapters cover both the last decade of Judah's existence and the early years after the defeat in 587. However, unlike prophetic historiography, to which they might seem similar, these biographies refer to this history by focusing on the vagaries of Jeremiah's existence. The "primary" story of Israel in the early sixth century B.C.E. involves life in the Babylonian exile. Thus, 2 Kings 24–25 narrates two deportations, the first (597) during which King Jehoiachin, along with other leaders, was taken to Babylon, and the second (587) when King Zedekiah and another group were taken into exile. Only brief mention is made of an exile in another direction, that is, to Egypt (2 Kgs. 25:26). In contrast, the way in which Judahites ended up in Egypt receives considerable attention in Jeremiah. Chapters 41–44 provide this account, which runs counter to Jeremiah's own words, for he prophesied on behalf of continued residence in the land. However, against his will, he was taken into Egypt, where he continued to work as a prophet, presumably until he died.

The author of these chapters seems as much interested in Jeremiah and his fate as he does in the larger historical issues. Such focus on the person, and not on the message, is a hallmark of ancient biography. Moreover, there is, as one should expect, a thesis or principle being addressed by the author, namely, that Jeremiah's words received a positive response neither before nor after the devastating defeat of Jerusalem. One might have expected that the Judahites would pay attention to him after his earlier words had been borne out, but such was not the case. Even now, though God "persistently" continued to send prophets (Jer. 44:4), the people did not respond. Such is the theme of this prophetic biography.

Divinatory Chronicle

The Hebrew Bible contains several texts that indicate the prophet could function like a diviner, an individual who could provide information or help from the world beyond that of normal human knowledge. Samuel functions this way in 1 Samuel 9. Ezekiel does as well. Ezekiel 20 presents a scene in which the prophet, living in exile, receives representatives from "the elders of Israel." They have come to "inquire from the LORD." Yahweh then speaks through the prophet, thereby responding to the elders. Perhaps the most straightforward case of a prophet receiving a request for a divine oracle and then providing the expected response occurs in Zechariah 7–8. The citizenry of Bethel empowered legates to ask: "Should I mourn and fast in the fifth month?" (Zech. 7:3). The prophet then responds: "[T]he fast of the fourth month, and the fast of the fifth, and the fast of the seventh, and the fast of the tenth, shall be to the house of Judah seasons of joy and gladness" (Zech. 8:19).

In these and other cases (e.g., Jeremiah and Zedekiah [Jer. 38:14]), prophetic literature attests to interaction between the intermediary and those who want information from the deity. The deity's response, which is communicated by the prophet, is only one, though important, part of the literary form. The prophet as diviner is clearly attested in the divinatory chronicle.

In sum, prose accounts as a basic type of prophetic literature occur in a number of subcategories. Moreover, the impulses for the creation of these accounts are diverse. They do, however, tend to focus on action, people's behavior, rather than speech, which comprises the other basic type of prophetic literature.

Poetic Speech

Important though prose accounts are, poetic speech is the predominant form of prophetic literature. Most, though not all, speeches are written as poetry. Hence, readers need to attend to the rules of Hebrew poetry in general as well as to the special features of prophetic speech.[15]

Parallelism

The dominant feature in Hebrew poetry, parallelism is, quite simply, the presence of several poetic lines of a roughly comparable length that stand in a semantic relationship. The semantic relationship between the lines can vary significantly; they can be similar, dissimilar, or sequential. Parallelism is more a comment about form than it is about semantics or meaning.

Readers of Hebrew poetry in prophetic books confront hundreds of speeches composed using parallel lines. One typical set of lines comes from the book of Nahum:

> The chariots race madly through the streets,
> They rush to and fro through the squares.
> (Nah. 2:4)

Earlier scholars would have identified these lines as examples of synonymous parallelism, emphasizing the essential similarity of the action described by the prophet. Chariots charging around in a city is the subject of both lines. Still, these lines do more than repeat each other. They are more than synonymous. James Kugel expresses the notion in an almost formulaic way: "A, what's more, B."[16] In the above-cited text, the first line focuses on the speed of the chariots, whereas the second line highlights the back-and-forth movement of the chariots in the city.

The horse-drawn chariots do not simply race through the city once; they churn around, like a disemboweling sword. Prophets who exploited parallelism were able to develop powerful images, particularly of military destruction or cosmic distress.

> The earth dries up and withers,
>   The world languishes and withers;
>   The heavens languish together with the earth.
>   (Isa. 24:4)

Here, three parallel lines work together to create a picture of total desiccation throughout the universe. Such descriptions regularly appear when a prophet envisions a scene in which God punishes Israel or its enemies.

Prophets also used parallel lines powerfully when they identified what was wrong in Israel.

> . . . because they sell the righteous for silver,
>   and the needy for a pair of sandals—
> they who trample the head of the poor into the dust of the earth,
>   and push the afflicted out of the way;
> father and son go in to the same girl,
>   so that my holy name is profaned;
> they lay themselves down beside every altar
>   on garments taken in pledge;
> and in the house of their God they drink
>   wine bought with fines they imposed.
>   (Amos 2:6–8)

These ten parallel lines provide a catalogue of travesties, including social, economic, religious, and sexual infractions. But as lines of poetry, they offer more than would a tabular list. The lines reinforce each other. The reader may focus on the verbs—sell, trample, push, go in (sexually), profane, lay, take, drink, impose. They create an image of aggressive, violent, wanton behavior, even apart from the nouns present in these lines. Moreover, one may also examine the relevant nouns: the righteous, the needy, the poor, the afflicted, girl, garments, people fined. Here too the parallel lines enable us to create a picture of those who have been violated. Parallelism provided a remarkable way for a prophet vividly to list charges against those who were being indicted. There was a remarkable fit between the needs of the prophets and the means offered by Hebrew poetry.

Figures of Speech

Many other elements characteristic of poetry the world over are also present in prophetic poetry. For the purposes of this introductory chapter, I offer one example, the figure of speech called a simile as used by Hosea. The book of Hosea offers a rich trove of poetic devices. That prophet uses two related tropes, the simile and metaphor, throughout his prophetic discourse. The following simile occurs in the indictment portion of an oracle:

> Your love is like a morning cloud,
> > Like the dew that goes away early.
> > (Hos. 6:4)

That which God expects from Israel, fidelity or life, vanishes quickly, as if it had never been there. The prophet uses this same image of dew to symbolize punishment:

> Therefore they [idols or people] shall be like the morning mist
> > or like the dew that goes away early,
> like chaff that swirls from the threshing floor
> > or like smoke from a window.
> > > (13:3)

Similes in Hosea are not limited to oracles of indictment and punishment. They can depict weal as well. Using faunal images in a positive way, the book describes a moment when God will summon Israel from exile.

> They shall go after the LORD,
> > who roars like a lion;
> when he roars,
> > his children shall come trembling from the west.
> They shall come trembling like birds from Egypt,
> > and like doves from the land of Assyria.
> > > (11:10–11)

Normally, God as lion evokes negative connotations (e.g., Hos. 5:14; 13:7). In Hos. 11:10, however, the lion's roar summons rather than devours. Israel becomes a lion's progeny rather than its prey. And then, the prophet moves from mammal to bird in order to develop the motif of "trembling" that occurs in verses 10–11.

To read Hosea's similes is to enter a world of complex imagery. But Hosea is not the only prophet to utilize such a figure of speech. Amos envisions God acting toward Israel in the following way:

> So, I will press you down in your place,
>   just as a cart presses down
>   when it is full of sheaves.
>
> (Amos 2:13)

In this and comparable prophetic texts, it can be difficult to do more than appreciate the primary significance of the image. In this case, God will act powerfully and negatively, but it is difficult to know how this image might work itself out in the life of Israel. Does "pressing down" equal military attack, drought, or political unrest? The reader cannot be sure. As a result, one must be careful to avoid using prophetic poetry as an obvious statement about prosaic matters. Poets do not provide reports or chronicles. They offer images calculated to achieve a particular emotional effect or rhetorical response. Hence, when reading prophetic poetry, one should in the first instance attend to the text as poetry and not immediately view the poem as data by means of which to reconstruct the social or economic history of the period during which the prophet lived.

Forms of Prophetic Speech

In addition to attending to matters of poetic technique, readers of prophetic structured speech should also consider the formal characteristics of those speeches. Scholars have invested considerable energy in understanding the form (hence the term *form criticism*) of speeches in prophetic books. They have identified speeches that are traced to the deity, that is, when the deity speaks in the first person (e.g., "I, the LORD, am its keeper; every moment I water it" [Isa. 27:3]). Though the prophet might mouth these words, he or she is clearly the rhetorical mouthpiece of the deity. Such speeches may be described as divine oracles. Some form critics have distinguished these divine oracles from those speeches in which the prophet speaks about God in the third person, such as, "My joy is gone, grief is upon me, my heart is sick. Hark, the cry of my poor people from far and wide in the land: 'Is the LORD not in Zion? Is her King not in her?'" (Jer. 8:18–19). Here a different rhetoric is at work. The prophet speaks on behalf of the deity's perspective but not with the voice of the deity. Hence, these utterances are known as prophetic speeches.

Those interested in the form of prophetic speeches or divine oracles have been particularly impressed and puzzled by texts such as Amos 1–2 or Isa. 10:5–19. Amos 1–2 is made up of a series of oracles that have a remarkably regular structure: "Thus says the LORD," followed by an indictment that is then linked to a judgment. Many of the oracles conclude with a brief formula: "says the LORD." Moreover, this basic form, known as the judgment oracle—an indictment followed by a sentence of judgment—appears in many other prophetic books (e.g., Jer. 5:10–17; Mic. 1:5–7). How should one explain such remarkable regularity? It seems very unlikely that Amos created such discourse, which was then copied by other prophets.

Form critics have observed the sorts of regularities we have just identified. They have then sought places in the ancient society in which such regular forms might have been created and preserved. In the aforementioned case, some form critics have argued that the language of indictment and sentence is most likely to have been at home in the law court. That social institution would have preserved such a form with great regularity, just as wills and contracts are preserved by our legal institutions today. Form critics suggest that prophets such as Amos "borrowed" forms of speaking from various sectors of ancient Israelite society in order to make their points. Elsewhere we find Amos using hymnic language, poetry created and preserved at the temple or other ritual contexts (e.g., Amos 4:13; 5:8–9; 9:5–6). Thus, some poems that we find in the prophetic books have been forged using structures known both to prophets and their audiences.

Readers of prophetic poetry will need to be alert to the various forms they will encounter. The following incomplete list is designed to be suggestive rather than exhaustive:

> judgment oracle (Jer. 6:16–21)
> woe oracle (Isa. 10:1–4)
> lawsuit (Mic. 1:2–7)
> lament (Jer. 8:18–9:3)
> hymn (Hab. 3:2–15)
> song (Isa. 5:1–2)
> allegory (Ezek. 17:2–10)
> acrostic (Nah. 1:2–8)

As noted above, the judgment oracle is a speech made up of two basic parts: an indictment and a sentence. The woe oracle includes these same elements, though it commences with the Hebrew word *hoy*, which has been translated in various ways (e.g., "Ah" [Isa. 5:8], "Alas" [Amos 5:18], "Ha" [Isa. 29:15], "Oh" [Isa. 30:1], "Woe" [Isa. 45:9]). The woe formula (woe plus a name) was probably used originally to refer to someone who had just died. Both the judgment and the woe oracles pass a sentence on some individual or group, with the woe oracle offering the connotation that the party is as good as dead. In a similar legal vein, the lawsuit attests to the legal process that would have resulted in the passing of such a sentence. Parties are summoned: "Hear, you peoples" (Mic. 1:2); interrogations are made: "What is the transgression of Jacob?" (Mic. 1:5); and judgments are offered: "Therefore, I will make Samaria a heap in the open country" (Mic. 1:6). As the notion of passing sentence or reference to a legal process suggests, these three forms of speech derive from Israel's law courts. The prophets used such legal forms of speech more than any other type. In contrast, the lament and the hymn derive from the world of ritual. The lament would have been used in funerary rites whereas the hymn was sung at the temple. Jeremiah used laments not only to express his concern for the people (Jer. 8:18–9:3) but to reflect about his own situation (15:10, 18). In addition, a number of prophets used the language of hymns (which typically begin with a plural imperative verb such as "sing" or "praise"), which is then followed by a statement expounding the character of the deity (e.g., Amos 9:5–6). This hymnic language attests to the character of the deity, who, despite judging the people, remains worthy of veneration and worship. Finally, the prophets used forms that one associates with the scribes or intellectuals: elaborate allegories (Ezek. 17:2–10) and acrostics (Nah. 2:1–8). Such formal variety attests to the broad cultural knowledge that the prophets possessed along with their rhetorical abilities, which enabled them to use such diverse forms of verbal expression.

Great value may be achieved by undertaking such a process of form-critical classification. It is terribly important to know what sort of literature one is reading. For example, a lament, which derives from the language of ancient funerals, bears certain connotations. To utter a lament over someone who is still alive would have jarred ancient readers (see Amos 5:1–2).

The Poetics of Prophetic Literature

Prophetic literature may be created as either prose or poetry. It is, therefore, possible to think about a poetics of prophetic literature that encompasses both prose and poetry. Yet prophetic prose and prophetic poetry each involve certain hallmarks.

Prophetic prose constitutes a type of literature appropriate to the experiences that it conveys. Robert Alter makes this case when he examines two forms of discourse: "the oracular vision" (e.g., Jer. 1:13–19), which I would prefer to label a vision report, and the direct speech of the deity to a prophet (e.g., Jer. 36:27–31).[17] In each instance, the medium suits the message. The contents of the reported vision are sufficiently vivid and forceful so as not to require poetic expression. Moreover, the complex report of direct speech—along with its narrative content—would be difficult to convey in poetry.

Prophetic prose also regularly, though not exclusively (so the legends), attends to the political world in which the prophets were active. This is true both for prophetic literature embedded in prophetic books and prophetic literature that belongs to the Deuteronomistic History. Alter discerns this element in arguing for the presence of "incremental repetition." He notes the subtle ways in which Nathan's speech differs from an earlier and similar one spoken by Bathsheba (1 Kings 1). Nathan "sharpens the general political aspects of the threat from Adonijah."[18] As prophet, he is especially sensitive to the political dimension of the controversy. In a similar vein, prose texts often set the context for poetic utterance. Such prophetic literature often defines that context in overtly political terms, whether by reference to a king's reign, to wars, or to matters of national purport. The world of politics suffuses much prose prophetic literature.

Further, prophetic prose often focuses on the person of the prophet and what that individual does, not simply what the prophet says. The legend and the biography offer classical examples. They attend to things other than verbal behavior. So too does the symbolic action report. As Gabriel Josipovici puts it, "The prophets, desperate for the people to see and understand, act out that meaning with their own bodies."[19] The word can no longer just be spoken (a la poetic speech); it must be embodied. The description of such embodied performance normally occurs in prose, a form of literature appropriate to the behavior of these intermediaries as "word-persons."

Finally, prophetic prose is tough literature. It manifests a hard edge just as much of the poetry does. Here we find an element shared by both prose and poetry. Ephraim Sternberg claims, "The irreverent treatment of the gods in Homeric epic has its counterpart in the rough handling of the audience in prophetic discourse, for a Jeremiah can afford to lash out where the storyteller would entice and manipulate."[20] Such "irreverent" discourse is particularly prominent in prophetic poetry, though it also appears in prophetic prose, though in different form. As Sternberg observes, the prophets not only handle their audience roughly, but the Hebrew Bible handles the prophets roughly. And this rough handling of the prophets appears primarily in prose. For Sternberg, Samuel—as he designates first Saul and then David as king—continues to lose status. Ultimately, in other prophetic literature, the downgrading occurs within the relationship between the prophet and the deity.[21] One could quickly add Isaiah, Jeremiah, Ezekiel, and Habakkuk to the list of prophets who have a problematic relationship with the deity. This tension between deity and prophet constitutes an important element in the poetics of much prophetic literature.

The poetics of prophetic poetry are, for the most part, the poetics of poetry in the Hebrew Bible. However, one may identify two specific features of prophetic poetry: its character as speech from the divine to the human world, and its tendency to set the world of human affairs in a broader context. Robert Alter has described the former feature by claiming that prophetic poetry is "powerfully vocative in character"; it is "devised as a form of direct address to a historically real audience"; it is presented as "divine discourse . . . represented speech rather than historical speech."[22] These judgments reflect formal features of the language such as imperative verbs or vocative expressions. Such analysis permits one to speak about prophetic poetry as guided by rhetorical concerns, namely, the concern to have an impact on an audience—whether the putative "historical" audience or the readers of prophetic poetry.

As for the second feature, Alter maintains that prophetic poetry includes distinctive strategies—"direct accusation, satire, the monitory evocation of impending disaster"—that distinguish it from other biblical poetry (and prophetic prose). The first strategy, direct accusation, differs from a harangue because it typically moves to a "second power of signfication," in which the accusation involves a depiction of the accused in terms that allow the reader to understand the issue as transcending the immediate historical context (e.g., Isa. 1:2–9).[23] In satire, the second strategy, Alter discerns a proclivity toward placing the individual or group being satirized in cosmic perspective (e.g., Isaiah 14 likens the king of Babylon to a star). Then with the final strategy, Alter argues that the nature of the poetic medium begins to take charge of the message. What is essentially an admonition, rooted in this-worldly concerns, becomes, by dint of the inherent ability of Hebrew poetry to allow elaboration through parallelism, something cosmic or mythic in scope (e.g., Isa. 5:26–30; and even more, Isa. 24:17–20). In all three strategies, one may find a common thread, namely, prophetic poetry moves beyond the quotidian condemnation—the sorts of things one might find in newspaper editorials today—and places them in broader perspective.

In sum, the poetics of prophetic literature includes the poetics of both Hebrew prose and poetry, but it is more than just a combination of those two elements. In a synthetic way, the poetics of prophetic literature explores the language of intermediation, with attention both to the nature of the intermediary, often in prose accounts, and to the direct discourse of that intermediary, often in poetic speeches. A poetics of prophetic literature must take into account character and speech, prophetic person and divine word, account and saying. The prophets are boundary persons, not quite *běnê hā'ĕlōhîm* ("the sons of God"), but often "men of God," specially related to the deity. Their ability to speak on behalf of the deity attests to this role. They are able to speak the deity's very words, which are often written as poetry. However, the prose accounts and narratives move in another direction, focusing on the person of the prophet, the embodied word of the deity.

THE GROWTH OF PROPHETIC LITERATURE

Collecting

The dominant model for understanding the composition of prophetic books is one in which various discrete units of discourse were preserved, collected, and edited. Various speeches or accounts could be combined to create collections. The legends collected about Elisha (e.g., 2 Kings 4–6) offer a good example of a prose collection, as does the assemblage of Zechariah's vision reports (Zechariah 1–6). The book of Jeremiah presents several compelling examples of collections that include both prose and poetry. Jeremiah 21:11–23:8 comprises sayings about Judahite kingship; the collection begins with the phrase "concerning the royal house of Judah." Jeremiah 23:9–40 offers a comparable collection of sayings, but about prophets; this collection bears the title "concerning the prophets" (23:9). These labeled collections provide graphic evidence for the ways in which prophetic literature came to be formed. Either the prophet or an editor placed sayings addressing a similar topic together.

A quite different mode of collecting lies behind Hosea 12–14. Though the sayings are all composed in poetry, they are not similar in their content. Rather, their very dissimilarity—some very negative, others hopeful—permits the creation of a collection that moves the reader from a sentiment of judgment to one of restoration. This and other sections of prophetic books represent the activity of an editor who confronted sayings of very different sorts. The result was an ordering that moved from punishment to promise. One can imagine oracles of admonition such as those in Hos. 14:1–3 originally spoken prior to oracles of judgment. Now, however, within the prophetic book, they are meant to be read after Yahweh has spoken: "Compassion is hid from my eyes" (Hos. 13:14). The new literary context of Hos. 14:1–3, namely, the oracle (Hos. 13:14–16) that stands immediately before it, elicits the call for Israel to "return."

Commenting

Other dynamics resulted in the growth of prophetic literature. Readers of earlier oracles often found them difficult to understand or otherwise problematic. As a result, scribes proceeded to interpret them and to include the interpretation as part of the biblical text. A comparison of the MT and LXX texts of Jeremiah presents a number of such examples.[24] The reader of the LXX form of Jer. 28:16 ("Therefore thus says the LORD: I am going to send you off the face of the earth. Within this year you will be dead") might have asked: Why does Jeremiah offer such a harsh and abrupt sentence? The MT answers that question by adding the following clause to the end of the verse: "because you have spoken rebellion against the LORD." Such commentary or explication contributed to the growth of prophetic literature.

Updating

But much more than collection and exegetical interpretation were at work. The original prophetic sayings and accounts possessed a generative power that resulted in the creation of new literature, which is particularly evident in the books of Isaiah and Zechariah. This new literature, sometimes called "deutero-prophetic," represents an attempt by Israelites to understand their own times by reformulating earlier prophetic words and accounts. In some cases, the new literature arose in the form of rather short comments. Another prophet might update something that had been said earlier: "On that day the Lord will extend his hand yet *a second time* to recover the remnant that is left of his people" (Isa. 11:11); "This was the word that the LORD spoke concerning Moab *in the past. But now* the LORD says . . ." (Isa. 16:13–14). These texts represent brief notes from the hands of those who preserved and venerated the words of the earlier prophets as they contemporized those earlier texts. However, these later figures composed not only compact sayings but also major compositions in their own right. This ability of prophetic literature to elicit newer prophetic literature is one of its hallmarks. The book of Isaiah contains two major exemplars of this process. The chapters that are often called Second (40–55) and

Third (56–66) Isaiah were based on the sayings and accounts attributed to Isaiah ben Amoz and were integrated into a composition that presents those earlier sayings and accounts as a response to Israelites living in the Persian period, long after Isaiah ben Amoz had died. In this process, major topics such as the role of Jerusalem/Zion and Babylon are explored over a long period of time.

The orientation of much prophetic rhetoric toward the future helps explain this kind of literary creativity. Deuteronomy 18 informed Israelites that one could rely upon a prophet's oracles if they proved true. To be sure, not all sayings were subject to clear verification. Nonetheless, one can imagine that when Jeremiah spoke of a seventy-year captivity (Jer. 25:11), some would have started counting to see if he would turn out to be correct. Both later prophetic (Zech. 1:12) and nonprophetic (2 Chr. 36:21) biblical writers reflected upon the nature and accuracy of that prediction. *50 yr. for Judah 587–539*

Linking

There is a final type of literary development in prophetic literature, which is exemplified by Hos. 14:9 and Mal. 4:4. The former text emphasizes the connection between Hosea's words and those who are wise, whereas the latter concludes the Minor Prophets, perhaps even the entire prophetic canon, by calling for obedience to Torah. In both cases, these components of prophetic books link that literature to another portion of the canon—wisdom literature as in Proverbs and the Torah, respectively.

All of these elements—collecting, commenting, updating, and linking—belong to the process by means of which the prophetic canon grew. Of these, the copious updating or contemporizing of prophetic words and traditions for a new generation seems to be a distinguishing feature of prophetic literature.

Ultimately, this process by means of which prophetic literature grew eventuated in the creation of prophetic collections and books. For much of the twentieth century, those who have studied prophetic literature have tried to discern the elemental building blocks of prophetic literature. For example, those who have written about Amos have taken pains to identify the constituent oracles in chapter 1. More recently, they have understood these oracles as part of a collection of oracles against nations, which makes up chapters 1–2. Now, most recently, they have studied the ways in which an entire prophetic book works. Such analysis has even moved to considering categories larger than an individual prophetic

book. For example, some scholars have begun to read the so-called
Minor Prophets (Hosea–Malachi) as one book, the Book of the Twelve.

To this end, some scholars have identified a "normative" form for a
prophetic book: oracles against Judah, oracles against the nations, hope
for Judah. However, whereas this pattern appears in Isaiah, LXX Jeremiah, and Ezekiel, it is absent from most other prophetic books. As a
result, it is clearly difficult to talk about the typical format of a prophetic
book. Still, most prophetic books do possess one typical element, the
superscription. This element often links the activity of a prophet to that
of a period defined by the reign of a king (this is true of Isaiah, Jeremiah, Ezekiel, Hosea, Amos, Zephaniah, Haggai, and Zechariah). In
other cases, the superscription simply characterizes the book as "word"
(Joel), "oracle" (Nahum, Habakkuk, Malachi), or "vision" (Obadiah).
Though some superscriptions do refer to their books as "words" (e.g.,
Amos), the use of a singular noun predominates. This use of a singular
noun to refer to books filled with diverse sayings and accounts may
indicate that the editors who composed these superscriptions thought
of them as literary entities, not simply collections. These entities have,
therefore, become the object of study, as scholars ask: How does Amos
work as a book? How does Hosea work as a book? Are they similar to
or different from each other?

The book of Habakkuk offers an interesting example for this kind of
analysis. The reader sensitive to the diversity of rhetoric in prophetic literature will read Habakkuk and experience the sharp moves from dialogue (1:2–2:5) through woe oracles (2:6–20) to theophanic hymn
(3:1–15) and prophetic response (3:16–19a). It would be possible to
think about Habakkuk as simply a collection. However, the reader may
move beyond the aforementioned variety to perceive an integrated
booklet. The prophet's voice continues even after explicit dialogue with
the deity has ceased. Instead of direct encounter, the prophet moves into
the temple (2:20), utters a prayer (3:2), sings a hymn (3:3–15), and then
reflects or meditates upon what he has just sung (3:16–19a). The book
of Habakkuk revolves around the prophetic voice, not a voice challenging the people but a voice speaking to or about the deity in various
modes: "O LORD, how long shall I cry for help, and you will not listen?"
(1:2); "O LORD, I have heard of your renown, and I stand in awe, O
LORD, of your work." (3:2); "GOD, the Lord, is my strength; he makes
my feet like the feet of a deer" (3:19). The book begins with complaint
and concludes with the language of vow and thanksgiving. Hence, one
may speak of the movement within and the coherence of this book. Such
is also the case with other exemplars of prophetic literature.

THEOLOGICAL AND ETHICAL ISSUES

The prophets occupied religious roles. Moreover, the literature they created or elicited offers theological claims. The prophets may not have been theologians, at least in the contemporary sense of that term, but prophetic literature shows them addressing numerous theological and ethical issues.

Covenant and Imperium

If prophets are best understood as intermediaries, those who act and speak on behalf of Israel's deity, then they should, in principle, reflect the religious affirmations and theological norms of ancient Israel. And such is the case. But the emphasis here must be on diversity—norms, not norm. As a result, it is difficult indeed to talk about a single prophetic theology or a sole prophetic ethical perspective. One of the great strengths of von Rad's treatment of prophetic literature was his ability to discern the remarkable variety of theological traditions within the various prophetic books.[25] For example, traditions about Zion are constitutive of Isaiah, whereas they are absent from Hosea; the exodus is important in Hosea and unimportant in the literature attributed to Isaiah ben Amoz (Isaiah 1–39).

Despite such diversity, scholars have devoted considerable energy in attempting to discern a common core or element to prophetic literature. For example, Blenkinsopp has argued that prophecy in a military context was an essential early feature that influenced prophetic discourse in general.[26] Even more prominent have been assessments of the covenantal background of much prophetic literature.[27] For example, it is difficult to read Hos. 4:2 and not hear echoes of the Ten Commandments, which are in some ways similar to the stipulations of a covenant or treaty. So too, curses as found in covenant texts (e.g., Deuteronomy 28) also appear in prophetic literature (e.g., Isa. 34:11–17). In a similar vein, the lawsuits brought by God through the prophets reflect the covenant relationship between God and Israel (so Mic. 6:1–8). Such observations have led many scholars to think about the prophets as spokespersons on behalf of Israel's covenant, calling Israel to obey that to which it had agreed at Sinai. Such a covenant background is difficult to deny, especially when some of the later prophets wrestle with a new way to understand Israel's relationship to its God and in so doing use the image of a new covenant (Jer. 31:31; cf. Ezek. 36:26). The image of Moses, the quintessential covenant spokesman, as prophet (Deuteronomy 18) adds further weight to this idea, which one might term the exodus perspective.

However, equally important is what I would term the imperial perspective of Israel's prophets. In prophetic literature, the image of God present in a theophany on Mount Sinai is complemented by that of God enthroned in the divine council. This, after all, is the scene portrayed in the call narratives of both Isaiah and Ezekiel. The case of Isaiah is telling. The prophet envisions the deity in the temple, which is the visible, earthly symbol for the heavenly divine council. In that context, Yahweh is surrounded by minor deities, to whom he speaks, "Whom shall I send, and who will go for us?" (Isa. 6:8), the "us" being the members of that council. Isaiah speaks up in that royal chamber, "Here am I; send me!" When he is given his "message" ("Go and say to this people . . .") Isaiah then becomes nothing less than a herald from the divine council, empowered with its words and its power.

Such a way of thinking about prophets helps explain the remarkable sweep of their vision, a sweep considerably broader than that of the language of covenant between Israel and its God. Jeremiah provides a case in point. In Jeremiah's commissioning narrative, God designates him as "a prophet to the nations" and says, "I appoint you over nations and over kingdoms" (Jer. 1:5, 10). The prophet's having an international role fits better with the notion of God as imperial and cosmic sovereign than it does with the God who is covenant partner with Israel.

The international aspect of the prophet's work cannot be overestimated. Though Jeremiah is the only prophet officially designated as "a prophet to the nations," each of the "major" prophetic books includes a sizable collection of sayings and oracles devoted to nations other than Israel (Isa. 13:1–23:18; Jer. 46:1–51:58; Ezek. 25:1–32:32). These chapters provide more than just jingoistic rhetoric. They exemplify a "plan" that God has for all people: "This is the plan that is planned concerning the whole earth; and this is the hand that is stretched out over all the nations" (Isa. 14:26).

Even among the Minor Prophets, this testimony to God's international imperium remains in place. The book of Amos begins with a short set of oracles concerning Israel's neighboring states. Joel is concerned with a northern army (2:20) and includes rhetoric proclaimed "among the nations" (3:9). Obadiah focuses almost exclusively on Edom and its relation to Judah. Jonah's eyes are set toward Nineveh. Micah sees both woe and weal from an international perspective: "Peoples shall stream to it [Zion], and many nations shall come" (Mic. 4:1–2). Nahum is titled "an oracle concerning [against] Nineveh" (Nah. 1:1). Habakkuk's vision is palpably international: "Look at the nations, and see! . . . For I am rousing the Chaldeans" (1:5–6). Zephaniah, like Amos, includes a short section devoted to foreign nations (2:4–15). Haggai, perhaps the most "domestic" prophetic book, understands Judah's weal and wealth to derive from God acting on a cosmic scale: "I am about to shake the heavens and the earth, and to overthrow the throne of kingdoms" (2:21–22). Zechariah too is written from a grand scale. The very first vision reports that the divine patrol has moved throughout "the whole earth" (Zech. 1:11). Finally, Malachi's theological perspective is international: "[M]y name is great among the nations" (Mal. 1:11).

The prophets lived in the world of politics, both international and domestic. They did not think that Israel, and more so Judah, could have an international policy (e.g., treaties, alliances) that did not take into account the divine king's imperial plans. In sum, Israel's prophets serve as heralds for a cosmic God. As such, they offer an international perspective for what happens to Israel even as they affirm the importance of God's covenant with Israel.

Ethical Norms

Ethical norms inform much of the critique offered by Israel's prophets. At the risk of oversimplification, one might suggest that there are two different levels of norms: those common to all humanity and those that Israel understands as specific to it. These two levels complement the aforementioned imperial and covenant perspectives. The former infuse those sayings and oracles devoted to foreign nations. One may read the judgment oracles that occur in Amos 1–2 and discover that those nations are indicted for behavior that all humans would normally find heinous: genocidal acts (1:6, 9), violence against noncombatants (1:13), acts of ritual degradation (2:1). Oracles against the nations also include indictments for prideful behavior that offended Israel's God. Isaiah 14 includes a dirge directed at an unnamed Neo-Babylonian emperor who, in the eyes of the poet, had attempted to "ascend to heaven." Finally, there is a strain of language according to which God had designated certain imperial powers—the Neo-Assyrians and the Neo-Babylonians—to act on his behalf to punish Israel. However, in both cases, Israel experienced such devastation that some prophets maintained these two countries had overstepped the roles assigned to them by Yahweh (Assyria: Isa. 10:12–15;

Babylon: Jer. 51:11–49). Hence, they are to be destroyed. But the norm is one common to Israelites and non-Israelites alike, namely, one should avoid excessive violence in time of warfare.

When the prophets move to discourse about Israel, things change. More specific ethical categories are at work. They are not unique to Israel, since they also appear on the stele that preserves Hammurabi's law code, but they pervade much of what the prophets say.[28] The norms are righteousness and justice. Quite simply, righteousness involves the principle of beneficence, doing the good thing (e.g., in Israelite language to aid the widow or orphan). Justice addresses the question of how. In concrete terms, should one offer ten pounds of wheat to one widow or one pound of wheat to ten widows? Considerations of justice are apt when one attempts to act out beneficence.

Still, less overt and more troubling values underpin much rhetoric in the Hebrew Bible, particularly involving the place of violence. Though some have viewed language of slaughter as simply a concomitant of ancient warfare, on occasion there seems to be an interest in graphic descriptions of terror for its own sake (Isa. 34:5–7; Jer. 46:10). Also, violence against women—often bordering on the pornographic—cannot be gainsaid (e.g., Ezekiel 23).

As the reference to Hammurabi's law code suggests, the king was theoretically responsible for administering justice in the ancient Near East. Such was the case in Israel as well. To be sure, prophets did address kings, but they also challenged the entire population. One could say that they democratized the responsibility for justice and righteousness. To act in such a fashion was, ultimately, the responsibility of all, not simply the job of those elders and judges who were most prominent in the legal system.

Israelite prophets during the Neo-Assyrian period seem concerned about a particular form of social and economic development in the eighth century, a style of life that stood in tension with the realization of basic norms. It was increasingly difficult to provide for economic justice as larger estates were being created. People's land was being taken away, high interest rates made it difficult to retain financial independence, and debt slavery was rampant. When addressing these issues, the prophets were indicting societal structures as well as the behavior of individuals.

Along with these categories known both to moral philosophers and religious ethicists, there is another norm. Micah 6:8 speaks of walking humbly with one's God. Just as there can be prideful behavior on the international scene, so too such arrogance can occur on the domestic front. As a result, some prophets argue on behalf of a proper relationship with Yahweh. What such a relationship involves is explored in various ways, but one important motif involves the absence of loyalty to any other deity. Hosea and Jeremiah, especially, attack the attraction of Baal, whereas Ezekiel 8 makes clear that the veneration of many other gods and goddesses was at stake. Only Obadiah, Jonah, and Haggai do not include overt polemics against the veneration of deities other than Yahweh. Of course, veneration of Yahweh alone is a characteristic feature of God's covenant with Israel (Exod. 20:3).

Later prophets wrestled with the realities of human behavior. References to a new covenant (Jer. 31:31) or a new heart (Ezek. 36:26) could be read as utopian solutions to the intractable tendency of humans to do the errant thing. The ethical norms had not changed, but one recognizes a realization in Jeremiah, Ezekiel, and Zechariah that to enact them is terribly difficult, requiring a moral and religious capacity not hitherto realized.

Hope

Despite the propensity of prophetic literature to identify the many ways in which humans have fallen short of both universal and Israelite ethical norms—along with the ensuing results—that literature also often strikes a hopeful note. However, the vocabulary and images of hope in prophetic books have troubled many scholars. How, they ask, could someone like Amos, who speaks about an end for Israel, also talk about a future of plenty (9:11–15)? The same question could be posed about Micah (2:12–13).

Scholars have offered a number of answers to explain this hopeful strain. Most prominent has been the judgment that the language of weal arises only after the disasters actually occurred. Hence, books like Micah, which speak of both disaster and hope for Judah, need to be read as composite compositions. According to these scholars, the negative material predates the assaults by the Neo-Assyrian and Neo-Babylonian empires, whereas the positive language (e.g., Mic. 4:6–8) was added after 587 B.C.E.

To be sure, as we already seen, various additions did make their way into prophetic literature. However, the language of hope is truly pervasive in prophetic literature and hence requires an explanation beyond that of scribal addition. Westermann has maintained that such hopeful discourse in prophetic oracles is far more prominent than many readers have thought to be the case. Moreover, Sweeney has assessed prophetic books in the following way: "In general, prophetic books tend to focus on the punishment and restoration of Israel/Judah, *with the emphasis on the latter*."[29]

The sources for hope in prophetic literature are multiple. The vocabulary of hope may stem from rudimentary knowledge of what happens when there is military destruction: Inevitably some people survive. The language of a remnant surely reflects this brute reality (e.g., Isa. 11:11; cf. 7:3). Despite the thorough destruction of Jerusalem and deportation of many Judahites, the land was not left uninhabited. This reality would have been apparent even prior to the various defeats Israel and Judah experienced. An "end" did not mean the cessation of all human life.

Judah's theological traditions would also have contributed to the notion that God could continue to act on behalf of his people. The language of the so-called Davidic covenant included the expectation that this polity would continue "forever" (2 Sam. 7:13). Hence, even well after the defeat of Judah, we hear about what "David" might mean for Israel, even when a prophet might mean something quite different from the restoration of the Davidic monarchy, as is almost certainly the case in Isa. 55:3.

Finally, as masters of poetic expression, the prophets attest to the power of new words, of language itself. It is striking that Isaiah, Jeremiah, Ezekiel, and the Book of the Twelve all acknowledge that the future will see a renaming of Jerusalem. The city that for many prophets personified all that was wrong with Israel (e.g., Isa. 1:21; Mic. 3:12) will undergo the same sort of transformation as did Jacob, who became Israel. A new name will signify a new fate. Jeremiah thinks Jerusalem will be called "the throne of the LORD" (Jer. 3:17). The book of Ezekiel concludes with a new name for Jerusalem: "The LORD is There" (Ezek. 48:35). Isaiah 62:4 refers to a new name that Yahweh will give, "Hephzibah," or "My Delight Is in Her." Finally, Zech. 8:3, as part of the Book of the Twelve, offers the final exemplar, "City of Faithfulness." In these diverse ways, prophetic literature attests to a future beyond the "end" that many of Israel's prophets foresaw.

CONCLUSIONS

Over time Israel was confronted with the task of thinking about prophets. To be sure, the people knew that individuals known as prophets had been in their midst, so they began to generalize about prophets, thinking about typical or ideal prophets. Moreover, as canonical literature—Torah and Psalms—began to emerge, Yahwists were

confronted with the question of the relation between prophetic literature and that of Torah and of the Writings.[30] Moreover, as Torah was
increasingly understood to be canon, that is, a body of literature that
was now essentially closed, how should one conceive of the relation of
prophetic literature to other parts of the canon? The phrase "the law
and the prophets," which postdates the formation of the Hebrew Bible,
hints at a way of addressing the matter in a later time.

Those biblical writers who depicted Moses as a prophet offered one
important way in which Torah and Prophets might be linked. If Moses
were a paradigmatic prophet (Deut. 18:15), and if Moses is responsible
for Torah, then prophecy becomes part of Torah, though still subordinate to it. Prophetic literature may consequently be understood as an
exposition or admonition based on Torah, rather than an independent
word of the deity. That is why Ezekiel appears to be such a dangerous
text, since it purports to be a new Torah, "the law of the temple" (Ezek.
43:12), which might stand in competition with the canonical Torah.

However, Moses was only one of several possible paradigmatic
prophets. Elijah is another; he had special credentials since, according
to biblical tradition, he had never died. As a result, writers both in the
Persian and Greco-Roman periods could look forward to the return of
Elijah "before the great and terrible day of the LORD comes" (Mal. 4:5;
cf. Matt. 17:10–13). Closed though the prophetic writings might finally
become, there was still an expectation that a prophet or prophecy would
appear in the future (cf. Joel 2:28–29; Acts 2).

Another important tradition about prophets as such involved the
notion that they suffered a violent fate. Though this may have occasionally been the case in ancient Israel (see the brief chronicle about the
death of Uriah son of Shemaiah in Jer. 26:20–23), the Persian (2 Chr.
24:20–22; Neh. 9:26) and Greco-Roman periods saw the development
of a notion that many prophets were treated in this way (e.g., Luke
13:34; Acts 7:52). Jeremiah's own rhetoric (e.g., 11:19) may well have
encouraged such an understanding. In contrast to this tradition, however, one may review the activities and speechs of Israel's prophets and
be surprised that they were not treated brutally more often.

Apart from traditions about prophets themselves, there were also
canonical formulations that attempted to integrate prophetic literature
with other portions of the canon. These texts are of several different types.
On the one hand, there is considerable psalmic language embedded within
prophetic literature (e.g., the so-called Amos doxologies [4:13; 5:8–9;
9:5–6] and the catena of thanksgiving and hymn in Isaiah 12). On the other
hand, there are texts at the end of prophetic books that call for the reader

to reflect on that text from the perspective of another portion of the canon (Hos. 14:9 points to wisdom texts, Mal. 4:4 to Torah). From this perspective, the Law and the Prophets were perceived by early readers as a far more coherent entity than has been supposed.

In this introductory chapter, we have seen that prophetic literature derives from the activity of Israel's prophets. Just as there were different kinds of prophets, prophetic literature is itself diverse. Primary forms occur as prose accounts (symbolic action report, commissioning report, vision report, legend, prophetic historiography, biography, divinatory chronicle) and poetic speeches (divine oracle and prophetic speech). Though prophetic literature is known elsewhere in the ancient Near East—most notably in Old Babylonian and Neo-Assyrian textual corpora—there are no extrabiblical exemplars comparable in size and sophistication to the biblical prophetic books, in considerable measure because of the generative power of Israelite prophetic literature. Prophetic literature is the product of creative speakers and writers who were influenced not only by contemporary events but also by a view of Yahweh as an international sovereign and by a profound understanding of God's relationship to Israel. These traditions contributed to a powerful theological and ethical amalgam. Phrases such as these embody some of the most enduring perspectives in prophetic, indeed all biblical literature:

> But let justice roll down like waters,
>   and righteousness like an ever-flowing stream.
> (Amos 5:24)

> They shall beat their swords into plowshares,
>   and their spears into pruning hooks;
> nation shall not lift up sword against nation,
>   neither shall they learn war any more.
> (Mic. 4:3)

> "I am the first and I am the last;
>   besides me there is no god."
> (Isa. 44:6)

Bibliography

Blenkinsopp, J. *A History of Prophecy in Israel*. Rev. and enlarged ed. Louisville, Ky.: Westminster John Knox, 1996.

Clements, R. *Old Testament Prophecy: From Oracles to Canon*. Louisville, Ky.: Westminster John Knox, 1996.

Gitay, Y., ed. *Prophets and Prophecy*. Semeia Studies. Atlanta: Scholars Press, 1997.

Gordon, R., ed. *The Place Is Too Small for Us: The Israelite Prophets in Recent Scholarship*. SBTS 5. Winona Lake, Ind.: Eisenbrauns, 1995.

Lewis, I. *Ecstatic Religion: An Anthropological Study of Shamanism and Spirit Possession.* Baltimore: Penguin, 1975.

Mays, J., and P. Achtemeier, eds. *Interpreting the Prophets.* Philadelphia: Fortress, 1987.

Nissinen, M. *References to Prophecy in Neo-Assyrian Sources.* SAAS 7. Helsinki: Helsinki University Press, 1998.

Orton, D., comp. *Prophecy in the Hebrew Bible: Selected Studies from Vetus Testamentum.* Leiden: Brill, 2000.

Overholt, T. *Channels of Prophecy: The Social Dynamics of Prophetic Activity.* Minneapolis: Fortress, 1989.

Parpola, S. *Assyrian Prophecies.* SAA 9. Helsinki: Helsinki University Press, 1997.

Petersen, D. *The Roles of Israel's Prophets.* JSOTSup 17. Sheffield: Sheffield Academic Press, 1981.

———, ed. *Prophecy in Israel: Search for an Identity.* IRT. Philadelphia: Fortress, 1987.

Rad, G. von. *The Message of the Prophets.* New York: Harper & Row, 1965.

Rofé, A. *Introduction to Prophetic Literature.* Sheffield: Sheffield Academic Press, 1997.

———. *The Prophetical Stories: The Narratives about the Prophets in the Hebrew Bible, Their Literary Types and History.* Jerusalem: Magnes, 1988.

Steck, O. *The Prophetic Books and Their Theological Witness.* St. Louis: Chalice, 2000.

Wilson, R. *Prophecy and Society in Ancient Israel.* Philadelphia: Fortress, 1980.

2

The Book of Isaiah

Our perception of the book of Isaiah has undergone a radical change during the past quarter century. The scholarly consensus that reigned in the mid-twentieth century is no more. As a result, much of what one reads in the "standard" study Bibles and commentaries on Isaiah is not as helpful as that associated with other prophetic texts. In order to clarify the radical changes that have taken place, I will offer a brief sketch of the prior scholarly consensus and then outline the challenges that have been offered to it.

Even with the aforementioned major changes, past study of the book of Isaiah still represents one of the great gains of critical biblical scholarship. The conclusion that portions of the book date to a time considerably later than that of Isaiah son of Amoz helped readers understand, especially, the differences between much of what appears in chapters 1–39 and chapters 40–55. For example, readers intuitively distinguished between the short woe oracles in 5:8–24 and the longer poems in chapter 42. For them to learn that the woe oracles in Isaiah 5 and 10 were probably composed during the time that Judah was threatened by the Neo-Assyrian Empire and that the poetry in Isaiah 42 stemmed from a time long after the Neo-Assyrian Empire had been defeated, from a time when the Persian Empire was ascendant, helped make sense of the significant literary (and theological) differences within the book known as Isaiah. Specifically, when reading Isa. 10:3, the reader can presume that the prophet is referring to the threat from Assyria when he uses phrases such as "the day of punishment" or "calamity." Similarly, when encountering Isa. 42:16, the reader knows that the exilic prophet is concerned about a "road" that will help those in exile move from Mesopotamia to Syria-Palestine.

Of course, claims that prophetic books contain texts that postdate the "authorizing" prophet were nothing new. What made the consensus concerning Isaiah so powerful was the claim that there were two coherent textual units rather than just a myriad of additions. In his classic commentary, Duhm distinguished between three major corpora (chaps. 1–39; 40–55; and 56–66).[1] In the work that followed, an almost formulaic consensus emerged, represented by the labels First, Second, and Third Isaiah. The argument ran like this: Chapters 1–39 derive primarily from the hand (or at least the time) of Isaiah of Jerusalem (ca. 740–700 B.C.E.), chapters 40–55 stem from middle of the sixth century B.C.E. (ca. 550–515), and chapters 56–66 are from the end of the sixth or the early part of the fifth century (ca. 515–480) after the temple had been rebuilt. The aforementioned labels were applied to each of these parts. Further, the labels began to serve a dual purpose: They referred not only to blocks of literature but also were used to refer, implicitly, to authors (or groups of authors). So, for example, one might speak of Second (or Deutero) Isaiah and mean either Isaiah 40–55 or the author of those chapters.

One might even adduce an image to convey the essence of the critical consensus. If one imagines an ancient tell, the bottom stratum could be called First Isaiah. Building on top of it, Second Isaiah added new material, sealing the earlier literature. Finally, Third Isaiah finished the construction by contributing even later structures. The image is of three temporally ordered, sequential strata. Following the archaeological image, each stratum was for the most part undisturbed by the others, though obviously the later ones depended on the earlier ones.

This notion of Isaiah as a book of three rather distinct sections has been challenged forcefully in the past quarter century. However, before we turn to those arguments, it is important to affirm that the critical consensus remains in force in at least one significant way. Few scholars would deny that the book of Isaiah is made up of texts deriving from diverse historical contexts. The argument is more about which parts of Isaiah derive from what periods along with the process by which the book grew than it is about the homogeneity of the book. For example, some scholars maintain that Second Isaiah was an independent body of prophetic poetry that was added to First Isaiah. Others maintain that Second Isaiah was designed to supplement First Isaiah and was never independent from it. But virtually no one maintains that the entire book (or even most of it) was written by one person.

One of the most telling challenges to the scholarly consensus involves the first chapter of the book. If one focuses on verse 1, the book's superscription, a certain historical horizon emerges, namely, that of the reign of the four kings mentioned by name: "The vision of Isaiah son of Amoz, which he saw concerning Judah and Jerusalem in the days of Uzziah, Jotham, Ahaz, and Hezekiah, kings of Judah." All four kings ruled during the so-called Neo-Assyrian period. The book dates the beginning of Isaiah's activity as prophet to the year that Uzziah died (742 B.C.E.), whereas Hezekiah's reign ended in 687. As a result, one reads Isaiah 1 anticipating that these chapters will reflect the period of 742–687. Indeed, certain portions of the chapter seem to work in that way. Verses 7–9 may allude to the campaigns of Sennacherib against Judah, a time during which many cities were destroyed, but Jerusalem was spared: "Daughter Zion is left like a booth in the vineyard" (v. 8). However, other sections of Isaiah 1 appear related to later portions of the book. They almost certainly postdate Hezekiah's death. For example, verse 27, with its focus on the redemption of Zion, sounds like the language that appears in chapters 40–55 (e.g., Isa. 52:3) or even chapters 56–66 (e.g., Isa. 59:17). Moreover, Isa. 1:27 should probably be translated in the following way: "Zion is to be ransomed by justice / And its returnees by righteousness."[2] Zion's ransom, defined by the notion of those who will return, probably refers to those who have been taken into exile by the Babylonians. So verse 27 really does belong to the world of Isaiah 40–55, long after the time of Hezekiah. A similar argument can be made about verses 28–31. These verses resonate with language in chapters 56–66. Reference to the "oak" (1:29–30) is similar to the charge about inappropriate worship made in 57:5. The same claim may be made about references to non-Yahwistic worship in gardens (1:29–30) and comparable charges in 66:17. The motif of inappropriate worship is relatively unimportant outside chapters 56–66.

To pursue this line of argument is to raise the question about the function of the first chapter of Isaiah. Spokespersons for the older critical consensus often read Isaiah 1 as the introduction to First Isaiah. However, when one attends to the similarities between this chapter and other, later elements of the book, such an approach is not satisfactory. Instead, one achieves greater explanatory power by contending that Isaiah 1 functions as a prologue for the entire book, introducing perspectives that appear throughout the book and not simply reflecting those in the first thirty-nine chapters. As a result of this and

comparable analysis, in this chapter we will address the entire book of
Isaiah, not simply Isaiah 1–39 or not simply those texts that might
derive from the activity of Isaiah son of Amoz.

HISTORICAL CONTEXT
OF THE PROPHET AND THE BOOK

When compared with Jeremiah or Ezekiel, Isaiah encompasses a far
broader chronological sweep. The vast historical scale may be symbolized by two names that appear in the book: Uzziah (also known as
Azariah) and Cyrus. The first was a Judahite king who reigned from
783 to 742, and the second a Persian emperor who reigned from circa
539 to 530. Since Isaiah 6 refers to the death of Uzziah, one may point
to a roughly two-hundred-year period represented by these two
chronological markers. Moreover, since the book alludes to the life of
the Judahite community after the temple had been rebuilt and rededicated (that rededication took place in 515), one may even assume that
the book reflects a period of around two hundred fifty years. In this
regard, the superscription that appears in Isa. 2:1 may be more ade-
quate than the one that appears in 1:1, since the superscription in 2:1
specifies no particular period of time. Even though the book covers
several centuries, Jerusalem remains a focal point from the first to the
final chapter.[3]

Although the historical horizon of the book extends from the Neo-
Assyrian through the Neo-Babylonian and on into the Persian period,
Isaiah does not offer a straightforward chronicle. Many decades receive
no attention at all. Moreover, it is difficult to identify the historical
background for many of the oracles in the book. For example, one may
surmise that Isa. 17:12–14 reflects a military assault. But it is not clear
who launched the attack, nor may one readily identify the object of the
assault—is it Judah or more specifically Jerusalem? Still, the book highlights certain periods as of special importance:

1. The Syro-Ephraimitic crisis and outcome (735–732)
2. The Neo-Assyrian assault on Judah and Jerusalem (705–701)
3. The threat of Babylon (ca. 610–587)
4. The time of Cyrus, "his messiah" (ca. 540)
5. Life in the rebuilt Jerusalem (ca. 520–480)

These five periods will structure the following discussion of the historical context of the book of Isaiah.

The Syro-Ephraimitic Crisis and Outcome

Judah Threatened

Several years after Isaiah experienced a vision of God in the divine council (Isaiah 6), his role as prophet led him to a direct encounter with the earthly king, Ahaz. Second Kings 16 offers one perspective on the situation in which Ahaz found himself. This Judahite king was being threatened by two nations to the north, Israel and Syria. These two states had wanted Judah to ally itself with them in order to create an even larger coalition, which would, they hoped, be able to surmount the threat posed by attacks from the Neo-Assyrians. Israel had already lost some land to the Assyrians and was desperate for help. Second Kings 16:5 refers to a military attack on Judah by Israel and Syria. Isaiah reports no such moment but does present a scene in which the king of Judah is reviewing Jerusalem's position, should an attack eventuate. Isaiah is instructed to take his son and to meet Ahaz at a place where he would be examining Jerusalem's water supply in time of siege. Isaiah offers an oracle admonishing Ahaz not to fear because of the relative insignificance of his enemies. In Isaiah's eyes, they are so insignificant that he does not refer to the king of Israel by name—the phrase, "the son of Remaliah" suffices. The oracle makes clear that this two-nation league will soon be destroyed—that is the good news. However, Isaiah tempers this good news by speaking an oblique threat to Ahaz: "If you do not stand firm in faith, you shall not stand at all" (Isa. 7:9). To "stand firm" means not seeking assistance from the Neo-Assyrian king, Tiglath-pileser. Such action would lead to disaster. The author of 2 Kings 16 reports that Ahaz did indeed travel to Damascus to meet with Tiglath-pileser, at which time Judah became a vassal state of the Neo-Assyrian Empire. Ahaz did not "stand firm." Israel was soon defeated by the Neo-Assyrians, who then attacked Judah in a matter of decades.

The Promise of Immanuel to Ahaz

Isaiah communicated in powerful ways during this period. His prophetic repertoire was wide-ranging. He conveys his message by referring to children with symbolic names (see Isa. 8:1–3; cf. Hos. 1:2–8). One such child is called Shearjashub (Isa. 7:3), the other Immanuel (Isa. 7:14). Ahaz is told about the first, the readers of the book of Isaiah about the second. As for the first, Isaiah invites Ahaz to ask for a sign, perhaps of divinatory significance. In a classic case of false piety, he responds, "I will not ask, and I will not put the Lord to the test"

(v. 12). Isaiah counters with an unsolicited sign, by announcing the birth of a child named "Immanuel," a name that means "God is with us." Consistent with much in the book of Isaiah, this name functions as a two-edged sword. Isaiah deftly transforms an oracle of salvation into an oracle of judgment. In the speech that follows, Isaiah tells Ahaz that Ephraim and Syria will vanish as a threat, and it will happen soon, before the child grows up. However, Judah will, because of Ahaz's lack of trust, suffer at the hands of the king of Assyria, who is being used as an instrument of Yahweh's power.

This issue of God's ambiguous presence with the people appears in the next chapter as well. On the one hand, the very words, "God is with us" (8:10), symbolize God's protection of Judah against foreign attack. On the other hand, the person Immanuel receives a woeful message. He is told that Assyria "will sweep on into Judah like a flood" (8:8). As we will see later, the primary notion of Immanuel was positive, but Isaiah could offer a theological variation on that theme. For this prophet, a motif of assurance could also function as a word of threat if the king or the people did not act as if they believed in that assurance.

The Demise of Israel

Second Kings 17 reports the demise of the northern kingdom. Isaiah, though alluding to this event, seems less interested in it than he does in its purport for his own nation of Judah. Isaiah 9:8–21 acknowledges the disaster wrought on Israel. Isaiah 28:1–4 offers a similar perspective, though suggesting more clearly that Assyria, "a storm of mighty, overflowing waters" (cf. 8:7–8), is the agent of Israel's destruction. This first oracle in chapter 28 introduces, however, perspectives on Judah's fate. Verses 7–8 suggest that what was true of Israel's incompetent leaders is also true of the ones in Judah, "you scoffers, who rule this people in Jerusalem" (28:14). In sum, Isaiah remains a true citizen of the South, primarily concerned about the fate of that people.

The literature in Isaiah that is associated with the years 735–732 contains a theme important to the book. God will protect his people. The deity's first word is one of assurance. However, if the people do not trust in that, then it becomes a word of judgment. For Isaiah, there is an inextricable connection between religious and political activity. Judah could demonstrate its fidelity to Yahweh by certain political action, namely, by not creating an alliance with the Neo-Assyrians. "Belief," or "faith," involves judgments and decisions concerning war, among other things; it is not simply assent to religious convictions (see also 30:15).

The Neo-Assyrian Threat to Israel and Judah

Literature Attesting Assyria

The activities of the Neo-Assyrian Empire had a profound impact upon the book of Isaiah. Scholars have identified a number of biblical texts that refer to the threat posed by Assyria, both to Israel, which it defeated in 733 and then subsequently destroyed in 721, and then later to the Assyrian assault on Judah and Jerusalem. Three Neo-Assyrian emperors were of critical importance during the latter half of the eighth century B.C.E.: Tiglath-pileser and Shalmaneser defeated Israel, and Sennacherib attacked Judah and lay siege to Jerusalem.

The most explicit references to Assyria occur in the prose accounts in chapters 7–8 and then again in chapters 36–38. Chapters 7–8 reflect the Syro-Ephraimitic crisis of 735–732 whereas chapters 36–38 derive from the Assyrian attack on Judah (ca. 705–701). One might even say that these two accounts were constructed in such a fashion as to highlight these events, and particularly the responses of the two Judahite kings, Ahaz and Hezekiah, to them.

Poetry in the book of Isaiah also attests to the Neo-Assyrian Empire. The poetic sayings are more ambiguous, befitting their literary character, than are the prose accounts. When Isaiah refers to "a nation far away, a people at the ends of the earth; here they come, swiftly, speedily!" (5:26), there can be little doubt that he is referring to the Neo-Assyrian armies. Less clear is Assyria's opponent. Does "his people" (5:25) refer to Israel or to Judah (or to both)? On the one hand, if one reads Isa. 5:25–29 along with 9:8–21 (the same refrain appears in 5:25; 9:12, 17, 21; and 10:24), then one might surmise Isaiah is referring to Israel, since the northern kingdom is clearly in view (9:8). On the other hand, the woe oracles that precede 5:25–29 more likely represent Isaiah's analysis of what is going on in Jerusalem. Hence, it is best to conclude that they set a Judahite perspective from which to read 5:25–29, which depicts the fate of Israel.

Isaiah on Assyria

Despite such ambiguity, the book of Isaiah holds some clear positions about Assyria and its role vis-à-vis Judah and Jerusalem. First, the threat by Assyria was divinely authorized. Isaiah deems the Assyrians to be Yahweh's instrument; they are not an independent political force. Yahweh is the one who "raises a signal for a nation far away" (5:26).

Second, though Assryia is not named explicitly in 9:8–21, Israel was destroyed by enemy troops; and we know that the troops were the Assyrians. Third, Isaiah focuses on certain moments, which may be associated with two Neo-Assyrian emperors, Tiglath-pileser III and Sennacherib. During Tiglath-pileser's reign, Israel was destroyed. Sennacherib was the emperor who attacked Jerusalem but whose siege stalled. To be sure, the history of the Neo-Assyrian Empire's activity in Syria-Palestine involved more than these two campaigns. For example, a reinvigorated Egypt encouraged Judah to break away from Assyrian vassalhood (see chaps. 18–20). Nonetheless, the book highlights the work of these Assyrian kings as of special significance for Judah. Fourth, even though Assyria was Yahweh's instrument, it acted in so malicious a way that it too would be punished. Yahweh asks of his agent, the Assyrian king, "Shall the ax vaunt itself over the one who wields it, or the saw magnify itself against the one who handles it?" (10:15). This rhetorical question—to which the obvious answer is no—yields to an oracle in which the true Sovereign, Israel's God, promises that the Assyrian troops will be destroyed by "a wasting sickness" (10:16). The divine response is made even more clear later in the book: "When you have ceased to destroy, you will be destroyed" (33:1).[4] This sentence upon Assyria seems to be more a function of Sennacherib's assault on Judah than it does Tiglath-pileser's destruction of Israel. Isaiah's loyalty to the southern kingdom may be reflected in these judgments.

Sennacherib's Assault

The book of Isaiah involves one very complex historical question related to the Assyrians. How many times did Sennacherib launch a major assault against Jerusalem? This historical issue has direct theological implications. It is possible to read Isa. 36:1–37:7 as if it reflects one attack, and then 37:7–38 as if it reflects another. Or one may maintain that these two texts reflect different traditions about one attack. If two attacks occurred, the first took place in 701 whereas the second would have transpired in 688, when, on other grounds, one may claim that Sennacherib campaigned again in Syria-Palestine. The Deuteronomistic History reports, regarding the siege of 701, that "the king of Assyria demanded of King Hezekiah of Judah three hundred talents of silver and thirty talents of gold" (2 Kgs. 18:14), which Hezekiah paid. This does not seem to square well with the miraculous reprieve reported in Isa. 37:36. One might postulate therefore that in the earlier campaign—if there were two campaigns—Sennacherib forced Judah to give up some of its wealth.

The historical ambiguity remains before us,[5] and it affects the way we read the book of Isaiah. On the one hand, Isaiah seems to think that Assyria will indeed attack and decimate Jerusalem.

> Your men shall fall by the sword
>   and your warriors in battle.
> And her [Jerusalem's] gates shall lament and mourn;
>   ravaged, she shall sit upon the ground.
> (3:25–26; cf. 29:1–4; 31:4)

On the other hand, some texts appear to reflect a belief that Jerusalem will be spared in a military attack.[6]

> The LORD of hosts will come down
>   to fight upon Mount Zion and upon its hill.
> Like birds hovering overhead, so the LORD of hosts
>   will protect Jerusalem;
> he will protect and deliver it,
> he will spare and rescue it.
> (31:4b–5)

If there were two attacks, the first text might reflect Isaiah's perceptions of what was happening in 701 and the second what transpired circa 688. If there were only one attack—the more widely held view—Isaiah's views about the nature of an Assyrian (or any military) assault against Jerusalem become more intriguing, presumably that Jerusalem would suffer a dire threat but would learn from it and be rescued. Our perceptions about Isaiah's theological interpretation of Judah's history depend upon our understanding of that history.

The book of Isaiah knows Assyria both as Yahweh's agent and as a dire enemy. Israel was destroyed by Tiglath-pileser. Judah was assaulted by Sennacherib. Isaiah was convinced Yahweh wanted to protect Judah but also that, should Judah not act on the basis of that divine protection, the people would suffer mightily.

Earlier in this section devoted to the Neo-Assyrian challenge we observed the presence of ambiguity. We need to conclude on such a note. The fate of Jerusalem itself is, in the book of Isaiah, unclear. On the one hand, it is the city in which the deity is present through temple and ritual. On the other hand, it is a city against which the deity may bring enemy troops. Such ambiguity is resolved in the next historical period reflected in the book.

The Threat from Babylon

Most introductions to the book of Isaiah focus on the historical periods that we have just examined, and for good reason. Isaiah ben Amoz probably died sometime early in the seventh century B.C.E. However, the book continued to grow after his death, such that attention to periods after his own life and work are necessary.

Prominent though Assyria was for Isaiah ben Amoz, Babylon is the truly villainous nation from the perspective of the book as a whole. Where and how we do find the book addressing Babylon? The first question is easier to answer than the second, since the second involves the complex history of Babylon and its relation to Judah.

As one of the two primary Mesopotamian powers, Babylon was always competing with Assyria. During Isaiah ben Amoz's lifetime, Assyria had dominated Babylon. Sennacherib attacked Babylon in 703, finally defeating that city in 689. But the end of the seventh century saw a resurgence of the Babylonians, such that they (and the Medes) defeated Nineveh, a major Assyrian city, in 612. Soon thereafter, Babylon, under Nebuchadnezzar, was able to control Syria-Palestine, defeating Judah in 587. Then, within a matter of decades, Babylon was defeated again (though not razed) by the Persian emperor, Cyrus (in 539). Both defeats of Babylon—in 698 by the Neo-Assyrians and in 539 by the Persians—fall within the purview of the book of Isaiah. So we again confront ambiguity whenever the book offers a threat to that city and nation. Between its two defeats, Babylon posed a constant threat to Judah and Jerusalem, which is reflected in the book of Isaiah.

References to Babylon occur in three places: the oracles against the nations (13:1–14:23), the prose accounts in chapters 36–39, and the poetry of chapters 40–55. The texts are quite different.

1. *Oracles against the nations (Isa. 13:1–14:23).* Isaiah's oracles against the nations (chaps. 13–23 and perhaps 24–27) commence with literature concerning Babylon.[7] The formulaic 13:1 introduces a poem announcing universal destruction as a part of "the day of the LORD." Only late in the poem (vv. 19–22) does Babylon figure in.

> And Babylon, the glory of kingdoms,
>   the splendor and pride of the Chaldeans,
> will be like Sodom and Gomorrah
>   when God overthrew them.
> It will never be inhabited
>   or lived in for all generations.
>   (13:19–20a)

The severity of the critique probably makes more sense when directed at the Babylon that destroyed Judah rather than the Babylon that opposed Hezekiah. The same may be said for the Babylon of chapter 14. Here the remarkable poem (vv. 4b–21) never mentions Babylon (the noun only occurs in the surrounding prose of vv. 4 and 22).

> How you are fallen from heaven,
>   O Day Star, son of Dawn!
> How you are cut down to the ground,
>   you who laid the nations low!
> You said in your heart,
> "I will ascend to heaven. . . .
>   I will make myself like the Most High."
> But you are brought down to Sheol,
>   to the depths of the Pit.
>   (14:12–15)

The cosmic imagery seems appropriate to depict the enemy that removed Judah from the map of ancient Near Eastern nations. Finally, the last reference to Babylon in the oracles against the nations (21:9) also refers to a defeated nation, a destruction more like the one in 698 than the one in 539.

2. *Isaiah 39.* This second text that alludes to Babylon is pivotal. Standing between the literature attesting Isaiah ben Amoz (much of chaps. 1–38) and that of a later prophet, namely, the author(s) of chapters 40–55, chapter 39 provides an account of Hezekiah's response to envoys from Babylon. Although the exact purpose of the envoys' visit is unclear—the more so since the Babylonian king (Merodach-Baladan) ruled for two different periods in the second half of the eighth century—Isaiah criticizes Hezekiah for revealing too much about Judah to them: "Days are coming when all that is in your house, and that which your ancestors have stored up until this day, shall be carried to Babylon; nothing shall be left" (39:6). It is difficult to hear these words and not think about the devastation that the Babylonians under Nebuchadnezzar wrought on Judah in 587. The book testifies that the interactions between Hezekiah and Merodach-Baladan will manifest themselves over a century later when two other kings are on the throne: Nebuchadnezzar and Zedekiah.

Babylon figures prominently at the end of these prose accounts that had initially focused on the threat posed by Assyria. However, the authors or editors have created a chapter that encourages the reader to think about a new nation, Babylon, and what it will mean for Judah.

3. *Isaiah 40–48*. The book of Isaiah affirms that the threat of Babylon will be surmounted, though only after the destruction of Judah and Jerusalem. Chapters 43, 47, and 48 refer to Babylon, with 47:1–15 offering the most important poem. Chapter 47 sounds as if it might belong in Isaiah's oracles against the nations, but it is of a piece with the poetry in this part of the book. The prophet indicts Babylon for the sin of pride. Personified as "virgin Babylon," she says, "I am, and there is no one besides me" (47:10). Yahweh charges Babylon with the indictment of overkill: "I gave them [Judah] into your hand, you showed them no mercy" (47:6). And, of course, Yahweh's new agent to punish Babylon (who will "strip kings of their robes" [45:1]) is the king of yet another ancient Near Eastern power—Cyrus the Persian.

Cyrus, Yahweh's Messiah

The face of the ancient Near East changed significantly during the sixth century B.C.E. Prior to this time, the powers of Mesopotamia had taken turns exercising the superior hand, both in Mesopotamia and in Syria-Palestine. This pattern ceased with the powerful appearance of a non-Semitic culture, the Persians. Led by Cyrus, the Persians conquered all of Mesopotamia, entering Babylon in 539. Soon thereafter, they held sway over Syria-Palestine as well. It suited the Persians to permit the reconstitution of those territories. To wit, a document known as the Cyrus edict was promulgated, one version of which is attested in Ezra 1:2–4. This royal decree permitted those who had been taken into exile to return to their homeland. As well, it mandated the reconstruction of the temple in Jerusalem, which had been destroyed by the Neo-Babylonians.

> Thus says King Cyrus of Persia: The LORD, the God of heaven, has given me all the kingdoms of the earth, and he has charged me to build him a house at Jerusalem in Judah. Any of those among you who are of his people . . . are now permitted to go up to Jerusalem in Judah, and rebuild the house of the LORD. (Ezra 1:2–3)

The book of Isaiah seems to know this mandate concerning the reconstruction of the temple:

> Thus says the LORD, your Redeemer,
>   who formed you in the womb:
> I am the LORD . . .
> who says of Cyrus, "He is my shepherd,
>   and he shall carry out all my purpose";

> and who says of Jerusalem, "It shall be rebuilt,"
>   and of the temple, "Your foundation shall be laid."
>   (Isa. 44:24, 28)

Just as the book of Isaiah had recognized earlier that Neo-Assyrian kings were instruments of God's activity, now Cyrus fills that role. He is described not only as "shepherd," a traditional symbol for kings throughout the ancient Near East, but also as Yahweh's anointed, or his "messiah." (The noun *messiah* means someone who has been anointed with oil; a king was normally anointed when the act of coronation took place.)

Parts of the book of Isaiah may thus be read in light of Cyrus's permission to let people leave the land of their exile and return to Judah. And, consistent with the edict, they are not simply returning to the land but going back to enable the re-creation of the temple and its rituals:

> Depart, depart, go out from there!
>   Touch no unclean thing;
> go out from the midst of it, purify yourselves,
>   you who carry the vessels of the LORD.
>   (Isa. 52:11)

Much in Isaiah 40–55 reflects the time just as Cyrus was defeating the Mesopotamian powers. The concrete realities of a rebuilt Jerusalem lay in the future, and these chapters offer ebullient rhetoric about the nature of that reconstituted city.

> I am about to set your stones in antimony,
>   and lay your foundations with sapphires.
> I will make your pinnacles of rubies
>   your gates of jewels,
>   and all your wall of precious stones.
>   (54:11–12)

This is truly an expectation about a city in which the streets would, as it were, be paved with gold.

Since these chapters know about Cyrus, seem to refer to Babylon about to fall, reflect certain aspects of the Cyrus edict, and do not know about the difficult realities that those who returned faced, we may situate this literature in the general period of 550–530.

Life in the Rebuilt Jerusalem

Although Cyrus ordered the rebuilding of the temple, work on that project foundered. The books of Ezra, Haggai, and Zechariah attest to this period. There were probably multiple reasons that the temple was not rebuilt immediately—few Yahwists may have returned, those who did may have faced opposition, financial resources for such work were limited. Nonetheless, due to the work of both Yahwists (e.g., the prophet Haggai) and Persians (especially Darius; see Ezra 6:1–12 [another imperial decree]), the temple was indeed rebuilt. The rededication ceremony took place in 515, a date that inaugurates the so-called Second Temple period.

Isaiah 56–66 probably derives from early in Darius's reign (522–486). If, from the perspective of Yahwists, the rebuilding and rededication of the temple was the significant moment during these years, then chapters 56–66 appear to surround that event. On the one hand, Isa. 66:1 seems to reflect a time before the temple has been rededicated ("what is the house that you would build for me?"). On the other hand, the references to sacrifices, burnt offerings, and the altar (56:7) suggest that the book seems to know the reconstituted temple ritual.

These chapters anticipate but do not reflect directly the issues addressed in Ezra-Nehemiah, especially the question of who may be counted among God's people. Isaiah 56:1–8 offers a strikingly inclusive position—one open to eunuchs and foreigners in particular ("my house shall be called a house of prayer for all peoples" [56:7]). In contrast, Ezra's emphasis on "the congregation of the exiles" (those Yahwists who had returned from exile in contrast to those Yahwists who remained in the land) and his demand that "foreign wives" be divorced from their Yahwistic spouses move in a different direction. Nonetheless, Isaiah 56–66 does not appear to know the acrimonious confrontations that took place between Israel's neighbors in the fifth century and those Yahwists who were rebuilding Jerusalem's walls. One may therefore safely infer that this book achieved much of its final form in the late sixth or early fifth century.

In sum, the book of Isaiah extends through much of Israel's history— not as much as the Book of the Twelve, but still over two hundred years. It covers the history of Yahwists during three imperial periods: Neo-Assyrian, Neo-Babylonian, and Persian. These years saw the decimation of the northern kingdom, the defeat of the southern kingdom, life in exile, and the early rebuilding of Judah and Jerusalem. Still, as we shall see later in this chapter, there are some important ways in which the book achieves a coherent perspective, despite the various hands that produced it.

LITERARY STRUCTURE AND FEATURES

The task of analyzing the literary elements and structure of Isaiah is more daunting than it is for either Jeremiah or Ezekiel. To be sure, Isaiah is a longer book, but the breadth of time during which it was composed adds to the complexity.

Literary Structure

At the outset, it is important to affirm that the division of the book into First, Second, and Third Isaiah no longer suffices as a means for understanding the structure of the book. That model permitted a division of the book into further segments, such as those in the following schema: 1–12 (oracles and narratives involving Isaiah ben Amoz), 13–23 (oracles against the nations), 24–27 (Isaianic apocalypse), 28–32 (oracles involving Isaiah ben Amoz), 33–34 (prologue to Second Isaiah), 36–39 (historical narratives), 40–55 (Second Isaiah), 56–66 (Third Isaiah). That way of classifying the book's content was useful, up to a point. For example, it made clear that the book included vastly different kinds of material. However, that classification did not point to a structure for the book as whole, a structure that some author or editor intended. The most that could be said was that the book was a compilation of earlier collections.

The search to discern structure in the book of Isaiah continues. Two models for understanding the book are now emerging. One model focuses on the book, the other on the role of Isaiah ben Amoz within the book. As for the former, scholars have noted that chapters 1 and (65–) 66 function as an envelope for the book. For example, Clements has maintained that the initial chapters of the book (1–4) share some important features with chapters 56–66, especially 63–66.[8] Both at the beginning and at the end of the book, we find indictments of injustice and a critique of ritual behavior (1:10–17 // 66:1–3). These chapters also attest to the glorification of Jerusalem along with the pilgrimage of nations to it. The clear implication is that some editor intended these chapters to frame the book.

Inside that book are a number of prior collections (e.g., prose accounts or series of woe oracles). These have been integrated into larger sections à la the earlier consensus. However, other chapters are transitional, and much of that material bears the marks of liturgy (chaps. 12; 33; 34–35; 55). Recent monographs and commentaries have stressed that the book grew and that specific moments after the time of Isaiah ben Amoz were of special importance. These include the Josianic reform, the appearance of Cyrus, the rebuilding of the Second Temple, and the time of Ezra-Nehemiah.[9] This redaction-critical perspective permits one to view the book as made up of a series of increasingly larger compositions that have been integrated by major transitional pieces.

Further, though later additions are present throughout the book, the book itself proceeds in something of a rough historical progression.

The greatest unevenness occurs in the middle chapters, especially 33–35. It is here—though the precise dividing point is difficult to discern—that a major change in the book takes place. One might say that the book changes either in chapter 33, between chapters 33 and 34, or between chapters 34 and 35. Chapters 34–35 cohere, with 34 offering words of woe and 35 containing words of weal. Chapter 33, by contrast, is something of a miscellany, in which Yahweh announces, "Now I will arise . . . now I will lift myself up, now I will be exalted" (v. 10). This statement recalls a similar announcement in Joel, attesting that Yahweh will now respond to the plight of his people (Joel 2:18–20). Chapter 33 breathes the air of the first part of the book, anticipating "the king in his beauty" (v. 17), whereas chapters 34–35 belong more to the rhetoric of the succeeding chapters, with language such as "strengthen the weak hands" (35:3), "a highway shall be there" (35:8), "the wilderness and the dry land shall be glad" (35:1). It is as if the book contains two transitional moments, one oriented to chapters 2–32 and another oriented to chapters 36–66. As with the two stories of creation in Genesis (1:1–2:4a; 2:4b–24), the reader is provided with several perspectives on how it is that the deity will act with Israel at a critical time. In Isaiah, that moment provides salvation for "the valiant in the streets" (Isa. 33:7) and/or "the ransomed of the LORD" (35:10).

If it is correct to think about Isaiah 33–35 as offering a complicated turning point, then the book itself becomes a grand diptych.[10] (A diptych is an altarpiece or work of art made up of two panels and joined by a hinge.) The first part, chapters 1–32, focuses on the travails of Zion—its sin, punishment, polity, and relation to other nations. The second part, chapters 36–66, continues with concern for Zion but in new ways, personifying the city as a person. Moreover, there is a historical move, with overt concern for a time beyond that of the Assyrian Empire. Babylon and the new messiah, Cyrus, achieve pride of place. In attempting to understand the book's structure, one should not look for a plot, but instead invest effort in comparing the complicated panels that make up each side of the diptych and, as well, focus on the major (chaps. 33; 34–35) and minor (chaps. 12; 55) points of transition in the book. Both redaction and literary criticism have important and appropriate roles in this endeavor.

A second model devotes attention to the role of Isaiah ben Amoz. Here, too, scholars have discerned a major point of transition—a strong demarcation between chapters 39 and 40. This view, consistent with the earlier consensus, is represented, though in different ways, by the recent commentaries of Childs and Tucker. Childs writes, "The sharp break between the collection of oracles in which the person of the eighth-century prophet is foundational for the tradition ends in chapter 39. Beginning with chapter 40, the message of the book functions in a different fashion apart from any role for the historical figure of Isaiah."[11] Tucker's work pushes in the same direction: "[T]here can be little doubt that the most distinctive break falls between chaps. 39–40. Isaiah 1–39 is not an arbitrary unit. Although some parts of the first half are similar to chaps. 40–55 (chap. 35 in particular), the shift beginning with chap. 40 is dramatic in terms of style, historical horizon, and message."[12] That which God had done through and with Isaiah ben Amoz constituted the early part of the deity's plan. Much of what appears throughout chapters 2–11 and 28–32, as well as portions of the oracles concerning the nations (14:24–27), attest to this stage of Yahweh's "plan that is planned concerning the whole earth." However, elements of that plan are, in chapters 40–56, construed as "former things . . . the things of old" (43:18). Those chapters that follow Isaiah 39 attest to the new thing that Yahweh is doing. Since both the former things and the new things belong to God's intentions, the book testifies to the deity's sovereignty over all history.

It is too early to know which of these models will prevail, or whether a new and more compelling one will appear. Still, both models attest to a twofold structure in the book. Readers can therefore test the alternative hypotheses for themselves to see which offers a more compelling vantage point from which to read the book.

Literary Features

This grand diptych of Isaiah is made up of many forms of speech. As we shall see, there is less homogeneity than is the case in the other two major prophetic books. Moreover, there are many instances in which the formal features of Isaiah's speech are shared with one or another of the components that make up the Book of the Twelve, particularly Amos and Micah, the latter of whom was a contemporary of Isaiah ben Amoz. Thereafter, we will examine the prose accounts, which depict the prophet in a unique way, more like a Hosea or Elijah than his southern compatriots.

Poetic Speech

Simply to offer an inventory of the poetic speeches that occur in Isaiah would demonstrate the remarkable variety present in the book. In what follows, I attempt to identify three significant forms of discourse in the book: polemical, promise, and liturgical, though such a classification cannot easily encompass all the poetic literature in the book.

Polemical Discourse[13]

Like other prophetic literature (e.g., Amos, Micah) the book of Isaiah includes many speeches that challenge, indict, and judge various entities. Scholars have regularly contended that such discourse derives from the legal processes of ancient Israel. That certainly may be the case. However, the origins of such discourse are not so much our concern here as is the need to appreciate the various types of polemical discourse that occur in the book. For the purposes of such analysis, I would identify six types of polemical discourse in the book: lawsuit, trial speech, judgment oracle, woe oracle, disputation, and exhortation.

Lawsuit. The Hebrew noun *rîb* has often been understood to mean court proceeding or lawsuit. Hence, scholars often think that those speeches in which this term appears—or texts that share similar rhetoric—should be termed lawsuits. One may discern several such speeches early on in the book. Isaiah 3:13–15 introduces the noun *rîb* in the very first colon: "Yahweh rises to argue a *rîb*" (or "case"). Here the deity appears to function as prosecuting attorney, offering an indictment against multiple parties for having made the condition of the poor worse than it had been before. Yahweh challenges the defendants with a question—"What do you mean . . . ?"—but there is no answer. This prophetic saying is less interested in offering a judgment than it is in challenging the people to reflect upon their misdeeds. Isaiah 1:2–3, which is normally viewed as a lawsuit even though the term *rîb* does not appear, presents the deity appealing to elements in the natural order: "Hear, O heavens, and listen, O earth." They are part of the jury who hears the testimony of the trial, which results in a judgment that the people lack knowledge. Isaiah 1:18–20 belongs here as well: "Come let us argue it out!" Finally, Isa. 5:1–7, though often termed a "love song" (see v. 1), really involves a legal process of judgment: "And now, inhabitants of Jerusalem and people of Judah, judge between me and my vineyard" (v. 3). Unlike some of the other texts termed lawsuits, Isa. 5:1–7 proceeds to the pronouncement of a sentence, which is uttered by the deity (vv. 5–7). One very interesting feature of Isaiah's lawsuits is that the deity can enact multiple roles, functioning as prosecutor, judge, and executioner!

Trial speech. Later in the book, particularly in chapters 40–48, the language that might derive from a trial between Yahweh and another party reemerges. These trial speeches involve two different trials, one between Yahweh and Israel, the other between Yahweh and other nations. Isaiah 43:22–28 and 50:1–3 attest the trial alluded to in the earlier lawsuits, namely, between Yahweh and his own people. In Isaiah 43, the legal imagery is overt. Yahweh challenges the people: "Accuse me, let us go to trial; set forth your case, so that you may be proved right" (v. 26). Earlier in the speech he offered an indictment: The people had presented him with sins, not proper offerings. And he alludes to a judgment that has already occurred: "I profaned the princes of the sanctuary [i.e., the priests]." In 50:1–3 there appears to be the sort of interrogation that would belong in a courtroom. Again, as with chapter 43, the poet alludes to a judgment that has already taken place: "because of your sins you were sold." The historical origins of these trial speeches betray themselves. Whereas the lawsuit anticipated a time of judgment, the two trial speeches between Yahweh and Isaiah reflect a time after judgment has been passed. However, polemical discourse is still in order to help the audience understand what has happened.

Isaiah 40–48 includes a striking number of trial speeches against foreign nations. These are quite different from the block of speeches in chapters 13–23, the oracles against the nations. The clearest instances of litigation against other nations occur in 41:1–7, 21–29; 43:8–13; 44:6–8. Isaiah 41:1–7 offers pointed questions to distant peoples ("O coastlands"). The questions ask about the identity of the one who "roused a victor from the east," surely a reference to Cyrus, and who has even "called the generations from the beginning." The author, portraying the deity in the first person, offers an answer: "I, Yahweh, am first and will be the last." Through the interrogation, the trial has adduced evidence sustaining the power of Yahweh to the ends of the earth.

The rhetoric of Isa. 41:22–29 is more pointed. Instead of presenting questions, the deity offers pointed challenges: "Tell us the former things. . . . Tell us what is to come." Not just the nations, but their gods are in the dock. And here too there is a sentence: "You, indeed, are nothing."

Isaiah 43:8–9 is very similar in tone to 41:22–29. Other nations are challenged to appear in the courtroom. What is new, however, is Yahweh's claim to have his own set of witnesses. "You are my witnesses," he says to the people. It is not too much to say that this trial speech has as one of its goals the proof of Yahweh's divinity ("I am God!"). Though these trial speeches convey a fictive world in which the world's peoples appear in a courtroom, the discourse appears designed for the ears of Yahweh's own people, the "witnesses," who, through this lens of legal imagery, learn about the power and purpose of their deity along with what that power can do for them. The challenging questions are, in this courtroom, addressed to the ends of the earth, but questions such as "Is there any god besides me?" are also intended for Israel to contemplate.

Judgment oracle. The judgment oracle, another form of structured speech that has been traced to the law court, is more of a summary of the legal proceeding than a record of the process. This form, which is particularly prominent in books such as Amos (e.g., chaps. 1–2), is less significant in Isaiah. Interestingly, judgment oracles are more frequent in the middle portion of the book rather than in the earlier chapters. Isaiah 28:14–22; 29:13–14; and 30:12–14 offer some of the clearest examples. Isaiah 29:13–14 exemplifies the bipartite structure of the judgment oracle, which normally offers an indictment or accusation followed by a sentence or punishment. In this particular oracle, Yahweh speaks *about* the people, not *to* them. He indicts them for worship that is not genuine and then reports that he will cause wisdom to vanish from among them. In the next chapter, one may find a judgment oracle (30:12–14) embedded in a larger composition (30:8–17). The formulaic introduction is longer, but the overall structure remains the same. Now God addresses the people directly. He indicts them for not attending to "this word," the true word that the prophets proclaimed, and instead trusting in deceit. The indictment takes up no more than one verse, whereas the sentence extends for two long ones. And it is replete with similes. Yahweh's judgment will be "like a break in a high wall, like the breaking of a potter's vessel" (vv. 13–14). Finally, Isa. 28:14–22 offers another indictment and sentence directed at the people. Here the rulers of Jerusalem are quoted as having made "a covenant with death." Thereafter, the oracle goes on to describe the deity's response to such idiocy (vv. 16–22). Though not all the imagery is clear, the final verse summarizes the point well: "for I [Isaiah] have heard a decree of destruction from the Lord GOD of hosts upon the whole land."

The judgment oracle represents a move within the polemical genres to a point at which the legal proceeding has been completed. Something is being announced; the sentence is being passed. And in this legal setting, there is no court of appeal. Yahweh decrees the fate of the party that has been indicted, whether it is the people of Israel, Judah, or a foreign country. (Many of the oracles against foreign nations offer just the sentence [e.g., the oracle about the fate of Egypt in 19:1–10]).

Woe oracle. The woe oracle plays a prominent role in Isaiah. The woe oracle bears the same basic structure as the judgment oracle but is introduced by a special word, *hoy,* which is translated variously in the book: "Ah" (1:4; 33:1), "Ha" (29:15), "Oh" (30:1), "Alas" (31:1), "Woe" (45:9), "Ho" (55:1). Its earliest meaning involved the call to lament when someone died. Hence, the basic grammar of the opening of a lament statement is a woe, followed by someone's name. This form of speaking was taken over by the prophets and applied not only to individuals but also to groups. If an oracle began with a woe, then the prophet seemed to be saying that someone or some group was as good as dead. The phrase containing "woe" foreshadowed the dire sentence that was to come at the end of a woe oracle. The book of Isaiah includes many woe oracles, some even in little collections (5:8–24; 10:1–11; those in chaps. 28–33 are not bound together).

The woe oracles replicate the same twofold structure of the judgment oracle. Immediately after the introductory formulae—woe + x—one regularly hears the language of indictment. If one were interested in knowing what the prophet thought was wrong in his own time, this is the place to look. Isaiah 5:22–23 offers a classic case:

> Ah, you who are heroes in drinking wine
> and valiant at mixing drink,
> who acquit the guilty for a bribe,
> and deprive the innocent of their rights!

Isaiah 10:1–2 offers a similar challenge:

> Ah, you who make iniquitous decrees,
> who write oppressive statutes,
> to turn aside the needy from justice
> and to rob the poor of my people of their right,
> that widows may be your spoil,
> and that you may make the orphans your prey!

One hears a prophet observing behavior in Jerusalem, the seat of government, a city in which political rulings are made by those in power. And one hears a defense of those who, by comparison, have minimal power, namely, the innocent, the poor, and the orphan.[14]

The rhetoric of woe appears in the latter chapters of the book as well. But here it seems to function differently. Now the language of woe (45:9–10) is addressed to those who challenge the authority of the deity and those who are unable to find appropriate sustenance (55:1).

The second part of the woe oracle either offers the expected sentence or challenges those addressed to reflect upon the behaviors described in the first portion of the speech. After observing that some Judahites harbor a secret plan, the prophet asks a series of probing questions

(29:16). After observing that Judahites seek help from the Egyptians, Isaiah reports that "shame and disgrace" will result (30:5). More typical are the elements in Isaiah 5, particularly those sections introduced by "therefore" (5:14–17, 24, 25). Here the language of death and destruction is more prominent:

> Therefore, Sheol has enlarged its appetite
>   and opened its mouth beyond measure;
> the nobility of Jerusalem and her multitude go down,
>   her throng and all who exult in her.
>   (5:14)

? Marduk

This verse reflects an image, known from Northwest Semitic mythology, according to which Death (Mot) can open his mouth with lips touching heaven and earth. No one could escape. In this case, however, Sheol, the land of the dead, is subservient to Yahweh.

As with other polemical genres, the woe oracles can serve multiple purposes, offering specific charges against identifiable groups, challenging those people to think about their behaviors, and offering sentences based on those behaviors. Though there is a basic form for the woe oracle, it can be deployed in multiple ways.

Disputation. Isaiah 40–55 includes a genre of literature that is similar to the legal forms but may reflect influence of the wisdom school. The form is flexible, often giving voice to only one party in an argument. Basic to the form, however, is one position that is identified and is then challenged by another. The rhetoric often attempts to seek common ground between those engaged in a controversy, with the goal of convincing the listener or reader, even if not the party engaged in the dispute. The form appears earlier in the book (8:16–23; 10:8–11; 28:23–29). In each text, it is clear that there is a party—those who consult ghosts, the personified Assyria, and those told to pay attention, respectively—whose views are challenged.

Apart from those earlier exemplars, a number of scholars agree that the following texts may be classified as disputations: 40:12–31 (in which there may be several disputations); 44:24–28; 45:9–13; 46:5–11; 48:1–11. Of these, the speeches in chapter 40 are typical. Questions are very prominent. At the outset (vv. 12–14), the prophet offers a number of rhetorical questions, the answers for which are as obvious as were those for the questions God asked Job (Job 38–41). And the rhetoric seems similar. The obvious answers attest to the power and unsurpassed knowledge of the deity. As the chapter progresses, we learn that some group, the "you" (plural), is being addressed: "To whom then will you liken God?" (v. 18); "Have you not known?" (vv. 21, 28). Only in the final section of the poem do we learn the identity of this collectivity; it is none other than Jacob (v. 27), who is then quoted: "My way is hidden from the LORD, and my right is disregarded by my God." Here is the nub of the matter: The deity is interested in dissuading the people from saying such things. Yahweh does this by asking a series of penetrating questions and by offering a list of theological affirmations:

> The LORD is the everlasting God,
> the Creator of the ends of the earth.
> He does not faint or grow weary;
> his understanding is unsearchable.
> He gives power to the faint,
> and strengthens the powerless.
> (40:28–29)

The disputation works in such a fashion that if the people answer the questions for themselves and if they give assent to these characterizations of the deity, then they will "know" and no longer say what they are quoted as having said. Clearly the goal of these disputations is to change people's minds, not to indict and sentence them for what they are thinking and/or saying. The genre, though still in the realm of the polemical, rarely, if ever, stops with a legal judgment.

Exhortation. The final example of a polemical genre is comparable to the disputation in that it seems interested in seeking a change in behavior and not primarily in what one thinks, as does the disputation. One hallmark of exhortations is the presence of imperative verbs. Such discourse may be found scattered throughout the book. It occurs early, in the first chapter:

> Wash yourselves; make yourselves clean;
> remove the evil of your doings
> from before my eyes;
> cease to do evil;
> learn to do good;
> seek justice,
> rescue the oppressed,
> defend the orphan,
> plead for the widow.
> (1:16–17)

After reading this speech, one hears echoes of other polemical genres. Acting badly toward the orphan and the oppressed occurs within the indictments of the woe oracles, and the positive tone of encouragement is shared by the disputation. It is as if the authors are wrestling with several basic issues but using various forms of literature to gain rhetorical purchase of one sort or another. It would, therefore, be a fundamental error to claim that the polemical or legal genres have as their essential goal the offering of a judgment. Rather, due to the tonalities of each form—from the death knell of a woe oracle to the encouragement of the exhortation—this set of poetic speech forms permits authors to work a broad set of variations on important themes.

The Discourse of Promise

The book of Isaiah includes a great many poems offering weal to Israel. Some of this poetry, particularly as found in chapters 1–39, has often been judged "non-Isaianic." Further, this poetry is often more difficult to categorize from a form-critical perspective than is that involving the polemical genres. Nonetheless, this discourse of promise is important for the overall configuration of the book. Though one might have supposed, based on the various historical contexts that lie behind the book, that the language of promise might be more prominent in chapters 40–55, it is very significant in earlier sections as well. As with the polemical discourse, one may discern several types of poetic utterance: poems concerning Zion, royal poems, oracles of salvation, promise of salvation, and a few miscellaneous compositions.

Poems concerning Zion. This is not a category for which one may identify a particular structure. Rather, Zion is featured in a number of poems throughout the book, and they are of such importance that to treat them as a set helps us understand some of the basis for Isaiah's language of weal. Gerhard von Rad observed that a number of these texts (primarily poetry) in chapters 1–39 (10:27b–34; 14:28–33; 17:12–14; 29:1–8; 30:27–33; 31:1–8) share some essential features.[15] One might even speak of a scenario in which an enemy assaults Jerusalem. Isaiah 10:27b–34 attests the route of march. An enemy appears to attack, even as a part of the deity's plan (29:1–4). However, such an attack will ultimately fail:

> The nations roar like the roaring of many waters,
>   but he will rebuke them, and they will flee far away,
> chased like chaff on the mountains before the wind
>   and whirling dust before the storm.
> At evening time, lo, terror!
> Before morning, they are no more.
>   (17:13–14a)

Though Yahweh may permit an assault, he will ultimately protect the place of his dwelling (31:5). Whether one characterizes this as a tradition about Zion, part of the national mythology, or even something embedded in the Northwest Semitic mindset about the dwelling place of a deity, this notion of Zion/Jerusalem as a place of safety is of major importance.

The book is, however, decidedly aware that Jerusalem was decimated. Moreover, Zion plays a prominent role in the poetry that was written after that destruction. However, there is a major change in the way in which the book treats Zion. Rather than a place, it now becomes a person. Zion the city is personified as a woman.

Zion speaks, as she does in the book of Lamentations, grieving over that which has happened to her.

> But Zion said, "The LORD has forsaken me,
> my Lord has forgotten me."
> (Isa. 49:14)

Yahweh immediately responds:

> Can a woman forget her nursing child,
>   or show no compassion for the child of her womb?
> Even these may forget,
>   yet I will not forget you.
> (49:15)

As a result, good news is promised to Zion:

> For the LORD will comfort Zion;
>   he will comfort all her waste places,
> and will make her wilderness like Eden.
> (51:3)

Here we see the language of geography making its way back into reflections about Zion, such that in the final chapters of the book, Zion becomes solidly both place and person (60:14; 62:1–12). In the rhetorical turn from Zion as place to Zion as person, the book is able to accommodate a continuing concern for Zion, as a woman who laments her plight. Personification and the discourse of lamentation—which always includes the potential for a response to the lament by the deity—help the Zion tradition move beyond the defeat of 587.

Royal poems. Content rather than form is of primary importance in identifying several poems that deal with the royal figure. There are two such poems in the early chapters: 9:2–7 and 11:1–9. Both reflect the ideals that Israel held for its monarch and both reflect a theology according to which the king is related to the deity in a filial manner. A member of the Davidic line who became a king was understood to be adopted by Yahweh on the day of his coronation, as in Ps. 2:7. Isaiah 9:2–7 reflects this same sentiment, though the speakers appear to be the members of the divine council (and not the people of Judah). The people are described in verse 2 as having lived in desperate straits. Moreover, the speakers note that "you" (v. 3), surely the deity, have broken the rod of the Judahite's oppressors (v. 4). Moreover, a son has been born, that is, a king has been crowned. Endless peace, justice, and righteousness will result from his reign. Isaiah 11:1–9 offers a very similar perspective, though emphasizing explicitly that such a king belongs to the Davidic dynasty ("from the stump of Jesse"). Here the king is "inspired" by the spirit of the deity. He will gain insight (v. 2) and judge appropriately (vv. 4–5), such that a reign of peace will ensue (vv. 6–9).

The historical background for these two poems is obscure. Some scholars have proposed that the first poem was written coincident with the coronation of Hezekiah. To be sure, the Deuteronomistic Historian assessed Hezekiah's reign in extraordinarily positive terms (2 Kgs. 18:5: "He trusted in the Lord the God of Israel; so that there was no one like him among all the kings of Judah after him, or among those who were before him."). However, the book of Isaiah itself attests to Hezekiah's foibles (chap. 39), which would lead to the nation's destruction at the hands of the Babylonians.

Oracles of salvation. This same attention to a "person" that we observed in the Zion poems also appears in oracles of salvation. A hallmark of these texts is the admonition "Do not fear," which was probably originally uttered by priests at the temple when responding to an individual who had sung a psalm of lament. In fact, these oracles of salvation in Isaiah are probably the missing piece in the psalmic literature of complaint. One may postulate that they enabled the individual to move from despair to hope, affirming that God had heard their prayer.

The following texts may be classified as oracles of salvation: 41:8–13, 14–16; 43:1–4, 5–7; 44:1–5; 54:1–8. In each, one finds the admonition "Do not fear," and the deity addresses an individual. In four of the six oracles, Jacob, who functions as a personification for all Israel, is that individual. In the last oracle, an unnamed female is addressed—no doubt the personified Zion whom the deity elsewhere calls by name.

The importance of naming this individual is underlined in the third and fourth oracles:

Do not fear, for I have redeemed you,
  I have called you by name, you are mine.
(43:1; cf. 43:7: "everyone who is called by my name")

This one will say "I am the LORD's,"
  another will be called by the name of Jacob.
(44:5)

It is as if when God tells an individual not to fear and calls that individual by name, the heart of the oracle of salvation has been created. For the deity to respond to someone by name is to set the stage for broadly redemptive words.

For I will pour water on the thirsty land,
  and streams on the dry ground;
I will pour my spirit upon your descendants
  and my blessing on your offspring.
They shall spring up like a green tamarisk,
  like willows by flowing streams.
(44:3–4)

Such language, redolent of fertility, is especially fitting when addressed to one of Israel's ancestors, since it was to those early progenitors that the blessing of progeny was initially made. The same issue of progeny is emphasized in the final oracle. Instead of Jacob, the deity addresses a barren woman, the unnamed Zion. Here too the poet no doubt alludes to that earlier time of barren women—the generations of Sarah and Rachel. Just as their wombs were opened, so too will Zion's.

For the children of the desolate woman will be more
  than the children of her that is married. . . .
For you will spread out to the right and to the left,
  and your descendants will possess the nations
  and will settle the desolate towns.
(54:1, 3)

The oracle of salvation, then, grows out of the world of lamentation. It is the deity's response to a call for help. The oracles are words spoken to individuals, often personified as Jacob, once as Zion, but they are truly words to all Israelites.

Promise of salvation. The promise of salvation focuses less on the one addressed and more on what Yahweh will be doing. There are many such poems of promise (41:17–20; 42:14–17; 43:16–21; 45:14–17;

46:12–13; 49:8–12; 51:1–8; 54:11–17). In fact, the first two promises do
not involve the language of direct address to another party but rather
announce that Yahweh will help "them." This strikes a note different
from the one in the oracles of salvation. The deity is now dealing with
the community as such, not just through a personified individual,
whether Jacob or Zion.

> I the LORD, will answer them,
>   I the God of Israel will not forsake them.
>   (41:17; see also 42:16)

When direct discourse does occur, it is set in the plural, a grammar that
emphasizes the communal character of the promises.

> Do not remember [plural verb] the former things,
>   or consider the things of old.
>   (43:18)

The prophetic poet now refers to the people as a whole to be the object
of the deity's promises:

> But Israel is saved by the LORD
>   with everlasting salvation;
> you [plural] shall not be put to shame or confounded
>   to all eternity.
>   (45:17)

In no clear case does the deity speak a promise of salvation to a named
individual. Zion does appear to be the feminine singular referent in
54:11–17, and a masculine singular verb is used in 49:8. But, particularly in 49:8–12, after the singular "you" has been addressed, the text
shifts to consider God's care of the prisoners. This plurality becomes
the subject of Yahweh's attention for the rest of the poem. And in the
former case (54:11–17), though Yahweh probably speaks to Zion, he is
promising to her that "great shall be the prosperity of your children"
(v. 13). Just as the oracle of salvation deploys language concerning the
individual, the promise of salvation works within communal language
and in various ways.

"*On that day.*" For the sake of completeness, I should note that there
are a number of brief poetic (e.g., 11:11–16; 17:4–6; 22:12–14) and
prose (e.g., 7:18–25; 10:20) texts introduced by a formulaic expression,
"on that day," and variant forms such as "at that time" or "in days to
come." This phrase appears elsewhere in prophetic books as a way to

introduce later, often eschatological, reflections, or simply as an editorial rubric (Zechariah 14). The literature associated with this phrase is less specifically Isaianic and seems rather to belong to a trove of prophetic poetry concerning future weal for Israel. For example, Isa. 2:2–4 is introduced by this formula, but it appears also in Mic. 4:1–3. Prophets were heirs to language of promise.

Promise and punishment. Isaiah is an unusual book in many ways. It includes a type of speech that rarely, if ever, appears elsewhere. Paul Hanson identifies what he terms a new genre, "the salvation-judgment" oracle, in Isaiah 56–66.[16] Poems such as Isa. 58:1–12; 59:1–20; 65:1–25; and 66:1–16 belong to a synthetic style of prophetic utterance that includes elements drawn from the judgment oracle and the promise of assurance. Isaiah 65:13–15 offers a wonderful example:

> Therefore thus says the Lord GOD:
> My servants shall eat,
>   but you shall be hungry;
> my servants shall drink,
>   but you shall be thirsty;
> my servants shall rejoice,
>   but you shall be put to shame;
> my servants shall sing for gladness of heart,
>   but you shall cry out for pain of heart,
>   and shall wail for anguish of spirit.
> You shall leave your name to my chosen to use as a curse,
>   and the Lord GOD will put you to death;
>   but to his servants he will give a different name.

Here, words of weal and words of woe are interwoven throughout one oracle, whereas in most places in prophetic literature these two elements appear in separate speeches. Hanson thinks that the prophet who created this literature was speaking at a time when the community was fractured, a situation during which some needed to be judged and others to be blessed. At other times, prophets normally addressed the community with either one or the other discourse.

Liturgical Discourse

A number of prophetic books include language that reflects the world of ritual. The oracles of salvation in Isaiah are an obvious case in point. In addition, prophetic books attest psalmic literature, such as the so-called doxologies in Amos (Amos 4:13; 5:8–9; 9:5–6). Also, Joel called the people to lament, using language similar to psalms of lament, whereupon the deity responded to them (see especially Joel 1:13–14;

2:18–20). In these and other instances, the prophets clearly were able to deploy the language and behaviors associated with the world of the priests. That should not be surprising, since a number of prophets bore priestly credentials.

Although there is no reason to think that Isaiah was a priest, the book itself contains considerable liturgical language. By liturgical language, I refer to the discourse present in the services that would have been held at the temple or in other communal settings.[17] When one reads through the book, it is possible to create a list of literature readily comparable to that in the book of Psalms. Such a list includes the following texts: 12; 25:1–5; 26:1–6; 26:7–21; 33:2–6; 35; 42:10–13; 44:23; 45:8; 48:20–21; 49:13; 51:3; 52:9–10; 54:1–3; 63:1–6; 63:7–64:12. At the outset, one should note that these texts differ vastly in length. Some are single verses:

> Sing for joy, O heavens, and exult, O earth;
> break forth, O mountains, into singing!
> For the LORD has comforted his people,
>   and will have compassion on his suffering ones.
>   (49:13)

Here we have a poem that should be classified as a hymn. It bears the hallmarks of plural imperative verbs, followed by a clause explaining what motivates the commands. The form is typical of the hymns of the Psalter, but the vocabulary ("comfort," "suffering") is rooted in the poetry of Isaiah. This liturgically styled poetry was probably written for this literary context and not simply appropriated from a source.

Other liturgical texts are long compositions. For example, 63:7–64:12 is an elaborate communal lament. Someone speaking on behalf of the community confesses its sins, decries the destruction of the temple, and petitions the deity for help. As was the case with the single verse, this longer poem belongs to the literature that surrounds it.

There are, however, different types of liturgical composition in Isaiah. These too are longer pieces, but they seem less to inhere in their contexts and, instead, to provide for transitions between major portions of the book. Chapter 12 provides a case in point. This chapter occurs just after the first collection attributed to Isaiah ben Amoz, which itself was concluded by two "on that day" sayings (11:10–11) along with a brief poem in which a prophet anticipates a return from exile (11:12–16), and just before the "oracles against the nations," the first of which commences in chapter 13 with the following formula, "the oracle concerning Babylon that Isaiah ben Amoz saw." Chapter 12 alludes to the previous chapter when it uses the phrase "on that day" (v. 1), and it foreshadows the oracles against the nations when it proclaims, "make known his deeds among the nations" (v. 3). Further, chapter 12 draws on both the book of Isaiah and other elements in Israelite tradition, such as the exodus.[18]

These six verses offer liturgical instructions—"you [singular] will say on that day" (v. 1), "and you [plural] will say on that day" (v. 3). Moreover, they are imbued with psalmic language. Verses 1–2 adumbrate an individual thanksgiving, whereas verses 3–6 offer a brief hymn. Together they suggest that Israel should respond in liturgical fashion to what Yahweh is doing for them. Chapter 12 is not, itself, a hymn or thanksgiving but a liturgical response to that which is being proclaimed both before and after it in the book.

Liturgical discourse is prominent in the book of Isaiah. Some scholars have suggested that it imitates rather than preserves the "real" language of worship. Others maintain the opposite. Both are probably correct. More importantly, the liturgical discourse functions in different ways, both serving the interests of discrete sections of the book and providing major points of transition between different portions of the book. Clearly, for those who created this book, the language of liturgy and the language of prophetic rhetoric belonged together. The same cannot be said for all prophetic books (e.g., Ezekiel), though Jeremiah's use of liturgical language—the lament—offers a case comparable to the prominence of liturgical discourse in Isaiah.

Prose Accounts

The book of Isaiah includes less prose than does Jeremiah or Ezekiel. Nonetheless, three portions of the book are constructed as accounts; two are lengthy, and one is brief.[19]

Isaiah 20:1–16

We begin with the shortest prose account. It belongs to the genre of the symbolic action report, a style of literature that becomes very important in the book of Ezekiel. We might be surprised to learn that the prophet Isaiah, who walks and talks with kings (see Isaiah 7), is here commanded to walk naked. This symbolic action report is set within the context of an Assyrian assault against a Philistine city, Ashdod. Isaiah is, presumably, walking naked in Jerusalem. According to verse 4, walking naked symbolizes the Egyptians, who will be defeated by Assyria and whose captives will walk naked into exile. The symbolism is designed to inform a party, referred to as "they," presumably political leaders in Judah, who might have hoped that Egypt would offer help to Judah in the face of

pressure from the Neo-Assyrian Empire. This portrayal of the prophet
is unusual and may derive from different authorial circles, such as those
interested in offering portrayals of the prophets that might fit within
Israel's historical record, the books of Kings.[20]

Isaiah 6–8

This block of prose bristles with difficulties. It has been viewed as a literary entity made up of originally separate elements but, nonetheless,
integrated into one essentially prosaic entity. The final product has
been described as a *Denkschrift* or "memorial account."[21] One of the
primary roles of the theory that lies behind this term was to explain
how it was that similar woe oracles in chapters 5 and 9–10 had been
separated. Those advocating the *Denkscrift* theory argue that this unit
had been inserted into poetic, oracular material. The issue of the relationship between chapters 5 and 9–10 remains vexed. Blenkinsopp, like
many before him, treats the material in the following order in his commentary—5:1–7; 10:1–4; 5:8–24; 9:27–20 + 5:25; 5:26–30—whereas
Childs attends to them in their canonical order. Regardless of these differences in the interpretation of the chapters that surround the
Denkschrift, one still confronts three chapters (6–8) made up primarily
of prose and concerned with the period between 740 and 730. In all
three chapters there is overt reference—using both first person (chaps.
6; 8) and third person (chap. 7)—to Isaiah. All three chapters allude to
the obduracy of Israel in the face of God's promise that it should have
faith in the deity and not in the might of Assyria. What might seem to
be a fruitful alliance against the Israelites and Arameans would ultimately spell destruction for the southern kingdom. That, at least, is a
summary of the message. But these chapters are accounts, not oracles
to be summarized. Each has a different point to make, and each
involves the prophet Isaiah.

Isaiah 6 is the first (in the canonical order) of three accounts in
prophetic books that have been labeled call/vocation/commissioning
narratives. (The others are Jer. 1:4–10 and Ezekiel 1–3; interestingly,
none occurs in the Book of the Twelve.) In a classic form-critical argument, Norman Habel identified five of the six components that pervade these call narratives: divine confrontation, introductory word
(6:1–2), commission (vv. 3–7), objection (v. 11a), and reassurance (vv.
11b–13). The sixth component, the sign, is missing from Isaiah 6.[22]
Habel discerned this structure not only in these three prophetic texts
but in the call of Micaiah ben Imlah (1 Kings 22) as well as the com-

missionings of Gideon, Moses, and Abraham's servant. To be sure, Isaiah 6 is more like 1 Kings 22 than some of the other texts. Both, in fact, could be properly described as a vision report. However, they are vision reports that depict the commissioning of a prophet for a task, that is, they share the form of a commissioning narrative, which is, of course, not common to all vision reports. Moreover, each of the call narratives in the major prophetic books has been significantly influenced by an important tradition or motif in that book—Isaiah by the *kābôd* (glory) of Yahweh in the temple, Jeremiah by the word of Yahweh, and Ezekiel by the proximate ("this was the appearance of the likeness of the glory of the LORD" [Ezek. 1:28]) *qādôš* (holiness) beyond the temple. Some, such as Blenkinsopp, have objected to the categorization of Isaiah 6 as a call narrative since, unlike Isaiah 1 and Ezekiel 1–3, this vision report does not occur at the beginning of the book. However, once one recognizes that a later editor has incorporated chapter 6 into the memorial account concerning the period 740–730, one can affirm the formal quality of the text as call narrative and also understand why it does not appear first in the book. Chapter 6 comprises a vision report in which Isaiah is commissioned as a prophet. This report has been integrated into the account of the Syro-Ephraimitic crisis, which is the first major moment in which Isaiah was active as a prophet. Much of the material in chapters 1–5 postdates those events. Hence, it is altogether appropriate to have the report about how Isaiah commences his work as prophet otherwise linked to his earliest dated activity.

Chapter 6 is, of course, a mystifying commissioning narrative. We understand well that Isaiah "volunteers" to participate in the work of the divine council—"Here I am, send me" (6:8). However, the deity presents Isaiah with a task that is counterintuitive:

> Make the mind of this people dull,
>   and stop their ears,
>   and shut their eyes,
> so that they may not look with their eyes,
>   and listen with their ears,
> and comprehend with their minds,
>   and turn and be healed.
>
> (v. 10)

Whereas Amos exhorts the people, "Seek good and not evil, that you may live" (Amos 5:14) or "Seek the Lord and live" (Amos 5:6), Isaiah is instructed to act in such a way as to prevent the people from having life.

It has been a commonplace to explain such a negative view of the prophetic task as retrospective reflection on how the people responded to the prophet's admonitions and judgments. However, it may be better to suggest, consistent with the role of the call narratives, that such language makes clear that Isaiah is not to blame for the assaults on and defeats of Judah. Rather, this was part of Yahweh's plan, an important theological notion in the book. Isaiah, like many other prophets, was unsuccessful, if what we mean by that is that the people did not change their ways. However, this call narrative indicates that we would misunderstand the role of this prophet were we to charge him with failure. The measure of his "success" was not his ability to help the people avoid disaster but to proclaim truly Yahweh's conciliar word. The very fact that he spoke Yahweh's words—once his lips were purified and he participated, though minimally, in the divine council—enfranchised him as one of Yahweh's prophets. The first chapter of the *Denkschrift* not only authorizes but also characterizes Isaiah as a prophet.

Chapter 7, the next element in the *Denkschrift*, is an account, including speech, the core of which lies in verses 3–17. The account derives from the Syro-Ephraimitic crisis. As we saw earlier in the chapter, Isaiah proclaimed a word of assurance that also bore a negative implication. God would save Judah from Israel and Syria. But if Judah appealed to Assyria, Judah would suffer at the hands of "the king of Assyria" (7:17). These verses attest to the first performance of Isaiah as prophet. There should be no surprise that the final word to Ahaz in the account is a negative one: "The LORD will bring on you and on your people and on your ancestral house such days as have not come since the day that Ephraim departed from Judah." This ominous forecast is utterly consistent with the notion of a desolate land (6:11) that inheres in the call narrative, one chapter earlier.

Chapter 8 presents Isaiah in a role similar to Hosea. He is commanded to father a child, whose name bears symbolic significance. The name of the child born to Isaiah and "the prophetess" is Maher-shalal-hash-baz, which may be translated, "the spoil speeds, the prey hastens." The significance of the child is spelled out in a way similar to that of Immanuel in chapter 7. Before either child reaches maturity, something significant will happen. According to chapter 7, before Immanuel eats solid food or develops the ability to make independent moral judgments, the Syro-Ephraimitic coalition will fall apart. According to chapter 8, before Maher-shalal-hash-baz learns how to speak, Assyria will have despoiled both Israel and Syria. The messages conveyed by both children are essentially the same. The demise of Judah's enemies is imminent. Moreover, in the two episodes in which we learn about these children, the prophet spells out the negative implications of what could have been utterly good news for Judah, namely, that it too will suffer at the hands of the Assyrians if it does not rely solely on Yahweh. The prophet has a creative role in explicating these two symbolic action reports.

The character of this three-chapter unit as a memoir becomes particularly pronounced at the end of the chapter 8. It now possesses a more personal focus. Whereas earlier in the chapter, as well as in the foregoing chapters, Isaiah was addressed about matters concerning all Israel, God now talks to him in a way that separates him from his countrymen. Isaiah is commanded not to act as others do, the presumption being that Isaiah will escape the fate decreed for those in both Israel and Judah.

Just as Isaiah was addressed as a part of the divine council, so now, in verses 16–22, he addresses others. In verse 16, he tells an individual to secure his teaching, presumably in written form. In verse 19, he refers to a group (the "you" is grammatically plural). The final element of the memoir offers an interpretation of Isaiah's testimony, construing it as torah or "teaching" (v. 16). It is the true message, as opposed to false "teaching" (v. 20), that people might seek. Isaiah's true torah will be available to those who seek it, since he has preserved it. In sum, the *Denkschrift* not only offers an account of Isaiah's commissioning but also his work during the Syro-Ephraimitic crisis and a report about the preservation of that message for future generations.

Isaiah 36–39

When moving to this other lengthy prose section, one is struck by some pronounced similarities between these chapters and the *Denkschrift*. The location described in 36:2—"the conduit of the upper pool on the highway to the Fuller's Field"—is identical with that of 7:3. In both texts, Assyria is the decisive imperial power. In both texts, Isaiah speaks directly with a king, now Hezekiah instead of the earlier Ahaz. In both, Isaiah admonishes the king "not to fear" the military challenge that is before him (7:4 // 37:6). In both texts, there is overt reference to "signs" (7:11, 14; 37:30; 38:7, 22; the noun also occurs in the first prose account as well [20:3]). In sum, it is difficult to read chapters 36–39 without hearing echoes of the *Denkschrift*. The similarities highlight the different ways in which the king responds to Isaiah. Ahaz does not fear, but Hezekiah does.

However, Isaiah 36–39 presents one problem that chapters 6–8 do not. Isaiah 36–39 virtually repeats 2 Kgs. 18:13, 17–20:19. The material

in Isaiah does not include 2 Kgs. 18:14–16, which reports that
Hezekiah humbled himself before Sennacherib and also gave him considerable amounts of gold and silver, including some appurtenances
from the temple. Apart from this omission, all other elements in the
Kings account have been included. Moreover, Isaiah 36–39 includes
material unique to this account, most notably, the "writing of King
Hezekiah" (38:9–20), which might be described form-critically as an
individual lament. Both the omission of 2 Kgs. 18:14–16 and the inclusion of this psalm portray Hezekiah in a more favorable light than does
the Deuteronomistic History, though he is one of the few kings to be
described positively (see 2 Kgs. 18:3). The Isaianic portrait of
Hezekiah further distinguishes him from his predecessor, Ahaz, with
whom Isaiah also spoke. This positive portrayal of Hezekiah permits
one to claim that the dynamics within these three chapters are rather
different from those behind chapters 6–8, which focus on Isaiah and
his "disciples."

In fact, the prose accounts in chapters 36–39 bear resemblance to
accounts about prophets elsewhere in the Deuteronomistic History.
The narratives about Elijah and Elisha also portray prophets who consult directly with kings (2 Kgs. 13:14–19; Isa. 39:1–4). These prophets,
like Isaiah, can heal a sick person (1 Kgs. 17:17–23; Isa. 38:21). They,
like Isaiah, can answer questions about the future (2 Kgs. 8:9–10; Isa.
39:5–7). They, like Isaiah, can affect the natural order in a miraculous
way (2 Kgs. 6:1–4; Isa. 38:8). They, like Isaiah, offer oracles or perspectives that affect military campaigns (2 Kgs. 6:8–23; Isa. 37:5–7).
There are, to be sure, some differences. Elijah and Elisha are termed
"men of God"; Isaiah is not. In addition, many stories focus on just the
persons of Elijah and Elisha; that is not the case with Isaiah. Still, the
similarities are strong enough to suggest that the prose in Isaiah 36–39
has its home in the Deuteronomistic History, and not the other way
round. (Jeremiah 52, which duplicates 2 Kgs. 24:18–25:30, offers an
excellent analogy of literature that arose as part of the Deuteronomistic
History and that later was introduced into a prophetic book.)

This material has a different function in Isaiah than it does in Kings,
however. In the latter case, it is part of the national history. In the former case, it attests to the working out of Isaiah's commission in a new
time and with a new king. The book claims that Isaiah was to be a
prophet not just in the Syro-Ephraimitic crisis but in a later period as
well, when the Neo-Assyrian armies are encamped against Jerusalem.
In addition, these chapters within the context of the book offer a transition—from concern with Assyria to concern with Babylon (chap. 39),

for it is this imperial entity that will influence much of the rhetoric in ensuing chapters.

Isaiah 6–8; 20; and 36–39 may all be construed as prose accounts that attest to the work of Isaiah as prophet. They include a vision report during which time he is given his first prophetic charge. Moreover, they tend to depict him as similar to other prophets, most notably Hosea, due to their symbolically named children, and Elijah and Elisha, as we have just seen. These similarities are striking, since these other three prophets were residents of the northern kingdom and Isaiah was a quintessential Judahite. One might not expect this image of Isaiah were one to create a characterization of the prophet based just on his poetic speeches. This medium of prophetic historiography offers a different perspective on Isaiah and his work than does the rest of the book.

ORACLES CONCERNING THE NATIONS

The book of Isaiah, like Jeremiah and Ezekiel, contains a collection of oracles about foreign nations. As is the case with these other books, Isaiah's collection possesses some distinctive features. First, the boundaries of Isaiah's oracles against the nations are indistinct. Though virtually all scholars agree that the section begins with Isa. 13:1, they are less certain about the terminating point. Heretofore there has been a consensus that the collection involves chapters 13–23. However, a number of scholars (e.g., Blenkinsopp, Clements) would include chapters 24–27 (which are sometimes known as the Isaianic Apocalypse), noting that no formulae set off chapters 24–27 from the foregoing material. Moreover, the scale of chapters 24–27 is global, even cosmic, a perspective that grows out of chapters 13–23. Yahweh will punish the kings of the earth (24:21). Yet, even on this broad canvas, specific nations (i.e., the Moabites) continue to receive attention (25:10). Chapters 24–27 extend and develop the ideas adumbrated in the oracles that immediately precede them. Clements contends that 27:12–13 culminates the oracles against the nations by anticipating the return of Israelites from exile just as 11:12–16 concludes an earlier collection by emphasizing this same theme of return. Second, oracles concerning foreign nations occur beyond the aforementioned collection. For example, the prophet offers an indictment and sentence of Assyria in 10:5–19. Chapter 34 reports that Yahweh is "enraged against all the nations" (34:2), mentioning Edom by name (34:9). Similarly, 47:1–15 offers a graphic account of Babylon's fate, personifying Babylon as a woman (virgin, daughter, mistress, widow). Third, the oracles against the nations, in their narrowest construal (i.e., chaps. 13–23), include oracles directed against or concerning Jerusalem, most notably 22:1–15. The book is concerned about nations far beyond the boundaries of chapters 13–27, and even in those chapters, the book attends to the fate of Jerusalem. Fourth, the oracles in chapters 13–23 have been integrated by a number of introductory formulae. (Without these formulae, the oracles are more heterogeneous than are those in Jeremiah and Ezekiel.) There are ten such formulae (13:1: " Babylon"; 14:28: "Philistia"; 15:1: "Moab"; 17:1: "Damascus"; 19:1: "Egypt"; 21:1: "wilderness of the sea"; 21:11: "Dumah"; 21:13: "the desert plain"; 22:1: "the valley of vision"; 23:1: "Tyre"). These formulae have been translated as oracles "concerning" these nations or places rather than oracles "against" them. And, in each of these formulae, the editor has placed a special word, *maśśa'*, which can be translated either as "oracle" or "burden," the latter meaning deriving from the standard etymology for this word (the verb means "to lift up").[23]

Babylon

Several features of the discourse about "nations" in the book of Isaiah require special comment. First, Babylon bears unique importance. The first formulaic introduction, "the oracle concerning Babylon that Isaiah son of Amoz saw" (13:1), functions in two ways: to introduce the oracles against the nations and to introduce the oracle against Babylon. Isaiah 13:2–16 does not expressly address Babylon. Instead, these verses set the stage for Yahweh's oracles concerning all foreign nations:

> I will punish the world for its evil,
>   and the wicked for their iniquity;
> I will put an end to the pride of the arrogant,
>   and lay low the insolence of tyrants.
>   (13:11)

But then we discover in verse 17 that Yahweh is sending the Medes against "them." The lack of a proper name degrades those who will come under attack—the Babylon about whom we hear explicitly in verse 19.

We might have expected to hear such an oracle directed against Assyria, about which we find only minimal material in these oracles against the nations (see 14:24–27). Instead, Babylon bears pride of place, both as the first nation addressed in this collection and as the one that receives the greatest amount of space (even outside chaps. 13–14; see 21:9). As we know from elsewhere in the book, Babylon is the foreign nation that will suffer Yahweh's assault (43:14; 47:1). These texts truly affirm the exclamation, "Look at the land of the Chaldeans! This is the people; it was not Assyria" (23:13).

The poetry of Isaiah 14 expresses well this vehement attack on Babylon. Verses 14–21 comprise a "taunt" or dirge, designed to be chanted at the demise of the king of Babylon. The king is not named. Hence, we do well to think about this king as a personification of all Babylon. This person/nation is guilty of the ultimate hubris, thinking that it could be like God (14:14). However, instead of dwelling in the heavens, instead of appearing like an astral object ("O Day Star, son of Dawn" [14:12]; cf. the reference to stars in 47:13)—appellations with mythic overtones—the dead king/destroyed nations will be greeted by Sheol (14:9— death personified) and deprived of the decent burial (14:18–20) appropriate to other kings. All this is due to the oppression and insolent behavior (14:4; 47:6, 8) committed by Babylon. Just as the deity had used Assyria (10:5–7) and had judged it for acting beyond the scope of Yahweh's punitive activity, so Babylon had gone too far—"I gave them [Judah] into your hand, you showed them no mercy" (47:6). These two imperial agents, but especially Babylon, will incur Yahweh's wrath.

Isaiah 24–27

What is the function of Isaiah 24–27 if it is a part of these oracles concerning the nations? These chapters are a miscellany. They begin with poetry (24:1–13) that is very similar to 13:2–16. (Both poems refer to Yahweh as a deity who is about to destroy the earth [13:5 // 24:1]. Both poems refer to the world of the heavens [13:10 // 24:4, 18]. Such similarities suggest that the initial portion of chapter 13 and chapters 24–27 frame the oracles concerning the nations.) Yet we read these chapters through the focus of an urban lens. The poet refers to "the city of chaos," which symbolizes foreign existence, not as nation but as urban entity. The negative image is of a city destroyed (24:10–12). Moreover, this image of the city appears elsewhere (25:2–3; 26:5; 27:10), a motif that suffuses these diverse texts. Chapters 24–27 take the language of oracles concerning nations and turn it toward the foreign city, while at the same time observing the special place of the "strong city" (26:1), presumably Jerusalem.

At the same time, these chapters include responses by the people. It is not too much to say that chapters 24–27 include liturgical responses both to God's actions toward Jerusalem but also toward other peoples. Chapter 26 offers words of the people, including both complaint and praise (vv. 1–15), a characterization of those words as lament (vv. 16–18), and then a divine response to those words (vv. 19–21). Chapters 24–27 demonstrate that oracles concerning foreign nations can be refracted in liturgical language, one of the book's primary discourses.

Further, Isaiah 24–27 undergirds language concerning the entire earth with mythic images. Given the power of myth, such a development is utterly appropriate. Cosmic topics deserve mythic expression. So when the poet talks about the deity "swallowing up death forever" (25:8), he alludes to imagery concerning two Northwest Semitic deities, Death (Mot) and Baal, in which Death swallows Baal, who symbolizes life. Israel's God, unlike Baal, is able to swallow Death. This ability of Yahweh to conquer death also receives expression in chapter 26. In response to the lament of the people, "the dead do not live; shades do not rise" (26:14), Yahweh affirms, "Your dead shall live, their corpses shall rise" (26:19). Such an affirmation drives global discourse almost to its extreme. The sovereign God—the one who rules not only Israel but the entire earth—can do what no other deity can do (a point made elsewhere in the book), and can even defeat Death and the power of death over his people.

Isaiah's International Vision

Such a vigorous assault on Assyria and Babylon and even the earth, as in Isaiah 24–27—along with the general tenor of these oracles concerning foreign nations—might suggest that the book of Isaiah is superpatriotic, even jingoistic in its rhetoric. However, to reach such a conclusion would be to do an injustice to Isaiah's international vision. Hints of that broader vision occur within the collection of the oracles concerning the nations, particularly in the oracle regarding Moab (15:1–16:14). The prophet knows about an attack that Moab suffered, one that resulted in a flight of refugees from that land. In recognition of their plight, the prophet pleads, apparently with the Judahite king, to provide assistance to them:

> Give counsel,
> 　　grant justice;
> make your shade like night
> 　　at the height of noon;
> hide the outcasts,
> 　　do not betray the fugitive;
> let the outcasts of Moab
> 　　settle among you;

> be a refuge to them
>> from the destroyer.
>> (16:3–4)

This is an unusual sentiment. However, it does represent what a prophet who had a high view of the Davidic king might expect from the ruler—as one who looks to the welfare of those beyond his borders. The Davidic empire had, after all, encompassed Moab at an earlier time.

This international dimension in the book is attested beyond the borders of the oracles concerning the nations. In the second "servant-song," we hear the servant speaking to distant countries:

> Listen to me, O coastlands,
>> pay attention, you peoples from far away!
>> (49:1)

Later in the poem, we find a divine oracle in which the deity dignifies the servant with the following role:

> I will give you as a light to the nations,
>> that my salvation may reach to the end of the earth.
>> (49:6; cf. 42:6)

What precisely this salvation involves is ambiguous. At a minimum, it would mean the salvation of Yahwists within those nations (see 49:22–23; 52:10). However, the book of Isaiah (along with other texts in the Hebrew Bible, such as Gen. 12:3: "in you all the families of the earth shall be blessed") looks to blessing for all peoples. This sentiment appears at several points in Isaiah. For example, in the prose addenda to the poetic oracles concerning Egypt, we find the following statement: "Israel will be the third with Egypt and Assyria, a blessing in the midst of the earth, whom the LORD of hosts has blessed, saying, 'Blessed be Egypt my people, and Assyria the work of my hands, and Israel my heritage'" (19:24)—all this after "The LORD will make himself known to the Egyptians" (19:21; cf. the similar sentiment in 18:7: "gifts will be brought to the LORD of hosts from a people tall and smooth," that is, the Ethiopians). Such a global religious perspective is complemented by a prophetic oracle (2:2–4; cf. 60:3) that occurs earlier in the book (and in the book of Micah as well [4:1–3], attesting to its importance in Judahite prophetic circles). In a poem that might be viewed as eschatological, we discern the motif of an international pilgrimage to Zion (a radically different version of the earlier Zion tradition, according to which nations would attack Zion):

> In days to come
>> the mountain of the LORD's house
> shall be established as the highest of the mountains,
>> and shall be raised above the hills;
> all the nations shall stream to it.
>> Many peoples shall come and say,
> "Come, let us go up to the mountain of the LORD,
>> to the house of the God of Jacob;
> that he may teach us his ways
>> and that we may walk in his paths."
>
> (2:2–3a)

This motif also appears in the last poem in the book: "all flesh shall come to worship before me, says the LORD" (66:23). Nations will come to receive Yahweh's torah (2:3b), and the result of such instruction will be global shalom: "nation shall not lift up sword against nation, neither shall they learn war any more" (2:4). This compelling notion revises not only the Zion tradition but also transforms the Davidic tradition, which elsewhere attributes the notion of peace to the work of the Davidic monarch. In 2:2–4, peace will be achieved by the work of the imperial deity, not by the work of an earthly king.

The Foreigner

In the final section of the book, we do not hear much about "the nations," but something new emerges—the possibility of the nations venerating Yahweh. We find language about the "foreigner," about citizens of other nations who might reside in the land of Israel. Chapters 56–66 sometimes refer to strangers or foreigners as servants who will work the land on behalf of the Israelites (e.g., 61:5), and in so doing there will be a reversal of fortune for Israelites, who were slaves in foreign lands. However, just as with the nations, the situation of the foreigner is not utterly negative. Isaiah 56:1–8 addresses the status of two groups of outcasts, the foreigner and the eunuch, both of whom would have been excluded from participation in some rites of worship at the temple. However, this oracle announces that foreigners will be able "to join themselves to the LORD" in a number of ways. For example, if they keep the Sabbath, then the deity will bring them to the temple and accept their sacrifices. As a result, the temple will be "called a house of prayer for all peoples."

In sum, discourse concerning the nations occurs throughout the book of Isaiah. Even though certain nations, especially Babylon, are judged severely, they are much more than just Israel's enemies. Rather, they, like Israel, belong to the earthly realm of the heavenly sovereign, a kingdom in which Isaiah expects shalom.

THEOLOGICAL ISSUES

The book of Isaiah includes one of the prophetic commissioning reports (chap. 6). This in and of itself does not distinguish Isaiah from other prophetic books, since one may find comparable documents in Jeremiah 1 and Ezekiel 1–3. However, each of these commissioning reports introduces a major theological perspective that suffuses the book. The report in Jeremiah 1 emphasizes the prophet as one who is entrusted with "the word of the LORD." Ezekiel 1–3 emphasizes the mobile and baroque character of "the glory [kābôd] of the LORD." Isaiah highlights the prophet as one who experiences the holiness [qādôš] of Yahweh. In so doing, Isaiah 6 sets the stage on which the phrase "the Holy One of Israel" appears prominently throughout the book.

The Holiness of Yahweh and Righteousness

Isaiah 6 presents a picture of the prophet in the temple compound. He sees Yahweh (not simply "the appearance of the likeness of the glory of the LORD" [Ezek. 1:28] as was the case with Ezekiel). The prophet responds with a cry of woe since he is a human, "a person of unclean lips." Immediately thereafter, one of the heavenly retinue purifies him: "your guilt has departed and your sin is blotted out" (6:7). This statement emphasizes that, according to the book of Isaiah, holiness is not morally neutral; it is not simply a powerful numinous quality. Holiness and righteousness belong in the same conceptual world.

Yahweh as "the Holy One of Israel" (qĕdôš yisrael) appears many places in the book.[24] The earliest attestations (chaps. 1 and 5) link the holiness of the deity with the norm of righteousness.

> Ah, sinful nation,
>   people laden with iniquity,
> offspring who do evil,
>   children who deal corruptly,
> who have forsaken the LORD,
>   who have despised the Holy One of Israel,
>   who are utterly estranged!
> (1:4)

One could imagine that Isaiah would indict Israel for improper worship as an offense before Yahweh (as does Ezekiel). Instead, he charges that the people's iniquity and doing of evil is what has causesd an affront to the Holy One. Isaiah 5:16 pushes in a similar direction, though in more positive language: "But the LORD of hosts is exalted by justice, and the Holy God shows himself holy by righteousness." In classic parallelism, the qualities of justice and righteousness, so prominent in prophetic discourse, are those elements that undergird the essence of Yahweh as deity. This claim is a hallmark in the book of Isaiah.

Later in the book, the phrase "the Holy One of Israel" becomes one of the standard ways in which the deity is identified. It occurs in formulae, introducing prophetic speeches:

> Thus says the LORD,
>   your Redeemer, the Holy One of Israel . . ."
>   (43:14)

> Thus says the LORD,
>   the Holy One of Israel, and its Maker . . ."
>   (45:11)

> Thus says the LORD,
>   your Redeemer, the Holy One of Israel . . ."
>   (48:17)

Here the holiness of the deity is linked with that deity's role as creator and redeemer of the people (cf. 43:3; 54:5).

The character of Yahweh as holy and righteous helps one understand what Isaiah thinks is wrong in Israel. Here he shares much with other eighth-century prophets, especially Amos and Micah. Isaiah, as we have seen, highlights the covenantal norms of justice and righteousness, and like his prophetic compatriots, he specifies infractions of them. Isaiah speaks on behalf of the poor (5:8–10) and the oppressed (3:15), particularly as they are symbolized by the most vulnerable in Israel, namely, the widow and the orphan (1:2–3). He indicts those who act unjustly to them—princes, judges, lawyers, those who take bribes, those involved in illicit real estate transactions—in sum, those of high status and with access to power in the society. However, unlike Amos and Micah, who appear to root those norms in God's covenant with the people, Isaiah understands the nature of the deity as holy as the authorization for these ethical principles.

Yahweh's Plan and Zion

Readers of this prophetic book need to be aware of its affirmation that Yahweh has an overarching plan (5:19; 25:1; 28:29; 30:1; 44:26; 46:11). This plan has various components and is of cosmic and international scale. In Isa. 7:7–9, we learn that the threat posed by Syria and Israel will simply vanish. The plan also lays the groundwork for life in Israel. God has chosen a place at which to be manifest, namely, Zion. And God has chosen not only a polity (monarchy) but a particular lineage (the house of David) that will rule forever. The notion of such an overarching plan had a long life, since it was used to address both the Syro-Ephraimitic crisis and life after the defeat of 587. Throughout the book, diverse authors affirm that Yahweh's plan is "of old" (25:1) and "from ancient times" (46:10).

Much has been and should be made of the prominent theological status that Isaiah gives to place (Zion or Jerusalem) and, though less so, to person (the Davidic king). Von Rad maintains that Isaiah of Jerusalem highlighted these two election traditions—Yahweh's choice of Jerusalem as the site for his residence and the Davidic monarchy as his earthly political representative—and rooted his theology to them.[25] Others have suggested that, as a Jerusalemite, Isaiah could do no other. Some have claimed that events during Isaiah's own lifetime, such as the reprieve of Jerusalem from Sennacherib's attack, helped create these traditions. Be that as it may, no one may gainsay the importance of Jerusalem and the king in this book.

As for the former, one may discern a number of texts in which Yahweh's special protection of Jerusalem is clear (see the earlier discussion of the discourse of promise). The notion of an instantaneous rescue for Jerusalem belongs to the core of this affirmation (see 29:7–8). Perhaps the most important asseveration concerning Zion occurs as a brief answer to a question, embedded in the oracles against the nations.

> The LORD has founded Zion,
>   and the needy among his people
>   will find refuge in her.
>   (14:32)

Here, as with the affirmation of Yahweh's holiness, there is an ethical valence. Zion is a place where the outcasts can find help. Isaiah may have thought that if Zion were not such a place of refuge, it would forfeit its special sanctity and protection.

This symbol of Zion was important in other ways. First, it exemplified an urban notion of Israel. Isaiah could point to Zion as a city where life had gone wrong:

> How the faithful city
>   has become a whore!
>   She that was full of justice,
> righteousness lodged in her—
>   but now murderers!
>   (1:21)

After a time of judgment, however, Jerusalem would be a place where a restored Israel might live and flourish (2:2–4; 30:19; 54:11–17).

Second, Zion was the place at which the temple and its system of worship was manifest. One might think, based on Isaiah 6, that Isaiah would have a rather high view of the temple service. There is, however, striking ambiguity about the world of worship at the temple. Isaiah 1:10–17, which sounds rather like something Amos might have spoken, assails the full range of activities normally associated with worship at the temple. Such negative judgments also occur in the final chapter of the book:

> Thus says the LORD:
> Heaven is my throne
>   and the earth is my footstool;
> what is the house that you would build for me,
>   and what is my resting place?
> . . . .
> Whoever slaughters an ox is like one who kills a human being;
>   whoever sacrifices a lamb, like one who breaks a dog's neck.
>   (66:1, 3a)

Such challenges to the world of worship are especially prominent in chapters 56–66.

Third, in later portions of the book, Zion is personified (as are other entities, including Israel as Jacob). Zion has a special role within the larger cohort of Israel. Zion is designated as "a herald of good tidings," a woman who is to proclaim good news to the other cities of Judah (40:9). Later, Zion, symbolizing those who live in captivity, is admonished to leave Babylon wearing beautiful, new garments. Moreover, God's future acts of weal are accomplished for Zion, even eventuating in a new name for the city/person—Hephzibah (62:1–4). In sum, Zion as place and person has multiple functions in the book, and these many functions are rooted in Yahweh's overarching plan.

Yahweh's Plan and the Davidic Monarch

Zion as a place has a complement in a person—David, whom Yahweh has chosen. This choice involves a dialectic. The choice was made in the past, but its true benefit will only occur in the future. Four texts help us understand how important the king was to the authors of this book. Isaiah 9:2–7 is to be read as a song sung by the members of the divine council. Using the language of divine adoption (cf. Ps. 2), "a son has been born to us" signifies the accession of a new king to the throne in Jerusalem. The text offers throne names, "Wonderful Counselor, Mighty God, Everlasting Father, Prince of Peace" (similar to throne names used in Egypt), to describe the marvelous power and authority of the new king. The concluding verses emphasize that the new king will, as was expected of all kings in the ancient Near East, administer justice properly.

Isaiah 11 elaborates this understanding of the Davidic king. Here, however, the poet emphasizes that Yahweh's "spirit" or vivifying power will inspire the king. The poet also elaborates the notion of king as a symbol of justice, affirming not only that the king will administer justice, but that, in a wonderful image, he will be clothed by it.

> Righteousness shall be the belt around his waist,
> and faithfulness the belt around his loins.
> (11:5)

Such a just reign will eventuate in an Edenic peace:

> The wolf shall live with the lamb,
> the leopard shall lie down with the kid,
> the calf and the lion and the fatling together,
> and a little child shall lead them.
> (11:6)

Isaiah 32:1–8 offers a reprise of these notions, again highlighting the realm of justice that will ensue and identifying the sort of rogues (the rash, stammerers, fools, villains) who will no longer have power in God's kingdom. Instead, only noble things will prevail.

When one compares the roster of kings who sat on the Davidic throne—even the ones who receive passing marks by the Deuteronomistic Historian—with these poems, it seems clear that Israel never experienced such a reign. The idealized rhetoric of royalty that made its way into this book remains an expectation about the future rather

than a report about past or present kings. It should, therefore, surprise
no one that Israel, after the defeat of 587, began to rethink the character of the Davidic covenant, the promise that Yahweh would always preserve a Davidic king on the throne of Judah. (See the classic statement
in Ps. 89:35–36: "Once and for all I have sworn by my holiness; I will
not lie to David. His line shall continue forever, and his throne endure
before me like the sun.") Such rethinking lies behind Isa. 55:3:

> Incline your ear, and come to me;
>   listen, so that you may live.
> I will make with you an everlasting covenant,
>   my steadfast, sure love for David.

Such vocabulary about love for David derives from the Davidic
covenant itself. That is not new. But the third line is truly innovative.
In Hebrew the "you" is grammatically plural and almost certainly refers
to the people whom the poet addresses. The exilic poet broadens God's
eternal covenant with David so as to encompass all the people, not just
the king. The prophet does not spell out the full implications of this
new understanding of the Davidic covenant. Though the notion
remains inchoate, its implications are revolutionary, involving a
democratization of the earlier royal grant to one person, the king.

Yahweh's Cosmic Plan and Faith

The overarching plan of Yahweh, which involves a specific place and
person, is in no way parochial. Indeed, it bears cosmic implications.
The book's first poetic verse uses the form of the lawsuit, convoking
"the heavens" and "the earth." This vast scale of discourse befits Israel's
imperial deity. He is the one who adjudicates between nations (2:4;
11:12–16). There will be a time of vast destruction (chaps. 13; 24; 34).
Yet, as a part of God's plan, "a remnant" will survive, a notion highlighted in the symbolic name Shear-jashub, which means "a remnant
shall return" (7:2; cf. 10:20–22). The good news is not simply that a
remnant will exist, since a remnant means that most of the population
has been decimated. The good news is that this remnant, living in exile,
will return to the land. This too is part of Yahweh's purpose, which
becomes particularly important in chapters 46–55.

If Yahweh has a plan, it is incumbent upon Israelites to trust in it, to
have faith. The book of Isaiah offers numerous indictments of a people
who did not have such faith. One classic statement derives from the

Syro-Ephraimitic crisis. When Isaiah confronts Ahaz, he tells the king, "If you do not stand firm in faith, you shall not stand at all" (7:9). Faith here does not mean simply to believe in God but to believe and trust in God's plan. Ahaz ultimately failed that test—by seeking help from the Neo-Assyrians—which resulted in a series of tirades from the prophet. In a later period (ca. 700), another king, Hezekiah, sought help from the Egyptians. Again the book records an indictment of the Judahites for not trusting in God to save them. The book also indicts those outside Israel (e.g., the Assyrians) who moved beyond the constraints of God's plan. "Shall the ax vaunt itself over the one who wields it?" (10:15). In sum, all humans are expected to recognize the character of Yahweh's intent.

Unlike most prophetic books, Isaiah defends the character of the deity, primarily in chapters 40–48. To be sure, Jeremiah and Habakkuk raise questions about whether the deity is just. However, in Isaiah the issue of God's justice is not so much at stake as is the question of whether or not Yahweh is truly God. The trial speeches, referred to earlier, have as one of their central points the claim that Yahweh is, indeed, God, and that there is no real competitor. Foreign deities are challenged directly. They are asked if they have a plan, as Yahweh has (41:21–24). Since they offer no evidence of such, they are judged to be worth nothing. Even here, appeal to the deity's plan remains important:

> See, the former things have come to pass,
> and new things I now declare;
> before they spring forth,
> I tell you of them.
>
> (42:9)

Other prophets may impugn the worship of foreign gods, but Isaiah is an apologist on behalf of Yahweh and his plan.

TEXT

The book of Isaiah is often viewed as particularly well preserved. There are far fewer text-critical problems than in Hosea, Jeremiah, or Ezekiel. However, unlike the case of Jeremiah, the scrolls discovered at Qumran have offered few new perspectives on this biblical book. IQIsa^a, a very well preserved document, generally offers few readings that differ in consequential ways from the MT.

Bibliography

Baltzer, K. *Deutero-Isaiah*. Hermenia. Minneapolis: Fortress, 2001.

Barton, J. *Isaiah 1–39*. Old Testament Guides. Sheffield: Sheffield Academic Press, 1995.

Blenkinsopp, J. *Isaiah 1–39*. AB 19. New York: Doubleday, 2000.

Broyles, C., and C. Evans. *Writing and Reading the Scroll of Isaiah: Studies of an Interpretive Tradition*. VTSup 70. Leiden: Brill, 1997.

Childs, B. *Isaiah: A Commentary*. OTL. Louisville, Ky.: Westminster John Knox, 2000.

Clements, R. *Isaiah and the Deliverance of Jerusalem: A Study in the Interpretation of Prophecy in the Old Testament*. JSOTSup 13. Sheffield: Sheffield Academic Press, 1980.

———. "The Unity of the Book of Isaiah." *Interpretation* 35 (1982): 117–29.

Clifford, R. *Fair Spoken and Persuading: An Interpretation of Second Isaiah*. Theological Inquiries. New York: Paulist Press, 1984.

Melugin, R. *The Formation of Isaiah 40–55*. BZAW 141. Berlin: de Gruyter, 1976.

Melugin, R., and M. Sweeney, eds. *New Visions of Isaiah*. JSOTSup 214. Sheffield: Sheffield Academic Press, 1996.

Muilenburg, J. "Chapters 40–66." In *The Interpreter's Bible*, edited by G. Buttrick et al., 5:381–773. Nashville: Abingdon, 1956.

Schoors, A. *I Am God Your Saviour: A Form-Critical Study of the Main Genres in Isaiah 40–55*. VTSup 24. Leiden: Brill, 1973.

Seitz, C. "Chapters 40–66." In *The New Interpreter's Bible*, edited by L. Keck, et al., 6:307–552. Nashville: Abingdon, 2001.

———. *Zion's Final Destiny: The Development of the Book of Isaiah*. Minneapolis: Fortress, 1991.

Sweeney, M. *Isaiah 1–39, with an Introduction to Prophetic Literature*. FOTL 16. Grand Rapids: Eerdmans, 1996.

Tucker, G. "The Book of Isaiah 1–39." In *The New Interpreter's Bible*, edited by L. Keck et al., 6:25–305. Nashville: Abingdon, 2001.

Whybray, R. *The Second Isaiah*. Old Testament Guides. Sheffield: Sheffield Academic Press, 1983.

Wildberger, H. *Isaiah: A Commentary*. Continental Commentary. 2 vols. Minneapolis: Fortress, 1991, 1997.

———. *Jesaja, Kapitel 28–39*. Biblischer Kommentar: Altes Testament. Neukirchen-Vluyn: Neukirchener Verlag, 1982.

Williamson, H. *The Book Called Isaiah: Deutero-Isaiah's Role in Composition and Redaction*. Oxford: Clarendon, 1994.

3

The Book of Jeremiah

Of the major prophets, Jeremiah is the most palpable character. Here is someone who suffered house arrest, was thrown into a muddy cistern, and apparently died in exile. His compatriots thought he was a deserter and traitor, even someone who spoke lies on behalf of God. Jeremiah complained bitterly—to the king, and even more to God. Yet though God compelled Jeremiah to serve as "a prophet to the nations" (Jer. 1:5), his problems arose primarily because of his role as spokesman to Israel, not to other nations.[1]

HISTORICAL CONTEXT
OF THE PROPHET AND THE BOOK

The book of Jeremiah offers ambiguous evidence about its historical context. The superscription (1:1–3), as do others that preface prophetic books, links Jeremiah to the reigns of several kings, in his case Josiah, Jehoiakim, and Zedekiah. The thirteenth year of Josiah marks the beginning of his work (although some have argued that it is the year of his birth). Following the chronology of the superscription (627–587 B.C.E.), one would think that Jeremiah's work concluded roughly with the destruction of Jerusalem. Such a supposition, however, runs contrary to other elements of the book. The final chapter, often termed a historical appendix and apparently drawn from the final part of 2 Kings (2 Kgs. 24:18–25:30), refers to the release of a Judahite king (Jehoiachin) from a prison in Babylon. This event occurred around 560. Moreover, other portions of the book clearly report events that occurred well after Jerusalem had been destroyed. For example, 43:8–44:30 narrates

97

Jeremiah's activity once he and other refugees had settled in Tahpanes, which was located in the northeastern part of the Nile Delta. Hence, readers may conclude that the book reflects activity in the early exilic period as well as during the late monarchic period.

The book presents Jeremiah as a native of a small village, Anathoth, approximately five kilometers north of Jerusalem. Unlike Jerusalem, which sat in the tribal territory of Judah, Anathoth was near the border of Judah and Benjamin; it actually sat in Benjaminite territory. Scholars have made much of this distinction, since Benjamin was part of the northern kingdom and heir to theological traditions that were not necessarily shared by those in Judah. As is the case with several other prophets, Jeremiah was a priest, perhaps stemming from the house of Abiathar, who was sent to Anathoth by Solomon (see 1 Kgs. 2:26–27) for having supported David's son Adonijah instead of Solomon. Jeremiah—as a citizen of a northern tribe and in all likelihood heir of a declassed priesthood—might have been viewed as marginal by those in Jerusalem.

Many of the narratives that occur in the latter half of the book are prefixed with chronological formulae (e.g., 32:1). Of these, a goodly number reflect the ten-year period between the first and second Neo-Babylonian attacks on Jerusalem. During these years, Zedekiah, a regent who consulted Jeremiah, ruled as king. In contrast, the oracles that populate the earlier chapters in the book seem to have their points of origin in the late seventh century (e.g., the reference to Egypt in 2:36 may presage Josiah's death at the hand of Egyptian troops). Attempts to date precisely the poetic material are, however, unlikely to be productive.

Jeremiah's attitudes to the events of his time are reasonably straightforward. Once it became clear that his admonitions would affect no change in the people's behavior, Jeremiah affirmed consistently that the Babylonians would destroy Jerusalem. Judahites should respond not by forming alliances with potential allies but by submitting to Neo-Babylonian rule, and in so doing remain alive. Jeremiah even addressed those, like Ezekiel, who had been forcibly moved to Babylon. They were to "seek the welfare of the city" (29:7) where God had sent them. Those in exile were to "build houses and live in them" (29:5). Even more, Jeremiah was concerned that life in the land should continue. Just before the destruction of Jerusalem, Jeremiah claimed some ancestral land. This real estate transaction bore clear symbolic significance: "Houses and fields and vineyards shall again be bought in this land" (32:15). Jeremiah hoped for something akin to a return to an earlier political and social order.

Though chapters 29 and 32 attest that Jeremiah was active after the destruction of Jerusalem in 587, most of the literature attesting to his work refers to his activity prior to that year. The book itself, however, was formed in the exilic and postexilic periods. Both eras—before and after the demise of Judah—are, therefore, important for study of the book of Jeremiah.

THE "BOOKS" OF JEREMIAH

Several features of the book of Jeremiah deserve attention. First, the book itself was preserved in two significantly different versions. Hence, the reader should begin by knowing something about these differences and be able to assess how they might affect our understanding of the prophet and his work. Second, the book of Jeremiah comprises various types of prophetic speeches and prose accounts. Each makes different interpretive demands. Finally, two sections of the book—the "Book of Consolation" (chaps. 30–33) and the oracles against the nations (chaps. 46–51)—merit special examination because of their unique subject matter.

There is more than one form of the book of Jeremiah. In fact, we can read two quite distinct books, and in so doing gain considerable insight into the formation of prophetic literature as a whole. On the one hand, there is the version attested in the Hebrew Bible (or Masoretic Text, abbreviated as MT hereafter). On the other hand, one may consult the book of Jeremiah preserved in the Greek version of the Old Testament, the Septuagint (abbreviated as LXX hereafter). The Greek version of Jeremiah is around 3,000 words (about 15 percent of the total) shorter than the Hebrew version. In addition, the ordering of the two texts is quite different.[2]

One critical point for comparing the two books is the location of the oracles against the nations. They occur as chapters 46–51 in the MT, whereas they follow the first half of 25:13 in the LXX, where they occur as chapters 26–31. Moreover, the Greek version of the oracles against the nations occurs in a different order from the MT. For example, the major section against Babylon, which occurs as the final element in the Hebrew oracles against the nations (chaps. 50–51), appears as the second portion of the oracles against the nations in the LXX (LXX chaps. 27–28). In addition, the oracles directed against Moab (LXX 31:1–44) provide the conclusion for the Greek oracles against the nations (cf. 48:1–44 [vv. 45–48 do not occur in the LXX]).

Both versions have been known for centuries, but the significance of
the LXX version was not fully appreciated until after the Dead Sea
Scrolls had been discovered and analyzed.[3] In earlier times, the LXX
was thought to be an abbreviated form of the Hebrew text, the abbre-
viation having occurred during the process of translation from Hebrew
to Greek. That at least was the theory until the scrolls at Qumran were
discovered. The world of Jeremiah studies changed materially because
several of the Hebrew scrolls represented the same length of text as that
in the LXX. It became clear that the difference in size was not due to
the vagaries of translation. Analysis of these ancient manuscripts has
made scholars reassess the significance of the LXX form of Jeremiah
and to grant it more prominence in any analysis of that book.

Emmanuel Tov, who has recently written a definitive introduction to
Hebrew Bible textual criticism, has described the LXX as something
like a first edition of the book, with the version included in our modern English translations as a second edition.

> In edition II changes were inserted in the order of the verses and in
> wording, but more frequently elements were added: sections now
> occurring twice (e.g., 8:10b–12 for which cf. 6:13–15; 17:3–4, cf.
> 15:13–14; 30:10–11, cf. 46:27–28); new verses and sections (the largest
> ones are 33:14–26 and 51:44b–49a); new details, brief explanations, in
> particular expansions of proper names; expansions on the basis of con-
> text; expansions of formulae, etc.[4]

In order to demonstrate the differences between these two editions of
Jeremiah, it is appropriate to print up one major section in which there
are significant differences. Jeremiah 10:1–11 will serve as the exemplar.
Those elements printed in bold are not found in the LXX. In addition,
verse 11 is written in Aramaic (italics), probably a sign that this verse is
a later addition. One may now read this text with at least two questions
in mind: (1) What is the point of the earliest form of the text (i.e., without the bold and/or italic texts)? and (2) what has been added by the
new material?

1   Hear the word that the LORD speaks to you, O house of Israel.
2   Thus says the LORD:
    Do not learn the way of the nations,
        or be dismayed at the signs of the heavens;
        for the nations are dismayed at them.
3   For the customs of the peoples are false:
    a tree from the forest is cut down,
        and worked with an ax by the hands of the artisan;

4   people deck it with silver and gold;
         they fasten it with hammer and nails
         so that it cannot move.
5   Their idols are like scarecrows in a cucumber field,
         and they cannot speak;
     they have to be carried,
         for they cannot walk.
     Do not be afraid of them,
         for they cannot do evil,
         nor is it in them to do good.

6   **There is none like you, O Lord;**
         you are great, and your name is great in might.
7   **Who would not fear you, O King of the nations?**
         For that is your due;
     among all the wise ones of the nations
         and in all their kingdoms
         there is no one like you.
8   **They are both stupid and foolish;**
         the instruction given by idols
         is no better than wood!
9   Beaten silver is brought from Tarshish,
         and gold from Uphaz.
     They are the work of the artisan and of the hands of the goldsmith;
         their clothing is blue and purple;
         they are all the product of skilled workers.
10   **But the Lord is the true God;**
         he is the living God and the everlasting King.
     At his wrath the earth quakes,
         and the nations cannot endure his indignation.
11   *Thus shall you say to them: The gods who did not make the heavens and*
     the earth shall perish from the earth and from under the heavens.[5]

Those verses present only in the LXX concern the inappropriateness
of the construction and veneration of idols (though that particular term
is not present in these verses). The prophet admonishes his audience
not to learn, not to be dismayed, not to be afraid (vv. 2, 5). Moreover,
the prophet provides a warrant for these negative admonitions, namely,
these objects are human constructions; they are not alive and they can
neither walk nor talk (v. 5). In contrast, the poetry added in the Hebrew
version seems rather like a hymn extolling the deity. Verses 6–8—in
both affirmation and question—affirm that none is like Yahweh. Verse
10 emphasizes as well the singularity of Yahweh as the sole deity.
Whereas the earlier poetry is primarily negative in its purport, demean-
ing humanly confected deities, the later verses are positive, affirming the
power of Israel's God, especially as it is manifest over the nations. The

earlier words have exercised a generative role in eliciting language about Israel's God. Such is one of the ways in which the book of Jeremiah grew ("and many similar words were added to them" [36:32]).

Although the verse written in Aramaic (v. 11) is present in both the MT and LXX manuscript traditions, it makes a new point. The Aramaic material develops a theological position about the deity as true/living/everlasting. In addition, this verse introduces a theophanic, perhaps even eschatological, perspective, highlighting the impact of Yahweh's wrath on the nations and, more broadly, the earth.

In sum, Jer. 10:1–11 provides a wonderful experiment in the biblical studies laboratory. One may discern a core of poetry about the creation of icons. To it have been added both asseverations about Israel's God and judgments about foreign gods, the latter absent in the Greek Jeremiah, the former present in both Greek and Hebrew books.

Differences in length offer one fruitful way by means of which to compare these two books of Jeremiah. However, even in those cases in which the length is roughly the same, the two books differ in considerable measure. A. R. Pete Diamond has compared the general tendencies of these two books when studying the so-called confessions of Jeremiah. He has discovered that, whereas the Hebrew text tends to indict God in a particularly virulent and ironic way, the LXX text conveys the lament in terms like those in biblical psalms.[6] For example, Diamond examines the quite divergent understandings of Jer. 12:1:

> Righteous are you, LORD, so that I will defend myself before you; still, matters for judgment will I speak with you. (LXX)

> Innocent are you, Yahweh, if I lodge a complaint before you; yet sentence must I pass on you. (MT)

Clearly the MT offers the harsher judgment on the deity. As a result, the reader of the MT receives quite a different picture of Jeremiah's complaints than does the reader of the LXX.

Scholars have not yet offered definitive comparisons of these two versions of the book of Jeremiah. However, some tantalizing prospects are in view, particularly regarding the character of the prophet himself. In the Hebrew book, Jeremiah seems more an irascible individual; in the Greek book, more a typical prophet.

Obviously, in order to practice textual criticism in this way, one must know both the Hebrew and Greek languages, among others. Still, the student who knows only English can consult both of these textual types in

English translations. On the one hand, the MT is present in its purest form in *Tanakh*, a translation of the MT that uses no readings from the LXX.[7] On the other hand, the LXX is available in a number of antiquated English versions (e.g., *The Septuagint Version of the Old Testament with an English Translation by Sir Launcelot Lee Brenton* [London: Samuel Bagster, 1844]). A critical translation of the LXX is soon to be published by Oxford University Press. Finally, there are some monographs that include major portions of the Greek form of Jeremiah in English translation.[8]

LITERARY STRUCTURE AND FEATURES

Each prophetic book presents a unique set of literary issues. As for Jeremiah, readers will be struck by the prominence of prose in Jeremiah when compared with the book of Isaiah. In addition, the poetry is different from Isaiah. It is difficult to offer a list of basic forms, since Jeremiah's poetry is so filled with metaphors that dominate the structure of the poems themselves. As a result, we will focus on two important elements in the poetry—metaphor and the enemy from the north—before turning to the most significant feature of Jeremiah's poetry, namely, its relation to the world of lamentation. But first, we begin with the vexing issue of discerning the book's structure.

Literary Structure

Scholars have been more interested in offering hypotheses about the book's growth than they have in identifying the structure of the book as it currently exists. Of course, identifying such a structure is problematic because of the existence of the book in two quite different forms. Nonetheless, scholars have proposed several ways to understand the structure of Jeremiah in its Hebrew form.

The first model focuses on the importance of collections in the book. Many of the poetic sayings have been preserved in collections, some even with titles (e.g., "concerning the prophets" in 23:9) but some without (e.g., the wisdom sayings in 17:5–11). There are even thematic collections; for example, Jer. 3:1–4:4 revolves around the word and idea of "return."

If collections are so prominent, then one may postulate the existence of even larger ones. Indeed, it is possible to read the book and discern a basic tripartite structure: an agglomeration of poetic oracles and brief prose speeches (chaps. 1–25), primarily prose narratives about Jeremiah's activities (chaps. 26–45), and primarily oracles against foreign nations (chaps. 46–52). When reading the book in this way, the reader may perceive a movement from indictment and judgment to hope and then to a placement of Israel within an international perspective.

Other organizations have, however, been recently proposed. For example, Stulman has argued that the book is made up of two "scrolls" (chaps. 1–25 and 26–52). Stulman focuses on the role of the prose sermons as structuring devices. He understands the first scroll to offer a picture of "death and dismantling of Judah's sacred world," whereas the second scroll enables the reader to see "new beginnings from a shattered world."[9] Such a view finds an analogy with the judgment that the book of Isaiah may be read as a diptych.

As was the case with Isaiah, no view has won a scholarly consensus. Here again, readers are encouraged to read the book of Jeremiah and to attempt themselves to discern an intent behind the final form of the book.

Poetry

Scholarly attention to the book of Jeremiah has, for the past several decades, focused primarily on issues of the book's formation, especially that involving the prose sections. As a result, there has been relatively little study of the poetry, the more so since earlier studies of the poetry often constituted forays to discover what the prophet actually said or thought, a search often eschewed today.

Minimal attention to the poetry is in some measure understandable; there is more prose than poetry in the book. However, Jeremianic poetry, along with Isaiah 40–55, comprises one of the last major poetic prophetic corpuses, and hence deserves a careful reading. For the moment, I intend to bracket the poetic sections in the oracles against the nations and to focus on the hallmarks of the poetry in chapters 1–25, and even more in chapters 1–10, wherein lies much of the poetry in the book. Later in this section, we will examine poetry in the so-called Book of Consolation (the poetry is limited to chaps. 30–31) and in the oracles against the nations (chaps. 46–51).

General Features

Compared to the poetry both in the book of Ezekiel and in Isaiah 40–55, the poetry in Jeremiah appears in far briefer oracles, beginning with the first oracle in the book (Jer. 2:2–3):

Thus says the LORD:
I remember the devotion of your youth,
    your love as a bride,
how you followed me in the wilderness,
    in a land not sown.
Israel was holy to the LORD,
    the first fruits of his harvest.
All who ate of it were held guilty;
    disaster came upon them,
                                 says the LORD.

These two verses are normally understood to be a complete poem, replete with simile ("as a bride"), metaphor ("the first fruits of his harvest"), and historical allusion ("disaster came upon them"). And there is dissonance—how could there be harvest in a wilderness, in a land not sown? Moreover, how could the people (Israel), eat the first fruits of the harvest—to which they have just been compared? What did the people do that resulted in their being held guilty? We are not told. Compact though it may be, the poem appears to offer no simple lesson from history. Yet those who hear or read these lines surely know that Jeremiah is offering a terribly negative assessment of Israel's relation with its God.

As this reading of Jer. 2:2–3 suggests, this poetry is wonderfully wrought. What then are the hallmarks of these oracles that pervade the beginning of the book?

Metaphor and Indictment

From a literary perspective, the metaphors in Jeremiah are prominent, as they are in Hosea. Take, for example, the following passage in which God speaks:

[T]hey [my people] have forsaken me,
    the fountain of living water,
        and dug out cisterns for themselves
    cracked cisterns
        that can hold no water.
                                 (2:13)

However, Jeremiah's oracles are also different from those one finds in other prophetic books, such as Isaiah, Amos, or Micah. They are unlike those in Amos because they are relatively uninterested in offering specific indictments of what either individuals or the nation as a whole has done wrong. Whereas Amos speaks of bribery in the courts or unethical real estate transactions, we find no comparable observations about social or economic life in late seventh or early sixth-century Judah. One might read Jeremiah 1–10, noting those verses in which Jeremiah talks about what people are doing wrong. Inevitably, one would find the statements vague. We hear about "the evil of your doings" (4:4), individuals "skilled in doing evil" (4:22), "scoundrels" (5:26), people who are "greedy for unjust gain" (6:13), and those who practice "oppression upon oppression, deceit upon deceit" (9:6). Although Jeremiah's view of his countrymen is gloomy, he does not routinely tell us precisely what their inappropriate behavior involves.

The same may be said for his comments about religious malpractice. On more than one occasion, we read that Judahites have "forsaken" their God (e.g., 2:17, 19; 5:7; 18:13–17). There are indeed hints that they have gone on to venerate other deities. But the names of competitors (e.g., Baal) are not nearly so prominent as they are in books such as Hosea or Zephaniah. The following claim is typical:

> Has a nation changed its gods,
> > even though they are no gods?
> But my people have changed their glory
> > for something that does not profit.
> > > (Jer. 2:11)

The poem clearly suggests that the people have stopped venerating Yahweh. Still, the precise manner in which the people have "forsaken" the deity is not at all clear. In sum, Jeremiah is not a prophet who offers a series of precise indictments. The ambiguity of poetry invites readers to reflect about what might lie behind the images that the prophet provides.

Enemy from the North and Punishment

The prophet, however, provides far more pointed language about what is about to happen to the people than do many of his prophetic forbears. They will be devastated by military destruction at the hands of an enemy coming from the north, a primary motif in Jeremianic poetry.

> Hear, a noise! Listen, it is coming—
> > a great commotion from the land of the north
> to make the cities of Judah a desolation,
> > a lair of jackals.
> > > (10:22)

This notion of an enemy from the north is important at various points in the book. The motif is particularly prominent in chapters 4–10, but it returns in the oracle against Babylon near the end of Jeremiah. Danger from the north is first mentioned in two brief vision reports (1:11–14). It then reappears in 4:6, and with increasing frequency. At the outset, "north" is simply the direction from which a disaster will strike. Jeremiah 1:15, though probably an addition to the second vision report, identifies this disaster with "all the tribes of the kings of the north." That hyperbole of many nations does not continue. Instead, the poetry refers to one nation. It is an "enduring, ancient" nation (5:15), "a great nation . . . they are cruel and have no mercy, their sound is like the roaring sea" (6:22–23), "he comes like clouds, his chariots like the whirlwind; his horses swifter than eagles" (4:13). Such an assault will result in terrible, cosmic destruction: "I looked on the earth, and lo, it was waste and void; and to the heavens, and they had no light" (4:23), a description that depicts something antithetical to the created order.

Who was this enemy from the north? At the outset, we must note that in his poetry, Jeremiah never answers that question. The very ambiguity of this force from the north enhances its terror. Scholars have suggested Jeremiah may have originally been referring to the Scythians, a nation of horse-riding warriors from the area of the Caspian Sea who made incursions in Syria-Palestine. More recently, there has been a tendency simply to identify this enemy with the Babylonians, who did indeed destroy Judah. This would be satisfactory, except that in Jer. 50:3, 41, Jeremiah refers to a nation or people from the north who will destroy the Babylonians. In fact, 50:41–42, an oracle against Babylon, is a virtual replica of an oracle spoken against Judah, according to which they will be destroyed by the Babylonians. We should probably understand "the enemy from the north" as a potent symbol, ever available to convey a new, or the latest, military threat in the ancient Near East.

Jeremianic poetry, by employing a powerful image, the enemy from the north, enables the book to move one step beyond the world of mundane history. The poetry could have specified one or another country, but the ambiguity of the image adds to its ability to invoke terror.

The Poetry of Lamentation

How should people respond to this calamity? Later in the book in the prose sections we hear Jeremiah admonishing the people to accept their fate. However, in the poetic sections, we find a response rooted in traditional religious practice, namely, the lament.

So-called psalms of lament are the most prominent liturgical form in the Psalter. These psalms are often made up of a series of standard features: invocation, call for help, expressions of trust, vows to sacrifice or pray. The lament was not simply a way to complain; it involved a petition for help, expressing confidence that the deity would respond to the conditions that had elicited the lament. Individuals could offer laments, but so could entire communities. We even have laments from other ancient Near Eastern societies, often addressing the defeat of a nation's capital. Such laments are readily comparable to those in the book of Lamentations.

Laments derive from the language of ancient worship. They reflect what an individual or the people would have spoken in worship, often at a temple. There is strong evidence that, during the lament ceremony, a priest would have offered an oracle affirming that the worshiper had been heard and that his or her concerns were being addressed. These oracles of salvation, especially as they occur in Second Isaiah (e.g., Isa. 41:10), would have been spoken after the people had described their plight and asked for help. Then, after the proclamation of such an oracle, the individual would have continued with the final portion of the lament, acknowledging that the prayer had been heard (e.g., Ps. 6:9: "The LORD has heard my supplication; the LORD accepts my prayer").

The language of lament pervades the poetry in the book of Jeremiah.[10] The prophet commands the people to engage in lamentation (4:8; 6:26; 7:29; 9:10–11, 17–22; 14:17–18) as a result of the imminent destruction. We even hear what personified Jerusalem (Zion) will say:

> How we are ruined!
> We are utterly shamed,
> because we have left the land,
> because they have cast down our dwellings.
> (9:19; see also 10:19–21)

Even more typical, laments appear on the people's lips (e.g., 14:7–9, 19–22; 30:5–7; 31:15) as they confront not only military devastation but drought.

> Yet you, O LORD, are in the midst of us,
> and we are called by your name;
> do not forsake us!
> (14:9)

The prophet reports immediately that this request (and presumably the ensuing one in 14:19–22) would not be honored. (Interestingly, non-Israelites also are described as lamenting their fate [48:34–39]). Though the people might lament, Jeremiah's poetry provides no oracle of salvation from the deity.

Along with these laments of the people, we find brief poetic pieces that seem to reflect the deity's voice (9:10 [MT: "I will take up wailing and weeping"]; 12:7–13; 14:17–18; 30:12–15; 31:20; 48:31–33) and that contain elements of lamentation. In the first one, the Lord more or less reports what has happened:

> I have forsaken my house,
>   I have abandoned my heritage;
> I have given the beloved of my heart
>   into the hands of her enemies.
>   (12:7)

However, overt imagery depicting the deity's deep emotion about and response to such destruction appears in the second poem:

> Let my eyes run down with tears night and day,
>   and let them not cease,
> for the virgin daughter—my people—is struck down with a crushing blow,
>   with a very grievous wound.
>   (14:17; see also 8:18–9:1)

Even as the deity administers punishment to the people, God also grieves at their suffering. The rhetoric of lament permits the deity to express such sentiments.

Given the prominence of such language drawn from the world of lament, it should occasion no surprise that Jeremiah uses this discourse as well. It has become a commonplace to suggest that Jeremiah achieves full voice in his laments.[11] Such may be the case, but expressions of Jeremiah's complaints are not limited to the classic expressions listed below. As early as the book's fourth chapter we hear the prophet respond to the martial activity in Judah:

> My anguish, my anguish! I writhe in pain!
>   Oh, the walls of my heart!
> My heart is beating wildly;
>   I cannot keep silent;
> for I hear the sound of the trumpet,
>   the alarm of war.
>   (4:19)

Jeremiah 8:18–9:1 (cf. 13:17) also includes the powerful poetry of lamentation:

> My joy is gone, grief is upon me,
>   my heart is sick.
> . . . .
> For the hurt of my poor people I am hurt,
>   I mourn, and dismay has taken hold of me.
> Is there no balm in Gilead?
>   Is there no physician there?
>   (8:18, 21–22)

Nonetheless, there is a special set of Jeremiah's laments or complaints that have elicited intense scrutiny. Scholars disagree about which poetry should be counted among these laments. This diversity of judgment is primarily a function of the prominence of lament rhetoric in the book. Jeremiah 23:9, for example, which is attributed to Jeremiah, is imbued with the language of lament. Yet it is normally not included in the roster of Jeremiah's laments.

The laments attributed to the prophet grow out of and belong to the aforementioned language of lament. But they provide a personal angle of vision that is more focused on the persona of Jeremiah and his experience than it is on national destruction. They seem to derive from his own life, first in Anathoth and then in Jerusalem and, especially, from his work as a prophet. Scholars have debated vigorously the extent to which the laments express Jeremiah's own feelings and perceptions. That they could be understood in some straightforward autobiographical sense had been a presupposition for many interpreters of the book. However, Reventlow proposed that these poems were essentially like those laments in the Psalter, that is, the traditional language of worship and not the expressive poetry of an individual.[12] Hence, they did not represent Jeremiah's particular situation but instead reflected the community's perceptions of the crisis of the early sixth century. As could any ancient Israelite worshiper, Jeremiah used the traditional forms of lament. Baumgartner poses another explanation, namely, that Jeremiah appropriated traditional language to express his own anguish.[13] Many other scholars agree with this position. There can be no easy resolution to the quandary, namely, the extent to which one might find Jeremiah's experience embedded uniquely in these poems. However, in this book, these laments are attributed to Jeremiah, the primary character in the book. And so, we must attempt to understand them, filled with traditional images though they are, as words appropriate to this prophet as well as to the community, for whom he could serve as a spokesman.

I enumerate eight laments that stem from the prophet: (1) 11:18–23; (2) 12:1–6; (3) 15:10–12; (4) 15:15–21; (5) 17:14–18; (6) 18:18–23; (7) 20:7–13; and (8) 20:14–18. Of these eight, the first four include not only the complaint of the prophet but also a response from the deity. To this extent, they are very much informed by the ritual pattern of Israelite lamentation. However, the last four present no word from Yahweh. Hence, they work more as soliloquies than dialogues. This pattern of lament followed by response and then complaint followed by no response suggests that the order of these laments is significant. It is appropriate to read these laments as a minicorpus, a microcosm reflecting not only Jeremiah's role as prophet but also a world that includes Israel's increasingly complicated relationship to its God. I offer the following vignette for each of the laments.

Jeremiah 11:18–23. In the initial lament, Jeremiah attests that Yahweh has informed him about the machinations of some opposing group—a "they," which will be prominent throughout the laments. Jeremiah charges that some group is out to get him. Moreover, the lament itself has been influenced by the language and form of lament known elsewhere. One standard element of psalmic laments is a description of the individual's crisis—the complaint. In this case, it is a plot against Jeremiah's life (cf. Ps. 59:3). Another standard element in laments, the request for help, often plays itself out as a request that one's enemies be defeated (cf. Ps. 58:6–8). A third feature typical of laments is an expression of confidence that God can and/or will help those who ask for it ("for to you I have committed my cause"; cf. Ps. 43:1–2). In sum, this first lament of Jeremiah includes at least three elements typical of the form as attested in other biblical literature.

The deity offers a comprehensive response: Those who seek to harm Jeremiah will die. God's speech to Jeremiah both specifies and interprets the context of Jeremiah's complaint. The people are localized, they are "the people of Anathoth," Jeremiah's home village. Moreover, just as the lament quoted the people, so too does the oracle of response. We learn that these people have challenged Jeremiah not to engage in prophetic activity. Though Jeremiah has not said so explicitly, his lament stems from the response to his work as prophet, not an unmotivated—or simply personal—attack on him. The response to Jeremiah's complaint therefore does more than simply answer his request; the response contextualizes and interprets it.

Jeremiah 12:1–6. The tone shifts in the second lament. Whereas Yahweh was the one who informed Jeremiah about the nature of his plight in the first, now God becomes the object of Jeremiah's complaint. We seem to be more in the world of Job and Habakkuk than Hosea and Amos. Throughout verses 1–4, Jeremiah raises the big questions of theodicy—"Why does the way of the guilty prosper?" Again, Jeremiah's language is general; we hear no reference to those in Anathoth. Instead, according to Jeremiah, God bears the responsibility for enabling treacherous people to thrive ("You plant them, and they take root"). Even the "how long" query is general (cf. Ps 82:2; 94:7), introducing a question about the duration of the suffering of "the earth" (cf. Hos. 4:3). We hear nothing about Jeremiah's specific suffering, only his legal case.

Yahweh responds to Jeremiah's questions with two questions (v. 5), both of which suggest that what Jeremiah experiences now will become more severe in the future. "Horses" and "thickets of the Jordan" probably allude to the difficulties awaiting Jeremiah in Jerusalem, whereas "foot-runners" and "safe land" refer to his home. Again, Yahweh (v. 6) interprets those in Anathoth—Jeremiah's kin—as dangerous. However, Yahweh does not respond directly to the questions of Jeremiah's legal case; instead he challenges Jeremiah to ponder the difficulties he faces.

Jeremiah 15:10–12. This lament might strike the reader as unusual, since statements of woe often occur early on in prophetic oracles of judgment (e.g., Amos 6:1 or Isa. 5:8, 11). However, such language is also at home in laments. Psalm 120:5, an individual lament, includes comparable rhetoric ("Woe is me"). The phrase "man of strife" could be translated "man of legal contention" (it is the same Hebrew word that appeared in the second lament as "case" [12:1]). One has the sense that by now the laments are beginning to build on or allude to earlier ones, thereby achieving a cumulative effect.

The reference to mother and birth drives one back to prior language about the significance of Jeremiah's birth. The call narrative explicitly states that Jeremiah was designated as prophet prior to his birth, thus suggesting that any reference to his birth becomes—at least metaphorically—a comment about the beginning of his activity as a prophet. Again, as with the first lament, Jeremiah's experience of his role as prophet becomes a ground for lament. Also typical of laments are the protestations of innocence ("I have not lent, nor have I borrowed").

The deity's response is ambiguous, though it continues the rhetorical strategy of posing questions, not quick affirmations. Verse 12 again seems to allude to the book's first chapter. Jeremiah 1:18 also characterizes the prophet as iron and bronze, though the point of the question in verse 12 is not entirely clear. Still, in the prior verse, the deity attests having acted on behalf of Jeremiah in the past (the latter half of the verse is difficult to translate). Ambiguity pervades both verses and may be intentional (the ambiguity gives way to negativity in vv. 13–14, which were probably added by a later editor).

Jeremiah 15:15–21. This lament commences with an invocation of the deity, "O LORD," a hallmark of individual laments, and it continues by referring to the deity's knowledge of Jeremiah's situation (cf. 11:18). Other typical elements include the call for vengeance (15:15), protestation of innocence (v. 17), and complaint (v. 18). Two less typical features are even more important than the standard ones in this lament. First, Jeremiah attributes his suffering at the hands of his opponents to his work as prophet. Verse 16 recalls Jer. 1:9, which reports the manner in which Jeremiah received God's words, namely, that God placed them in Jeremiah's mouth. Second, Jeremiah challenges God even more directly than he did in the second lament, now using two similes: a deceitful brook and waters that fail. The image is consistent—something that one expects to provide help but that then disappears, as do seasonal streams in Syria-Palestine. Here too Jeremiah seems to appeal to the call narrative, in which God had affirmed, "I am with you to deliver you." Jeremiah claims that no such deliverance has been forthcoming.

Verses 19–21 constitute the last time God answers one of Jeremiah's complaints. As with the response to the second lament (12:5), the deity uses conditional language ("If you . . ."). God appears to challenge Jeremiah to stop mouthing words of complaint and instead to "return" to the task of uttering God's own words. And, with some irony, God says to Jeremiah: "return," which is what Jeremiah had been saying to the people (cf. the section with "return" as a motif [3:1–4:4]). The final portion of the oracle picks up imagery, the wall of bronze, and the promise of deliverance, which appeared as early as Jeremiah 1. The deity offers no new word to Jeremiah, but challenges him to act as prophet. Within the context of the eight laments, the deity now becomes silent.

Jeremiah 17:14–18. The fifth lament operates on two levels. On the one hand, these verses include stereotypic lament language. Verse 14 offers the imagery of being healed from disease and being saved from some tribulation. Verse 18 presents the call for retribution upon one's opponents, even "double destruction." On the other hand, the poet interweaves the concrete issue of Jeremiah's activity as prophet. His opponents say, "Where is the word of Yahweh?" suggesting that this word was not always immediately forthcoming (see 28:10–12 for an example of Jeremiah having to wait for Yahweh's word). Jeremiah then pleads with God, "Let it [the word] come." Moreover, Jeremiah claims that what he said in his role as prophet is known to Yahweh. Hence, he should be provided with his prophetic ammunition—God's words—in order to do his job. No word is forthcoming, either as a response to Jeremiah's lament or as a word that he might proclaim.

Jeremiah 18:18–23. The sixth lament presents the plotters at work, which is reminiscent of the first lament (11:19). They appear to quote from a Jeremianic oracle of judgment, that the various leaders of Israelite society will no longer be able to offer that with which they have been charged: no torah from priests, no counsel from the sage, and no word from the prophet. The last of the three issues picks up directly on the issue of the absence of the prophetic word, as that was addressed in the fifth lament. The issue of words and who is the author of words concludes the speech of the opponents. They claim that Jeremiah is speaking "his words" and, presumably, not the words of the deity. Hence, he can be challenged, even destroyed.

Jeremiah then challenges God to respond, using a play on the verb "heed" (vv. 18 and 19). Jeremiah appeals to one type of prophetic role, that of intercessor, to prove that he has acted on the people's behalf. Interestingly, the book offers no report of such intercessory activity. In fact, the traditions preserved in prose recollect that Jeremiah was prohibited from speaking to God on behalf of the people (7:16; 11:14; 14:11; cf. Amos 7:1–6 for an example of prophetic intercessory activity). The deity proclaims that even if the great intercessors of the past (Moses and Samuel) implored him on behalf of Israel, they would not succeed (15:11; cf. Ezek. 14:14, which makes a comparable claim but refers to different ancient heroes). Since Jeremiah is being hunted (both the pit and the snare were methods of hunting [vv. 20, 22]), it is difficult to imagine that Jeremiah would be enacting an intercessory role at this point. So it comes as no surprise that the remainder of the lament is filled with the call for vengeance upon his opponents, a feature prominent in many laments. We hear nothing from Yahweh's side.

Jeremiah 20:7–13. A subtext of sexual violence pervades the initial portion of this lament. The verb translated "entice" can also mean "seduce." And when coupled with vocabulary of being overpowering, the meaning moves toward rape. Such a judgment is confirmed by the prophet's shouting "Violence and destruction!" since Israelite law concerning rape involves the notion of crying out for help (Deut. 22:25–27). But another subtext also operates, namely, that of Jeremiah as purveyor of God's word, as prophet. He is a laughingstock, quite a different image from a victim of rape. He is a laughingstock, someone mocked, a subject of reproach and derision because of what he says. And what he says is "the word of the LORD."

Jeremiah claims that he has tried to avoid the prophetic role of speaking these words, but to no avail:

> Then within me there is something like a burning fire
>   shut up in my bones;
> I am weary with holding it in,
>   and I cannot.
>
> (20:9; cf. 6:11)

Due to the people's response to Jeremiah, he would prefer not to be a prophet, but he has been incapable of not speaking Yahweh's words, a claim that would be consistent with the logic of someone called to be a prophet before birth.

Much of the rest of this lament reprises earlier lament material, such as the reference to plotting, quotations from his opponents, confidence that Yahweh will act on Jeremiah's behalf, and the call for retribution. The final verse is unusual, however, if indeed it belongs to this lament. Verse 13 is the first line of a hymn. In the Hebrew language, it is a plural imperative ("You sing!"). That command is based on an appreciation of what God has done for someone (i.e., delivered someone in need). The verb "deliver" is the same verb as that present in the final of God's responses to Jeremiah (15:20–21) as well as in the call narrative (1:8). Moreover, the verb is in the past tense; deliverance of some sort has already occurred. The hymnic piece presumes the oracle of salvation, which is otherwise missing. Jeremiah still operates in the realm of the standard lament practice, even though in this case Yahweh has not responded to him.

Jeremiah 20:14–18. Any interpretation of the final lament must wrestle with the question of whether Jeremiah is calling for a curse or describing something as cursed. Put another way, should one translate "Cursed be . . ." or "Cursed is . . ."? Elsewhere in the book the latter option seems the appropriate translation (17:5; 48:10). Hence, one may understand Jeremiah to be viewing as accursed both the day of his birth and the one who announced it to his father. Again Jeremiah, as in the second lament, enters the world of Job (cf. Job 3:3: "Let the day perish in which I was born, and the night that said, 'A man-child is conceived.'" Here too the day and the "messenger" are viewed with radical negativity.)

Job's day of birth was, however, different from Jeremiah's day of birth. The latter event allowed what was happening in the womb to come full term, namely, the birth of someone designated as a prophet before he was born. Hence, in this last lament, Jeremiah turns back to his "preexistence" and expresses the wish that he had been killed before being born (v. 17). The final word is a question. This rhetoric is unusual in a lament, which normally asks for assistance, not for an answer. That Jeremiah lived in shame has been attested earlier in the laments (17:18), and it comes as the final words—"shameful days"—here. After posing this question, Jeremiah, as did God earlier, falls silent.

In sum, lament is *the* response to the disaster that Jeremiah proclaims. The language of lament plays out prominently throughout Jeremianic poetry, appearing on the lips of the deity, people, and prophet, even non-Israelites. The language of lament is essentially hopeful; those who use it expect a response. The laments in Jeremiah, however, make clear that a response—at least the hoped for response—was not, finally, forthcoming. The cry for help was allowed to stand on its own, a rhetorical response surely appropriate to the defeat and devastation of the period 597–587.

To affirm the centrality of laments offers Jeremiah and the people a way to think beyond the destruction of Judah. Laments move inevitably to life beyond the lamentable present. The hymnic fragment in Jer. 20:13 attests to this dynamic. As a result, the theo-logic of lament allows one to move from pronouncements of disaster to the poetry of life beyond destruction, just as laments are juxtaposed with—and sometimes even include elements of—thanksgivings in the Psalter.

Prose

In contrast to poetry, there has been considerable recent research on the prose literature in the book of Jeremiah, much of which is still influenced by Mowinckel's classic study. He maintained that the book was made up of four primary bodies of material: *A*—poetry, *B*—the prose story (biography) in chapters 26–45, *C*—prose speeches scattered throughout the book, and *D*—oracles of hope in chapters 30–31.[14] To these basic types of literature, one might add autobiographic prose (e.g., 14:13–16), though there is relatively little of this genre. Scholars have continued to use Mowinckel's alphabetic language, especially *A–C*. Further, its use has evolved into claims about authorship: *A* described as poetic oracles, with Jeremiah as the presumed author; *B* understood as biographic prose, with Baruch as the presumed author; and *C* as prose sermons, with various authors, including Deuteronomistic scribes.

All of these descriptions, as well as claims about authorship, need to be examined carefully. Is the poetry oracular (i.e., sayings of the deity), or are prophetic sayings prominent as well? Are chapters 26–45 bio-graphical or, more simply, third person narration? Moreover, do chap-ters 26–45 make up one long biography or several smaller ones? Are the prose sayings really sermons? (Were there "sermons" in ancient Israel? What are their essential features?) Moreover, all claims about authorship are increasingly viewed as difficult to justify and, perhaps, not all that important, since it may be possible to understand the liter-ature in question without knowing who wrote it.

I suggest that one may classify the prose in Jeremiah into essentially four basic types: reports, narratives, prophetic biography, and speech. This typology focuses less on the point of view—whether it is bio-graphical or autobiographical—and more on the literary style or genre of the literature in question.

Reports

The book of Jeremiah includes a number of reports, most of which depict—either in first or third person style—Jeremiah engaged in prophetic behavior. These are not stories; there is no arc of narrative. No narrative tension is created and then resolved. Instead, these texts chronicle action or behavior, in one case behavior that Jeremiah sim-ply observes (chap. 18).

Symbolic Action Report

Styles of literature known in other prophetic books make up part of this set. For example, there are symbolic action reports (e.g., chaps. 13; 18; 19; 20; 25; 32; 43; 51) in which the prophet is commanded to carry out a task, that behavior is then reported, and an interpretation of the behavior ensues. Jeremiah 13:1–11 offers a textbook example. Yahweh commands the prophet to buy and wear a loincloth, to bury it, and then to retrieve it many days later. When he does so, he finds that the loin-cloth has been ruined. Verses 8–11 then provide a divine oracle that explains the significance of this behavior, namely, that Israel is like a loincloth that God will now ruin.

Such texts in Jeremiah often involve the use of everyday objects (the linen loincloth, 13:1; wine jars, v. 12; clay and earthenware jug, 18:4; an ox yoke, 27:2; a deed, 32:10; large stones 43:8). But they can also involve the presence or absence of relationships in Jeremiah's life (i.e., the com-mand in chap. 16 that Jeremiah remain celibate). One symbolic action clearly exists essentially in the visionary world, one in which the prophet receives "a cup of the wine of wrath" from the hand of the deity (25:15–29).

Vision Report

Also typical of other prophetic literature are the vision reports that appear in Jeremiah (1:11–13; 24:1–10). Here, as elsewhere, the text reports that which is seen and then offers an interpretation of it. The message and the envisioned object are not coterminous. In Jer. 1:11–14, although Jeremiah reports seeing an almond branch, Yahweh, using a Hebrew pun, reports that the significance of the branch involves the way in which the deity is overseeing his word. What Jeremiah saw and what the deity intends as the meaning are entirely different matters. So, too, Jeremiah sees "a boiling pot, tilted away from the north," which Yahweh interprets as a military invasion. And, as with the symbolic action reports, the visionary objects—almond branch, boiling pot, and baskets of figs—are part of everyday life in Syria-Palestine. (The visionary world of Zechariah is far more bizarre!) Given the prominence of verbal and auditory imagery in Jeremiah (e.g., 6:17–18; 10:22; 19:3; as well as the call narrative), it is not surprising that visions are relatively infrequent in this book.

Other Reports

Other prose reports fall outside these standard genres of prophetic literature. They include the command to speak to the people, followed by the speech—again in prose—itself. Jeremiah 7:1–8:3; 17:19–27; and 22:1–5 are typical of this format. In none of these cases do we hear that the command is carried out, nor are we told about how the people responded, assuming that the words were in fact proclaimed. Such prose reports regularly include a command to speak, and they may identify a location (e.g., the temple or a city gate). But such descriptions about the occasion are overpowered by the speech(es) that follow. So, with the exception of the first two verses, all of Jer. 7:1–8:3 comprises a series of brief prose speeches. In sum, prose reports focus on the message of the deity as conveyed by the prophet, not on the prophet or the circumstances in which he worked.

Narratives

The book includes a number of stories about Jeremiah. These occur in two basic blocks—chapters 26–29 and 36–45. In no case are they told in the first person. Someone is writing about Jeremiah. Although Jeremiah's words or prophetic actions are frequently cited, they do not make up the bulk of the text. Prose narration or the speeches of others (king, opponents) are important building blocks. Finally, the prose possesses narrative structure, that is, a complication develops out of the present, whereupon some resolution is brought to the crisis. In many of these stories, the point of interest is the plight in which Jeremiah finds himself (e.g., having been thrown into a muddy cistern [38:6]).

The so-called temple sermon (26:1–24) provides an interesting example, the more so since this incident also occurs in the form of a prose report (7:1–8:3). The incident begins with Jeremiah able to move about the town freely (cf. the limitations reported in chap. 36). He is told to deliver a divine oracle at the temple (vv. 2–6), which he apparently does. One key element in his proclamation is that the temple in Jerusalem may well be destroyed, as had the Yahwistic shrine in Shiloh. This statement was apparently viewed as treasonous by "the priests and the prophets." As a result, Jeremiah is put on trial for his life. The resolution of the crisis transpires during the course of the trial, as a set of litigants—"the officials and all the people"—allude to the treatment of an earlier prophet, Micah, who also spoke disturbing words but who was not put to death. The trial speeches conclude with the elders' questions (v. 19). They seem designed to prevent the people from killing Jeremiah. Still, at story's end, the reader is not told what will happen. In an aside, the author reports a related episode about Jehoiakim's decision to kill the prophet Uriah. Finally, the author returns to the Jeremianic tale in the final verse of the chapter, in which we are told that Jeremiah was saved from the people by Ahikam, a court official (see 2 Kgs. 22:12, 14), who apparently still had considerable power under a new king. We are not told explicitly what the sentence of the court was, but we may infer that since Ahikam was forced to rescue Jeremiah, he had received the death sentence.

This story focuses less on Jeremiah's words than it does on what happens to him when he proclaims such words. Put another way, Jeremiah has become the message. Of the twenty-four verses in chapter 26, only eight convey Jeremiah's words. Clearly, story outweighs speech. The political and religious conflicts in which Jeremiah was embroiled had caught the attention of an ancient narrator. Unlike the author of Jeremiah 7, this individual offers a dynamic story as the context for the temple sermon, and not just the temple sermon itself. Jeremiah and the people around him, not just their words, have pride of place. The story about the encounter between Jeremiah and Hananiah (chap. 28) is equally compelling. These narratives explore what happens to the person of the prophet as a result of his prophetic activity.

Biography

The most extensive prose document devoted to Jeremiah is contained in chapters 36–45. Chapter 36 has received significant attention, since it purports to describe the creation of at least one form of the book of Jeremiah. However, it, like chapter 26, is one story—both have a beginning, middle, and end. The final portion, chapter 45, though composed in prose, reports Jeremiah delivering a divine oracle to Baruch. However, the situation with chapters 37–44 is different. Many scholars have maintained that they constitute one long narrative, though it is difficult to discern an overarching narrative structure.[15]

How should we understand this eight-chapter long section (much of which Mowinckel had described as his *B* source)? The categories we may use to analyze this material are not always carefully defined. Narrative, story, prophetic historiography, and prophetic biography constitute some of the important options. Narrative and story are virtually coterminous. Alexander Rofé has argued that prophetic historiography focuses on the role of prophets in the affairs of peoples, states, and their leaders, whereas prophetic biography addresses the prophet himself. According to these criteria, Jeremiah 37–44 looks more like biography than historiography. Rofé writes:

> A biography is a narrative account of the stages of a person's life, an account that aspires to authenticity and historical accuracy. It records the actions of a particular individual and his experiences in his struggle to achieve his principles. An examination of the narrative sections of Jeremiah reveals that they conform to this definition.[16]

This judgment is eminently sensible, though it does reflect a fairly modern notion of biography. By contrast, if one examines the set of literature known as ancient biography, one would expect biographic prose to depict an individual's life in order to demonstrate a point or prove a thesis (some have called such literature *biographie à thèse*). Following this notion, one would read the Jeremianic biography looking not only for the life of Jeremiah but for some larger theme as well. As we shall see, chapters 37–44 do embody such a theme.

Jeremiah 37–44 flows chronologically, from the beginning of the second Babylonian siege (ca. 589) to the time that some Judahites had settled in exile in Egypt (sometime in the first decade after the fall of Jerusalem in 587). The material is divided into episodes, which reflect diverse conflicts: Jeremiah versus "the officials," Jeremiah versus Zedekiah, Jeremiah versus those who want to leave the land, Jeremiah versus Judahite idolaters in Egypt. These chapters describe Jeremiah acting as prophet in utterly diverse conditions. They possess no overt narrative structure as a whole, nor do they convey Jeremiah as a fully fleshed-out character, though there are hints, (e.g., Jeremiah as someone who is afraid [37:10; 38:15]). Instead, these chapters focus around a theme or thesis: Jeremiah, no longer free, presents Yahweh's words, but no one follows those words, even after Jerusalem has been destroyed and the people are in exile.

The biography is really rather complicated. Nebuchadnezzar is a key player (see 37:1; 39:11; 44:30). In a significant portion (40:7–41:18), Jeremiah is not even present, perhaps suggesting that the biographer included some historical source material that had nothing explicitly to do with Jeremiah (as is also the case with chap. 52, the historical appendix to the book). Moreover, the biographer has created two basic panels (37:1–41:18 and 42:1–44:30), each of which begins with a request for Jeremiah to intercede with Yahweh on behalf of the people (37:3; 42:2). The fall of Jerusalem stands at the chronological center (chap. 39). But the fate of various people, rather than the destruction of the city or temple, receives pride of place. The description of the defeat is remarkably laconic ("when Jerusalem was taken" [39:3]). The first panel presents far more action than does the second, which includes two long speeches by the prophet (42:9–22; 44:2–14). It is perhaps appropriate that the biography ends with Jeremiah in full voice, offering a sign act to those in Egypt about the fate of Pharaoh Hophra.

If we were to look for a theme underlying these chapters, what might it be? For an answer, we should look to the words of the biographer, who presented the theme at the outset of his work: "Neither he nor his servants nor the people of the land listened to the words of the LORD that he spoke through the prophet Jeremiah." Never was there a less successful prophet.

Chapter 45 strongly suggests that Baruch was Jeremiah's biographer. He knew about the extent of Jeremiah's suffering—and apparently shared in that misery (45:3). Baruch would survive the degradation that the remnant of Judah would suffer. And, though not accorded the status of a prophet, Baruch would create prophetic literature, Jeremiah 37–44, a prophetic biography.

Speeches

The book of Jeremiah is infused with prose speeches, what Mowinckel termed source C (Mowinckel's primary exemplars were 7:1–8:3; 11:1–5, 9–14; 18:1–12; 21:1–10; 25:1–11a; 32:1–2, 6–16, 24–55; 43:1–17; 34:8–22; 35:1–19; 44:1–14). These prose sayings often include some reporting as well, identifying those to whom Jeremiah is speaking as well as their reactions to him (e.g., 44:15, 20). In addition, two of these texts present what we have earlier described as symbolic action reports (chaps. 18 and 32). Most distinctive from a formal point of view, however, is the absence of prophetic speech, which was quite prominent in the poetry. There we hear Jeremiah's voice (e.g., 9:17–19), with remarkable frequency. Once we move into the prose speeches, however, divine oracle predominates. The "I" of Yahweh seems to preclude the presence of the prophetic voice in this literature.

Mowinckel maintained that this material should be viewed as of a piece, a source. Similar features might be observed in many of these verses. They comprise rather long speeches, composed with a limited vocabulary. A number of phrases recur regularly (e.g., "to walk after other gods") as do certain topics (e.g., idolatry). "Ethical" indictments are a minor element, except in the temple speech. The texts are even comparable in form, often possessing a tripartite structure: call to repentance (11:6–8), indictment for lack of repentance (11:9–10), and judgment (11:11). Mowinckel thought they were monotonous in tone and without contextualizing circumstance. Moreover, he argued that there was a striking similarity between the elements common to these texts and so-called Deuteronomistic prose.[17] The phrase "walking after other gods" occurs throughout the Deuteronomistic History as a standard way in which to characterize sinful behavior. In addition, certain turns of phrase that appear in C (e.g., 11:4: "I brought them out of the land of Egypt, from the iron smelter") bear striking similarity to diction in the book of Deuteronomy (e.g., Deut. 4:20).

In essence, Mowinckel offered two distinct arguments: that certain prose texts comprise a corpus and that they are related to or derive from Deuteronomistic prose. Though these views held sway for decades, the second one has come in for serious challenge, as should the first. As for the second, Helga Weippert has maintained that the prose speeches derive from the poetry.[18] They represent the prose form of what was or could have been said in poetic form. Moreover, despite similarities in diction between Jeremiah and the Deuteronomistic History, the controlling ideas and literary contexts are often different. Consequently, Weippert argues that many of these speeches do not reflect the hand of the Deuteronomists. Instead, she insinuates that Jeremiah was responsible for these prose speeches, since they represent what she deems to be an essential feature of prophetic activity, namely, the attempt to convince people to change their behavior.

McKane has pushed in a similar, though not identical, direction. He maintains that the poetry is a "reservoir" from which the prose was composed.[19] Various elements of the prose elicited new literature, although probably not from Jeremiah himself. McKane's view challenges the notion of a *C* source. Rather than seeing the book as the conflation of a series of sources, he speaks rather of a "rolling corpus," that is, a collection of both poetry and prose that grows over time. Hence, to approach the prose speeches in the book of Jeremiah is to encounter greater diversity of literature than Mowinckel and others might have us suspected, that is, greater diversity than one source would present, even the set that Mowinckel outlined including oracles, sayings, and symbolic action reports.

We need to examine several exemplars of these prose speeches. Jeremiah 3 includes two speeches whose brevity probably prevented Mowinckel from including them in his analysis. The first one (3:6–10) is a private oracle from Yahweh to Jeremiah. It concerns both Israel and Judah, as well as the fact that Judah did not "return," even after seeing what happened to Israel. Although this private oracle shares the "return" motif with the oracles that both precede and follow it, and although Israel is addressed in the ensuing section (at least in v. 12), verses 6–10 seem to provide their own distinctive point, namely, that Judah did not learn from Israel's example. The two nations are personified as sisters, and their error is conveyed using the metaphor of adultery (cf. Ezekiel 16 and 23 for a comparable perspective). There is nothing particularly Deuteronomistic about this assessment. Moreover, Jeremiah frequently uses the metaphor of adultery in his poetry. The speech does seem to reflect the demise of Judah—she did not return "with her whole heart, but only in pretense" (v. 10). Such a speech addresses those who might have wondered about the equity of Judah's fate, who might have heard that Judah had attempted to "return." This author was concerned to explain, to help those who had survived understand what had happened. Not all "returning" is true returning.

Jeremiah 3:15–18 is another prose speech of similar length. It, too, clearly presupposes the demise and exile of both Judah and Jerusalem. Moreover, it is composed in three sections; formulae (v. 17: "at that time"; v. 18: "in those days) introduce the second and third parts. Together, these elements anticipate the restoration of Jerusalem, but things are moving in a more creative direction. In the early Persian period, Yahwists in Judah were concerned about the ways in which to order their political and religious lives. Should the old order be restored? This speech offers a negative answer—the ark, a constitutive symbol of early Israelite religion, is not to be restored. Instead, Jerusalem itself will be understood as Yahweh's throne. This prose oracle almost certainly postdates the earlier one in this chapter. These two prose speeches—both divine oracles—reflect different perspectives and backgrounds, and neither betrays what some have called Deuteronomistic influence. Such evidence must be included in any assessment of prose speeches in the book of Jeremiah.

Unlike the exemplars drawn from chapter 3, Jer. 11:1–17 routinely appears in lists of Jeremiah's prose sermons. Here the language and perspectives seem to be more resolutely Deuteronomistic, with references to covenant, the iron smelter (see Deut. 4:20), and "going after other gods." These verses are something of a pastiche. Verses 1–8 offer a retrospective judgment ("I brought upon them . . .") and the reason for it. In contrast, verses 9–13, equally Deuteronomistic, anticipate a judgment in the future ("I am going to bring disaster. . . ."). There follows the final portion in which poetry—verses 15–16 (though not so conveyed in English translations)—is surrounded by prose in verses 14 and 17. The poetry points to inescapable doom for Judah, whereas the prose forbids Jeremiah from attempting to intercede and offers further indictment. Here again, the "prose sermon" is in reality less a sermon than a collection of sayings from different times and with different themes.

In sum, most of the prose speeches are couched in the form of oracles from Yahweh. However, they reflect diverse theological perspectives—sometimes that of the Deuteronomist and sometimes not.

Conclusion

After examining both the poetry and the prose literature in Jeremiah, two distinctive features of this book emerge. First, the world of Jeremiah is a private or interior one. The introductory phrase, "the word of the LORD came to me," is strikingly prominent. The laments are embedded in this same world of communication, which involves dialogue between the deity and his prophet. Second, and almost a corollary, writing, as such, is particularly prominent in this book. To be sure, the imagery of a scroll is prominent in Ezekiel. However, the act of writing prophetic words is perhaps even more significant in Jeremiah, particularly as it involves the production of a prophetic book. The book itself attests to its own process of growth. Jeremiah 36 describes the destruction of one collection of the prophet's words along with the creation of a new one, in which more words were present than in the old one. Jeremiah 51:64 ("thus far the words of Jeremiah") obviously refers to a collection that ended at this point, perhaps before the historical appendix, chapter 52, was added to the book. In addition, we learn that the book was made up of a series of prior written collections. Jeremiah

51:60, while referring to a scroll that will be thrown into the Euphrates, almost certainly refers to what we find in chapters 50–51. In addition, Jer. 30:2 ("write in a book all that I have spoken to you") prefaces the collection in chapters 30–31, a separate collection of sayings (cf. also 25:13 and 45:1). And even when there is no specific reference to a scroll (*mĕgillāh*) or book (*sēper*)—both words no doubt refer to a scroll—one may identify collections that could be so identified (e.g., 21:11–23:8 and 23:9–40). Jeremiah may have been a speaker of Yahweh's word, but for a variety of reasons—including the ban of Jeremiah against appearing in public at certain points in his career—we are privy to the ways in which words that might have been declaimed were inscribed and/or organized. Jeremiah as prophet depended on his scribal colleague Baruch for the inscription and preservation of much of this work.

ORACLES CONCERNING THE NATIONS

The book of Jeremiah includes six chapters of oracles "concerning the nations" (Jer. 46:1). In this regard, Jeremiah is similar to the other major prophetic books, each of which includes such a section. This book, however, differs from its cohorts in several ways. This is the smallest such collection, which is, in itself, surprising (Isaiah has eleven chapters, Ezekiel eight). Unlike his compatriots, Jeremiah was called to be a "prophet over nations and over kingdoms" (1:10). So one might have expected more such oracles than are present in Isaiah and Ezekiel. Further, a more complicated textual history lies behind Jeremiah's oracles than is the case in the other books. As has already been noted, the oracles against the nations in the LXX occupy a different, and probably more original, position. (They also occur in a different order.) In the LXX, the oracles against the nations follow immediately upon Jer. 25:13a: "I will bring upon that land all the words that I have uttered against it, everything written in this book." Since Nebuchadnezzar and Babylon have been the object of concern in chapter 25 up to that point, we might expect an oracle against Babylon. But in the LXX, the oracle against Elam appears first, which is then followed by the oracles against Egypt and Babylon (chaps. 50–51 in the MT). Put another way, the oracles against the nations in the LXX commence with those against three major powers and then continue with those against Syro-Palestinian states, concluding with the one against Moab (what is 48:1–44 in the MT [48:45–47 are missing from the LXX]). Then in the LXX, the Hebrew material found in 25:15–38 becomes chapter 32, a prose conclusion to the oracles against the nations. In contrast, the oracles against Babylon conclude the MT version of the oracles against the nations. It is difficult to say which ending is the more original or, for that matter, more appropriate. In either case, Jer. 25:29—"See, I am beginning to bring disaster on the city that is called by my name, and how can you [plural] possibly avoid punishment? You shall not go unpunished, for I am summoning a sword against all the inhabitants of the earth"—conveys the logic of Jeremiah's oracles against the nations.

As a prophet "over nations," Jeremiah is empowered through a symbolic action (25:15–29). He is to take "a cup of the wine of wrath" and make all nations drink from it. A long list follows, and at its head stands Judah. Interestingly, the list in Jer. 25:19–26 does not match the list of nations in the oracles themselves. For example, Damascus is included in the oracles (49:23–27) but is not in the prose list, and Philistia is included in the list but not in the oracles. The list concludes on a subtle note, referring to "the king of Sheshach," which is a cryptic expression for Babylon. The list at this point, therefore, mirrors the general order in the MT, emphasizing that Babylon too will suffer during this universal judgment.

Several elements in these oracles stand out.

Egypt

The two oracles against Egypt are rooted in specific historical moments, interactions between Egypt and Babylon, which Jeremiah interprets from a theological perspective. The first (46:2–12) focuses on Egypt's attempt to deter Nebuchadnezzar's forces from entering Syria-Palestine. In 604, the Egyptian forces were defeated, events about which Jeremiah must have known. Verses 5 and 12 seem to reflect knowledge of the battle after it happened. Rather than a moment in the Neo-Babylonian chronicle, Jeremiah sees these events through the lens of an Israelite tradition—"the day of the LORD" (46:10). Rather than a victory of Nebuchadnezzar, these defeats are a sacrifice to Yahweh. In the second oracle (46:13–26), we hear about another military conflict between these two powers, circa 568, almost twenty years after the fall of Jerusalem. Jeremiah anticipates a Babylonian attack and the defeat of Egypt. Though we know that Jeremiah was taken to Egypt, there is little evidence from elsewhere in the book that he was active up to this time. Moreover, there is extrabiblical evidence for such an attack, though not for a devastation of Egypt by the Neo-Babylonian forces. Curiously, Jeremiah is not so much interested in indicting Egypt as he is in interpreting from an Israelite perspective what has happened to that country. He does this with wonderful images, such as Egypt slithering away like a frightened snake (46:22).

Babylon

The oracle against Babylon is truly monumental, from both literary and theological perspectives. At the outset, one is jarred by the new tone present in chapters 50–51. Earlier in the book, Jeremiah had viewed the Babylonians as the instruments of God's punitive action against Israel (and against Egypt for that matter). But now Yahweh's "vengeance" (e.g., 50:15; 51:11) will come against Babylon. But why, particularly if their action against Israel was at Yahweh's behest? There is no easy answer. The book itself points to that which Babylon had done: "Babylon must fall for the slain of Israel" (51:49). And yet that too was foreseen by Jeremiah. Some scholars have suggested that these chapters represent a hand different from Jeremiah, that of a later poet/prophet. Indeed, there is considerable evidence for such a claim. Still, before pursuing that line of argument, it is important to note that the role of Babylon in the book is not uniform, even apart from chapters 50–51. Babylon is not even mentioned in the first nineteen chapters of the book. Those chapters, many of which probably stem from the early period of Jeremiah's career, reflect the deep conviction that Judah will be defeated at the hand of the enemy, but Jeremiah speaks of an enemy from the north, not Babylon per se. Over the course of time, it apparently became clear that Babylon would serve as that enemy, then that Babylon itself would suffer attack at the hands of yet another enemy of the north (50:3; 51:41), which, fittingly, is not defined. Clearly the role of Babylon changes throughout the course of the book. In the final chapters, "arrogant" Babylon, rather than Yahweh's agent, becomes the object of the deity's assault.

Chapters 50–51, though titled "the word that the LORD spoke concerning Babylon," are diverse. Chapter 50 soon becomes a series of poetic oracles separated by those written in prose; after the poetic oracle in verses 11–16, they alternate without exception. Even with this literary variation, the dominant motif is that of a military attack on Babylon. It is almost as if what they had done to others (e.g., bring a sword against Judah) will be acted out against them with even greater intensity, as suggested by the repeated use of "sword" in verses 35–37. Things change with chapter 51, however. With the exception of verses 11, 24, and the concluding symbolic action report (vv. 59–64), the remaining fifty-six verses are all poetry. Moreover, the poetry is different from that in chapter 50, and with a new rhetoric.

Chapter 51 includes poetry that is hymnic (vv. 15–19), often condemning the veneration of images or idols (vv. 47, 52–53). In that poetry, the prophet commands those in Israel to flee from Babylon (vv. 6, 45). Woman Zion speaks of the disaster that befell her (vv. 34–35). All these sound very much like the poetry in Isaiah 40–55, something that could not be said of chapter 50. In sum, these chapters probably reflect multiple hands, perhaps Jeremiah, but certainly later ones, particularly those who were part of the Babylonian exile.

Hope

Jeremiah's oracles against the nations have been suffused by a motif of hope, which is present elsewhere in the book. One is not surprised to find language of promise to Israel (46:27–28, which also appears as 30:10–11). However, there are words of weal to foreign nations as well. With one exception (Edom), they come at the end of the material devoted to a particular nation: Egypt (46:26), Moab (48:47), Ammon (49:6), Edom (49:11), and Elam (49:39). Three of these (Moab, Ammon, and Elam) are virtually identical—"I will restore the fortunes of x," suggesting that they have been appended to the earlier collection. Although such a late redactor may have been interested in good fortune for many nations, that individual did not see fit to add such a sentiment to the final oracle, which is against Babylon. That nation shall "sink, to rise no more" (51:64). Ultimately, the final word in the oracles against the nations in the MT is one of doom.

AFTER JUDGMENT

Though Jeremiah, like Ezekiel, lived after the defeat of Judah, the book attesting his activity is far less engaged in the life beyond defeat. There is no program for restoration as there is in Ezekiel 40–48. Nonetheless, there are intimations about a life both in the land and in exile, several of which have exercised a profound influence on later writers (e.g., the notion of a new covenant). It is to this material that we now turn.

Although scholars normally point to chapters 30–33, often known as the Book of Comfort or the Book of Consolation, as the place where Jeremiah addresses a time beyond the destruction of Jerusalem, there are a number of other places where a message of weal is proffered

(3:15–18; 4:27 // 5:18; 12:14b–15; 16:14–15 // 23:7; 23:5–8; 46:27–28 // 30:10–11). One may offer several literary judgments about this material. First, with the exception of 46:27–28, which repeats 30:10–11, where it almost certainly originated, all these texts are written in prose. Many seem to be later additions to the earlier portions of the book. For example, 12:14b–15 is clearly a later addition; it concerns a plucking up of Judah with a positive intent and has been interpolated into an oracle dealing with Judah's neighbors, who will be plucked up for destruction. The word "pluck" has served as a link that allows this later addition. Second, several motifs appear in a number of these texts; there is almost an expected chain of events. Yahweh will not make "a full end" of the people. Those who have been taken into exile (in the land of the north) will return to the land. Such a return encompasses not only the most recent exile—that of Judah—but Israel as well. These nations will be reunited under a Davidic king (shepherd) who will rule with justice and righteousness. As a result, Jerusalem will become (again) "the throne of Yahweh," a place where all nations will gather. Of these elements, perhaps the most unusual is the presence of Israel, the northern kingdom, and the reunified nation.

When examining Jeremianic poetry, we explored the language of lament. Remarkably, this discourse remains prominent in the so-called Book of Consolation (chaps. 30–33). The vocabulary or types of lamentable conditions that have appeared earlier in the book recur here in the following oracles: 30:5–7, 12–17; 31:7–9, 10–14, 15, 16–17. However, now, instead of admonitory questions or conditional challenges, the poetry envisions the deity acting on Israel's behalf. Yahweh rescues (30:7); restores health and heals wounds (30:17); brings and gathers (31:8); ransoms, redeems, comforts (31:11, 13); rewards and gives hope (31:16, 17). Chapters 30–31 include a series of oracles that anticipate or report that God has responded to Israel in crisis. The ancient ritual of lament has been successful, though it has not averted the radical crisis of 587. Attending to the language and form of lament helps explain the language of hope and deliverance in the book, which is part of the process of lamentation and would have been well-known by the priest Jeremiah.

Chapters 30–33, though often offering a message beyond that of punishment, are not a body of homogeneous material. It is probably a misnomer to construe them as "a book," despite what is said in 30:2: "Write in a book all the words that I have spoken to you." Chapters 30–31 are primarily a collection of oracles written in poetry, though they culminate in prose describing a "new covenant." However, chapter 32 is a prose chronicle recounting a symbolic action, namely,

Jeremiah's purchase of a field in Anathoth, his ancestral home. This chronicle is followed by a prayer and more oracles, now in prose. Chapter 33 is introduced as "a word," one that has come a second time to Jeremiah, but in fact the chapter offers an anthology of words, most of which are introduced by a formula such as "thus says the LORD." I shall treat chapters 30–31, 32, and 33 as separate entities in this larger collection.

Jeremiah 30–31 roots words of weal in the disaster that has overtaken "Jacob." The first oracle (30:5–7) speaks of terror, panic, and distress, but concludes by affirming that this person representing Israel will be "rescued." Such an oracle is utterly appropriate, since it makes the transition from destruction to reconstruction. The same may be said for 30:12–17, which likewise focuses on the wound that Jacob has suffered but from which he will be healed. Just as the oracle against Babylon seems to be related to Isaiah 40–55, the same may be said for much of the language and ideas in chapter 30 (cf. 30:10–11 with Isa. 41:8–10). The rescue and healing that Yahweh promises are given specificity as the chapter develops: The people will return, the city will be rebuilt, a ruler will emerge from the people, people will have flocks.

In reading through these chapters, the prominence of references to Israel, the northern kingdom, are impressive. One could even term chapter 31 the "Ephraim" chapter. (Chapter 30 might be called the "Jacob" chapter.) Jeremiah 31:2–6, though it concludes with reference to Zion, seems focused on God's care for the mountains of Samaria. Jeremiah 31:7–9 focuses explicitly on Ephraim, a symbol of the northern kingdom. One can even read 30:18–21, asking: Could this oracle have been uttered by an Israelite prophet who hoped for the restoration of the northern kingdom (the city in v. 18 is unnamed)? Might Jeremiah have been such a prophet, particularly early in his work, when under the impetus of Josiah's political reforms, an integration between the north and south was in the air? Whatever their origins, these oracles now address the future of God's people who have been exiled, whether by the Neo-Assyrians or by the Neo-Babylonians. Though the oracle concerning the new covenant is the most famous portion of this chapter, one could argue that 31:21–22 should be equally well-known. In this poem, directed to "virgin Israel," the people are commanded to return, and this because "the LORD has created a new thing on the earth; a woman shall embrace a man," an image that reverses gender roles with regard to human affection. Such imagery concludes on a remarkable note: Jeremiah awakes from a pleasant "sleeping vision" (31:26). In contradistinction to earlier visions of destruction (1:13), the visionary world now offers words of weal.

The most famous part of the Book of Consolation ensues (31:27–40). This appendix comprises three prose and one poetic saying. Several things are striking. The sayings all share elements with texts in other prophetic books: Verses 27–30, which void the proverb concerning parents eating sour grapes, are directly related to Ezek. 18:1–32; verses 31–34, which involve a new covenant, seem similar to Ezek. 36:25–27; verses 35–37 share imagery of God as creator with Second Isaiah (e.g., Isa. 42:5–9); and verses 38–40, with their concern for the rebuilding of Jerusalem, resonate with Zech. 14:10–11. Further, verses 31–34 speak of a new covenant. Jeremiah and his followers were not the only prophets interested in the viability of covenant traditions after Judah had been destroyed. Isaiah 55:3–4 offers a democratic reworking of the Davidic covenant so that the blessing formerly associated with the Davidic house now becomes available to all Israel. Jeremiah works out of the older traditions as well, but with special attention to the Mosaic tradition. The Torah itself will apparently not change, but the way in which Israel knows that Torah will; it will be inscribed on their heart, not on stone. This idea was already present in principle in an earlier articulation of the Mosaic covenant: "Keep these words that I am commanding you today in your heart" (Deut. 6:6). Similarly, the language about "knowing" the deity is rooted in the diction of Hosea, whose oracles were available to Jeremiah. So it is inappropriate to speak of Jeremiah's new covenant as of a radically new type (as von Rad claimed); rather, it is a recasting of earlier ideas.

Jeremiah 32 borders on being incoherent. The chapter commences with King Zedekiah asking Jeremiah a question: Why do you say that I will be taken into exile and defeated? (vv. 3–5). Thereafter, Jeremiah reports about a symbolic action, a real estate transaction, which signifies that "houses and fields and vineyards shall again be bought in this land" (v. 15). The chapter then cites a prayer of Jeremiah (vv. 16–25), which though not explicitly including a petition, observes that the land is under siege. The deity then responds that nothing is too hard for the Lord (v. 27)—a point Jeremiah had already confessed (v. 17)—but the vast bulk of the deity's speech involves a catalogue of the people's sins. Then, at the end, we hear about an everlasting covenant, which reverberates with the previous chapter, and an allusion to real estate transactions. This sense of disjointedness is even more pronounced in chapter 33, which is an anthology of sayings. It is useful to note that verses 14–26 are not present in the LXX, suggesting that the collection was formed over a long period of time (e.g., vv. 19–22 appear to be a prosaic version of 31:35–36). One might view chapter 32 as multivocal, with speeches from Zedekiah, Jeremiah, and the deity. Ultimately, the chapter points to a hopeful future, but the pattern of communication is murky, still affected by the sins of the people and the radicality of their punishment.

In sum, the book of Jeremiah offers no single picture of a time after the destruction of Jerusalem. One and another motif undergirds separate oracles. However, the logic of such assurance is rooted in the primary rhetoric of the book, that of lament. When someone performs a lament in a religious setting, a response is expected. The God who hears laments is the God who offers an oracle of salvation. Just as the book of Isaiah, working with the Davidic and Zion traditions, can anticipate a time of weal, so too can the book of Jeremiah, though on the basis of liturgical tradition rather than political ideology. Jeremiah's closer prophetic kin, Hosea, also espoused a rhetoric of weal, but his was more theological, growing out of Baal/Yahweh imagery rather than from the ritual world that served Jeremiah so well.

THEOLOGICAL ISSUES

The book of Jeremiah presents an unusual problem for those interested in its theological dimensions.   Much in the book is similar to other literature in the Old Testament. Such overlap occurs most powerfully between Jeremiah and Hosea as well as between Jeremiah and the Deuteronomist. To the extent that the religious dimensions in Jeremiah are similar to these other literatures, they are obviously not peculiar to Jeremiah. However, at the same time, we may note that one characteristic of Jeremiah's book is the extent to which it is linked to broader theological streams. He is not always idiosyncratic!

Jeremiah and Other Biblical Traditions

What are the primary elements that Jeremiah shares with Hosea and the Deuteronomist? One may answer this question in various ways. Like Hosea, Jeremiah indicts Israel for veneration of deities other than Yahweh, especially Baal. Like Hosea, Jeremiah deploys the analogy of marriage between Yahweh as the male spouse and Israel as the female spouse. There are more general similarities; for example, both prophets use the notion of covenant to articulate the relationship between Yahweh and Israel. And there are very specific links; for example, Jer. 14:10 cites portions of Hos. 8:13.[20] These areas of overlap have led many to suggest that Jeremiah knew some form of the book of Hosea. After the defeat of Israel in 721, an early form of the book may have been preserved in Judah, though in the northern area. Anathoth, Jeremiah's hometown, was, after all, located in the tribal territory of Benjamin, one of the tribal holdings that belonged to the northern kingdom. Jeremiah inherits some of the legacy of the North as embodied in the book of Hosea.

The case with Deuteronomy and the Deuteronomist is more complicated.[21] Holladay has surveyed the relationships between Deuteronomy and Jeremiah. He concludes that Jeremiah knew and used some portions of Deuteronomy, namely, chapters 5–26 and 32, but that the prophet did not use material from the entire book. Moreover, it appears that redactors of Deuteronomy used some of Jeremiah's words. Put another way, each book influenced the other, though obviously at different points of time. Other scholars would maintain that some members of the Deuteronomistic "school" were responsible for many of the later prose additions to the book of Jeremiah. In particular, Nicholson has argued that the prose in Jeremiah reflects the theological concerns of the Deuteronomists. He identifies two themes present in that prose that are characteristic of the Deuteronomistic History: Judah's rejection of the word of Yahweh spoken by a prophet and the prophet as spokesman of Yahweh's torah. Moreover, Nicholson thinks that one essential purpose of the Deuteronomistic History is also present in the book of Jeremiah, namely, that if Israel returns to Yahweh, then Yahweh will restore the people. Jeremiah's notion of a "new covenant" grows naturally out of such an idea.

In a related vein, some biblical scholars have claimed that the theological understanding of Jeremiah's prophetic role is informed by the book of Deuteronomy. Both books share the notion of there being "a prophet like Moses."[22] These scholars suggest that Jeremiah inherited religious traditions from the North, traditions in which Moses played a more prominent role than he did in the South. According to the Deuteronomic code, "The LORD your God will raise up for you a prophet like me from among your own people; you shall heed such a prophet" (Deut. 18:15). Immediately thereafter, the deity says, "I will put my words in the mouth of the prophet, who shall speak to them everything that I command" (Deut. 18:18). It is difficult not to hear a resonance with Jer. 1:9. The notion of the prophet as one who conveys the deity's word is prominent in both books. Nonetheless, one of these books, Deuteronomy, concludes with the observation that there really has never been a prophet truly like Moses: "Never since has there arisen a prophet in Israel like Moses, whom the LORD knew face to face" (Deut. 34:10). Such a view clearly declasses someone like Jeremiah. Similarly, one essential arena of Moses' role as prophet involved intercession on behalf of Israel. Such activity was forbidden to Jeremiah (Jer. 7:16). So the book Jeremiah may have one foot in a theological stream that honored Moses in special ways, but other currents were equally important, if not more so.

Jeremiah and the Rhetoric of Lament

Jeremiah's own perspectives appear with special prominence in the rhetoric of lament. Some might suggest that Jeremiah uses this discourse because of his priestly heritage (Jer. 1:1); priests heard and responded to laments. However, the language of lament was available to all Israelites, though due to his priestly background, Jeremiah may have been especially familiar with it.

The prominence of lamentation in Jeremiah provides a valuable clue to the theological perspectives that undergird the book. Lament, which as we have seen grows out of traditional religious practice, enables people to give voice to their experiences during times of crisis. The book of Jeremiah attests that Yahweh hears such laments and even engages in them. The deity does not always offer an immediate response to the laments, however. The deity may be silent, but the prophet and the people continue to lament in the conviction that the deity indeed hears what they say. Moreover, the book attests that such conviction is well-founded. According to chapters 30–31, lament finally leads to words of weal from the deity. Yahweh now takes up the cudgel on behalf of the people who have suffered so grievously. A new covenant will be made as a response to the process of lamentation.

Bibliography

Bogaert, P.-M., ed. *Le Livre de Jeremie: le prophete et son milieu, les oracles et leur transmission*. BETL 54. Louvain: Peeters, 1981.

Bright, J. *Jeremiah*. AB 21. Garden City, N.Y.: Doubleday, 1965.

Brueggemann, W. *A Commentary on Jeremiah: Exile and Homecoming*. Grand Rapids: Eerdmans, 1998.

Clements, R. *Jeremiah*. IBC. Atlanta: John Knox, 1988.

Diamond, A., K. O'Connor, and L. Stulman, eds. *Troubling Jeremiah*. JSOTSup 260. Sheffield: Sheffield Academic Press, 1999.

Herrmann, S. *Jeremia: Der Prophet und das Buch*. EdF 271. Darmstadt: Wissenschaftliche Buchgesellschaft, 1990.

Holladay, W. *Jeremiah: A Commentary on the Book of the Prophet Jeremiah*. Hermenia. 2 vols. Philadelphia: Fortress, 1986; Minneapolis: Fortress, 1989.

Lundbom, J. *Jeremiah 1–20*. AB 21A. New York: Doubleday, 1999.

McKane, W. *A Critical and Exegetical Commentary on Jeremiah*. 2 vols. *Jeremiah*. Edinburgh: T. & T. Clark, 1986, 1996.

Miller, P. "Jeremiah." In *The New Interpreter's Bible*, edited by L. Keck et al., 6:553-982. Nashville: Abingdon, 2001.

Nicholson, E. *Preaching to the Exiles: A Study of the Prose Tradition in the Book of Jeremiah*. New York: Schocken, 1971.

O'Connor, K. *The Confessions of Jeremiah: Their Interpretation and Role in Chapters 1–25*. SBLDS 94. Atlanta: Society of Biblical Literature, 1988.

Perdue, L., and B. Kovacks, eds. *A Prophet to the Nations: Essays in Jeremiah Studies*. Winona Lake, Ind.: Eisenbrauns, 1984.

Stulman, L. *Order amid Chaos: Jeremiah as Symbolic Tapestry*. BS 57. Sheffield: Sheffield Academic Press, 1998.

4

The Book of Ezekiel

The book of Ezekiel continues to confound readers. The fantastic visions and long allegories make this some of the most difficult literature in the prophetic canon. Yet at the same time, we find Ezekiel offering hard-headed logic otherwise infrequent in prophetic literature. This combination of vision, symbolic action, ornate symbolism, and logical discourse stands without parallel in the Old Testament prophetic corpus.

Ezekiel presents other challenges. Paramount are the nature of Ezekiel's priestly background and the book as a document redolent with priestly imagery. Many commentators have explored the latter issue at length. However, Ezekiel's relation to things priestly has been less fully appreciated. Those who read the book need to appreciate how these dynamics are related. In this chapter, we will discover that the literary variety in the book reflects the activity of Ezekiel as a prophet who had been trained to be a priest.

HISTORICAL CONTEXT
OF THE PROPHET AND THE BOOK

Ezekiel lived astride the momentous historical events associated with the demise of Judah and the destruction of Jerusalem (587 B.C.E.). To that extent, he was a true contemporary of Jeremiah, whose work is also attested both before and after that fateful year. Ezekiel, along with other Judahites, was taken into exile in Babylon in 597, when Nebuchadnezzar ordered that leaders of Judah be deported. During the next ten years, there were, in effect, two Judahs, one in the land of Judah and one in exile. There were even two kings: Jehoiachin in exile and

Zedekiah in Jerusalem. The book of Ezekiel presents us with a picture according to which Ezekiel addresses both groups of people. He is present in Judah through visionary transport, but he speaks in a more mundane way to those among whom he lives in exile.

The historical period during which Ezekiel lived had a profound impact on his own life. He was born into a priestly lineage. Ezekiel 1:3 states "the word of the LORD came to Ezekiel, son of Buzi, the priest." (The verse can also be translated, as it is in the NRSV, "the word of the LORD came to the priest Ezekiel, son of Buzi.") Despite this ambiguity, we know at a minimum that Ezekiel *could* have been a priest. He was eligible because he was born into a family of priests. However, to be eligible to become a priest is quite different from preparing for the priesthood and, subsequently, being ordained to that status. The mysterious reference to "the thirtieth year" in Ezek. 1:1 offers significant evidence about Ezekiel's potential role as priest. According to Num. 4:3, a priest could begin his work as priest at the temple when he reached the age of thirty. And though we have limited evidence, the career of Samuel suggests that prior to their ordination, priests in training worked at the temple but in a subsidiary capacity. The "thirtieth year" in Ezek. 1:1 may well refer to his age, the year during which he would have been ordained. Such ordination, however, had become impossible, since five years earlier Ezekiel had been taken into exile. Ordination was a complex rite (see Exodus 29 and Leviticus 8) that included several burnt offerings, and these could only take place at the temple. Although Ezekiel could be present at the temple through visionary transport, he could not appear there for a service of priestly dedication. Thirty years was, then, a propitious moment for Ezekiel to experience his inaugural vision. He was unable to exercise the role of priest at the temple. However, Yahweh offered Ezekiel a new option, one in which he could exercise some of his priestly concerns but now in the role of prophet.[1]

Thus, one way to understand this prophet is to construe him within the context of his priestly heritage. There is another way, however, provided by the prophet himself. Two texts depict the role that Ezekiel will exercise as a *sopeh*. Translators have offered various English nouns for this Hebrew word, such as "watchman" or "sentinel." This is not the first occasion that a prophet is described using this term. Hosea is the first: "The prophet is a *sopeh* for my God over Ephraim" (Hos. 9:8; see also Jer. 6:17; cf. Isa. 21:6; Hab. 2:1). However, the book of Ezekiel presents two divine oracles in which the role of the *sopeh* is spelled out. Ezekiel 33:1–6 roots the work of the sentinel in warfare. Such an individual was responsible for warning the populace of a military attack. He is to sound a trumpet in order to enable people to survive the onslaught. If he does this and the people do not pay attention, it is their own fault. However, if he utters no warning, he will be culpable. The deity uses this image to explain to Ezekiel the seriousness of this role, which the deity has conferred on Ezekiel ("I have made you a sentinel for the house of Israel" [33:7]). But Ezekiel is an unusual sentinel. He is not called to speak to all Israel, but only to the wicked. Still, as sentinel, Ezekiel has the option of warning them about what Yahweh is saying: "O wicked ones, you shall surely die" (33:8). If he does not warn them and they persist in their behavior, both Ezekiel and the wicked will die. However, if he warns them and they still persist, they will die but he will live. Such is the case adumbrated in both chapters 3 and 33. Chapter 33 offers a fuller set of options, which include addressing the righteous along with the wicked. The results remain essentially the same. Ezekiel's work as sentinel may not necessarily change the behavior of others, but he can at least affect his own fate.

This understanding of the role of the sentinel is unusual. Normally, the fate of the watchman is bound up with that of the people on behalf of whom he works. If a guard sounds the alarm and the people respond successfully, that guard will indeed have saved his own life. However, if a guard does not sound the alarm, with the result that the city is defeated, he would normally suffer the same fate of the people whom he did not warn. This is the key distinction between Ezekiel as sentinel and the normal watchman. Ezekiel's fate can be different from that of the rest of the people if he conveys Yahweh's word to the people. This picture of the prophet's role is decidedly different from that of Jeremiah's, in which the fate of the prophet seems bound up inexorably with that of the people. In this contrast, one senses that the different theological underpinnings of the two books have affected significantly the ways in which the activity of the prophet is to be understood.

According to the book of Ezekiel, the prophet was active from 593, the year of his call, to at least the year 571, the date attested in Ezek. 29:17, a period of twenty-two years. Of this time, no more than seven years came before the fall of Jerusalem, whereas two-thirds of Ezekiel's life as prophet occurred after that formative event. Still, far more than one-third of the book itself is devoted to that initial period, before Jerusalem was destroyed. It is, therefore, no wonder that the scroll described in Ezekiel's inaugural vision is filled with "words of lamentation and mourning and woe" (2:10). Yet, as we shall see, woe is, finally, not the dominant tone of the book.

The book of Ezekiel, as we have just noted, includes specific reference to a date sixteen years after Jerusalem's fall. During the intervening years, Ezekiel was addressing, especially, issues of importance to those with whom he was in exile. And, as we shall see at the end of this chapter, there are good reasons (both redaction-critical and text-critical) to think that this process continued with hands other than Ezekiel's. The basic form of the book was, however, probably complete by the end of the sixth century B.C.E.   *500 BCE*

LITERARY STRUCTURE AND FEATURES

Literary Structure

The book has traditionally been divided into three basic parts: judgment on Israel (chaps. 1–24), judgment on the nations (chaps. 25–32), weal for Israel (chaps. 33–48). These divisions are useful general categories, but one should recognize that oracles of weal also occur in the first section of the book (e.g., 17:22–24). Moreover, chapter 33 does not primarily offer weal. Only with the vision of restoration in chapters 40–48 does Ezekiel move consistently into the realm of affirming speech.

Pohlmann regards the tripartite division of the book as more than just an ordering of materials. Rather, he believes that it provides an eschatological structure that involves movement over time, not just thematic divisions.[2] One may continue this line of argument by focusing on the major vision reports (see below). They occur at the beginning (1:1–3:15), middle (chaps. 8–11), and end of the book (chaps. 40–48). They too offer a tripartite structure, but one that does more than simply construe the content of the book. As we will see, the first vision establishes the notion of God's mobility in and through the language about wheels. The second vision depicts the people in idolatrous behavior, which warrants God's departure from the temple. Finally, the third vision reports the deity's return from exile. The visions provide a structure of theological movement in the book.

Prose in Ezekiel

Prose predominates in the book of Ezekiel. However, Ezekiel's prose is hardly prosaic. The date formulae surely are bare-bones prose, but the Hebrew Bible knows no real analogue to the baroque vision reports or the complex prose essays. The German term *Kunstprosa*, if we may mean by that "artful prose," seems apt.

Dates

The book of Ezekiel possesses a number of structures and structuring devices. Dates and chronological markers for prophetic activity appear prominently (e.g., 1:1; 1:2–3; 3:16; 8:1; 20:1; 24:1; 26:1; 29:1). There are fourteen such date formulae, though they do not occur in chronological order. Perhaps the best explanation for this odd feature is that the literature with which the formulae are associated has been moved from its original context in an earlier form of the book to its present location. Or, alternatively, there may have never been an attempt to present the formulae in chronological order.

The date formulae do, however, offer significant evidence concerning Ezekiel and his sociopolitical context. With the exception of Ezek. 1:1, which refers to Ezekiel's own age, the rest of the formulae reflect a chronology based on the year in which the Judahite king, Jehoiachin, was taken into exile, namely, 597. This point of reference bears great significance for at least two reasons. First, Ezekiel was almost certainly taken into exile at that same time. He and Jehoiachin thus, in all probability, belonged to a group of Yahwists who now shared a communal fate, namely, constructing life by the proverbial "rivers of Babylon" (Ps. 137:1). Second, that communal experience differentiated Ezekiel and his community from those who remained in the land. The Judah that remained even had a new king, Zedekiah, whom Nebuchadnezzar put on the throne. Moreover, we know that the people who remained in the land began to appropriate property that had been vacated by those taken forcibly to Mesopotamia (Ezek. 11:15). Hence, for the book of Ezekiel to be structured according to the date of Jehoiachin's exile attests to the prominence of that date and those who were in Mesopotamia. Within a little more than one hundred fifty years, the reconstruction of Judah will stem in large part from the efforts of those who had been in exile—as the power of "the congregation of the exiles," mentioned frequently in Ezra-Nehemiah, attests (e.g., Ezra 10:8).

Vision Reports

Another structuring device is even more important—the three major visions (we will discuss the fourth and less cosmic vision [37:1–14] in due course). These are the inaugural vision (1:1–3:15), the visions of indictment and judgment (chaps. 8–11), and the vision of temple renewal (chaps. 40–48). Ezekiel 43:3 makes it clear that these three visions are integrally related.

Though vision reports appear prominently in other prophetic books, most notably in Zechariah 1–6, Ezekiel's visions provide an architectural structure—beginning, internal pivot point, and ending—for that book in a way shared by no other biblical prophetic literature. Further, these three visions offer a consistent theological emphasis on the "glory" (*kābôd*) of Yahweh.

Ezekiel 1:1–3:15

The inaugural vision has captured the imagination of many readers. Moreover, a line in an African American spiritual—"Ezek'el saw the wheel 'way up in the middle o' the air"—captures several seminal features of the vision, namely, that the vision was not of this world (1:1: "the heavens were opened, and I saw visions of God"). Moreover, the wheels denoted mobility, which, as we shall see, is of fundamental importance to Ezekiel's visionary logic.

What is truly important in Ezek. 1:1–3:15? In order to answer this question, we need to approach these verses from a variety of perspectives. First, they bear strong similarities to other biblical texts according to which a prophet is commissioned. The most noteworthy points for comparison are Isaiah 6 and Jeremiah 1. By the end of the vision, Ezekiel has become a prophet (*nābî'* [2:5]). He will use standard prophetic speech: "Thus says the Lord GOD" (2:4). Yet, despite these words, that which Ezekiel experiences in this vision seems to be more important than what he utters by way of prophetic formula.

Second, one element of the typical form for the commissioning of a prophet has been blown out of proportion, namely, the description of the deity who encounters the prophet (Ezek. 1:4–28). As one reads through these verses, one glimpses images—four creatures, four wheels, fire, a dome, a throne, a human form—but it would be difficult indeed to depict what it is that Ezekiel actually sees. The picture is more surrealistic than realistic. He continually emphasizes that his description is "like"—"in the middle of it was something *like* four living creatures" (1:5), "there was something *like* a dome" (1:22), "there was something *like* a throne" (1:26).

Readers do well to compare Ezekiel's vision with Isaiah's commissioning vision (Isaiah 6). Isaiah makes a far more audacious claim, namely, that he "saw the Lord" (Isa. 6:1), and part of that visionary presence filled the temple. Ezekiel is far more nuanced; instead of claiming to see God, Ezekiel states, "This was the appearance of the likeness of the glory of the LORD" (Ezek. 1:28). This statement makes clear to the reader what Ezekiel apparently already knows: Ezekiel is several steps removed from actually seeing God. Such is the theological nuance this prophet offers. He specializes in the language of analogy, describing the unseeable with reference to that which can be seen.

Ezekiel reports that he had encountered "the glory of the LORD." Astoundingly, this happened not in Israel but in Babylon! What in Isaiah had been a vision in and of the temple is with Ezekiel a vision in and of exile. The deity is available to those outside the land, a theological affirmation that would be of great import to Ezekiel and the community with him in Babylon. Both the motif of wheels and that of the gale force wind (*ruaḥ sĕʿārāh*), which at the surface level of the vision indicate motion, involve mobility, a mechanism for God to leave the temple.

Third, Ezekiel is in some measure a prophet without a message, at least at this point in the book. The text narrates that he will go around saying "Thus says the Lord GOD," a phrase that appears in many other prophet texts (e.g., Amos 2:1). However, in Amos and other prophetic books, that formula introduces an oracle that the prophet as herald is called to declare. By way of contrast, in Ezekiel nothing follows the formula in 2:4 and 3:11; there is no oracle. To be sure, the people will know that a prophet is in their midst (2:5), but we do not know much about what he will say other than the words of "lamentation and mourning and woe" (2:10) written on the scroll. So the vision elicits speech and recognition of Ezekiel as prophet. But it does more; it makes clear that the deity previously worshiped in Jerusalem could be venerated in a foreign land. There is, therefore, a degree of ambiguity about this inaugural vision. On the one hand, the overt theological motifs constitute good news, in a way. Those in exile do, indeed, have access to the deity. On the other hand, that which Ezekiel is commanded to say, though ambiguous, appears dire, involving words of woe. Interestingly, we are told that those to whom Ezekiel will speak will hear only the prophetic messenger formulae: "Thus says the Lord GOD."

Ezekiel 8–11

The vision of indictment and judgment occurs in these chapters. Here again the prophet perceives the deity while he is in exile, but the prophet is now taken in visionary transport ("in visions of God" [8:3]) to the temple in Jerusalem. This text, though a vision report, does not share the form of the first one, which is part of a prophetic call narrative. Instead, the language and logic of the judgment oracle (indictment and sentence) are the driving forces, at least for the first part of this report. In 8:5–18, the reader is informed about the "abominations," a noun Ezekiel uses to describe religious misdeeds that are being practiced at the temple. The text also makes it clear that "bloodshed," "violence," and "perversity" are all significant problems.

The people are worshiping foreign gods from all over the ancient Near East. Such is the indictment. Thereafter the deity pronounces judgment: "I will act in wrath" (8:18). Ezekiel is then privy to the working out of Yahweh's wrath, as angelic executioners kill all those save individuals who have been marked as contrite. Despite Ezekiel's attempts at intervention, the deity persists in the slaughter.

After the slaughter, the author returns to the imagery of divine manifestation, which introduces the imagery of fire. Coals from the deity's theophanic appearance become the source for a conflagration in Jerusalem, whereupon "the glory of the LORD" continues its stately departure from the city (chap. 10). The final components of the vision report include indictment and punishment of leaders ("princes") in Jerusalem and a promissory note to those who have been exiled. Both the glory of the Lord and Ezekiel leave Jerusalem. The vision concludes: "I told the exiles all the things that the LORD had shown me" (11:25).

This vision report is far less coherent than the first one. One may posit a number of additions (e.g., 11:1–21). Moreover, the concluding sentence offers a significant statement, since it differs from anything we find in the first vision, namely, that Ezekiel reported to the people all that he had seen. The vision *is* reported, not just inscribed.

Again, though the text invests considerable effort in describing the deity, the point of the vision report moves in a different direction, namely, offering a reason for judgment and then not only announcing that judgment will ensue but that it has begun, at least at the cosmic level. The slaughter and destruction envisioned here in 592 is still some five years off. But it was important, Ezekiel maintains, for those in exile to know that Jerusalem would, indeed, be destroyed, contrary to what some both at home and in exile hoped for or anticipated.

Ezekiel 40–48

The final nine chapters of the book comprise a remarkable vision of temple renewal. When compared with vison reports in other prophetic books, this one is less similar to them than are Ezekiel's first two reports. In Ezekiel 40–48, we seem to be more in the world of the Pentateuch than we are in typical prophetic literature—in Exodus, with instructions for the design of the tabernacle; Numbers, with tribal boundaries; Leviticus, with its statements about priestly activity; and Deuteronomy, with its concerns for civil behavior. Were we to focus on some of Ezekiel's other oracles of weal (e.g., chaps. 34–39), we might feel as if we were more in the world of prophetic literature. But not so with chapters 40–48. How are we to understand the special character of these chapters?

Ezekiel 40–48 combines the vision report with the presentation of a new "law." The vision report includes a term that can be used to describe its contents—*torah*, which may be translated "law" or "instruction," an apt label given the similarities between these chapters and nonnarrative portions of the Pentateuch that we have just identified. Just as the first vision offers a statement of identification—"This was the appearance of the likeness of the glory of the LORD" (1:28)—so this final vision as well indicates what the prophet has been experiencing: "This is the law [*torah*] of the temple," a statement that appears twice in Ezek. 43:12.

Ezekiel and his followers apparently wanted to do more than affirm that God and the people would exist in a new and positive way. That had, after all, been suggested by Jeremiah, à la the new covenant, and earlier by Ezekiel himself, in similar terms (Ezek. 34:25; cf. 16:60). Moreover, Ezekiel had, in an earlier chapter, promised that the temple would be rebuilt (37:26). However, this final vision presents architectural plans and polity—what is to be built and how the people are to be organized. As we will see when we approach the books of Haggai and Zechariah, plans for the future appeared prominently among those who thought about the future after the fall of Jerusalem. Zechariah, too, talks about walls and about political order, but one would not confuse his visionary statements on these matters with portions of the Pentateuch. One could with Ezekiel. It is almost as if Ezekiel thinks that the old torah had not functioned properly in certain areas (a view consistent with the claim that some of the older stipulations were "not good" [20:25]) and that a new torah in certain areas was necessary. Obviously these are radical, one might say "utopian," claims and proposals.

The heart of the vision occurs early in the chapters.[3] Ezekiel confronts another individual, "a man whose appearance shone like bronze" (40:3), no doubt a minor deity. This creature leads Ezekiel through a floor plan of the rebuilt temple. It is unlike the old temple, a fact that underlies the bankruptcy of the old polity and emphasizes the need for a radically new basis for the restored community. This temple is distinct because it has gates that mirror the defensive structures that were otherwise part of city walls. These new gates contain several rooms through which people would pass on their way into a city. The people no longer need to be defended; rather, Yahweh's holiness must

be protected from the profane world. After this tour, Ezekiel is shown
the holy of holies (41:1–4). With this appurtenance in place, the vision
moves to its climax: the return of the glory of the God of Israel (43:1–5).
Here we participate in the world of the previous visions: What the glory
is was revealed in the first vision, and the reasons for the departure of
the glory were made clear in the second. Now that glory returns to the
rebuilt temple and to be with the people. Once the deity has entered
the temple, the gate that permitted such entry is closed ("it shall remain
shut" [44:2]), emphasizing the permanent presence of the deity in
Israel's midst.

As with the second vision, Ezekiel is more than a witness. Once he
has experienced this new edifice as well as the presence of the returned
deity, he is instructed to write down the plan, since it represents "the
torah of the temple." What Ezekiel sees is to be preserved for others.
Interestingly, the deity thinks that the people will "be ashamed" of their
misdeeds once they see the glorious pattern for the future. It may be
that the people will remember their misdeeds at the previous temple
when prompted by plans for the new one.

Ezekiel was not the first individual to whom plans for the divine
dwelling had been revealed. Moses too had been on a mountain and had
been told how to design the tabernacle along with the rituals and
priestly functions appropriate to it. All this reinforces the picture of
Ezekiel as one who offers (new) torah to Israel.

These chapters continue with elucidations—some of which almost
certainly were added at a later time—of various priestly responsibilities, reflection on the minimal role of the civil leader (called here a
prince), admonitions about proper behavior (45:10–12), ritual instructions, mention of a gloriously fructifying river (47:1–12), and a new
configuration of the land that includes new settlement patterns.
Though there is no conclusion to the vision (cf. 3:14–15 and 11:24–25),
the vision report and the book end with a motif shared with other
prophetic literature, namely, the renaming of Jerusalem (cf. Isa. 60:14
and Jer. 33:16 for other instances in which Jerusalem will receive a new
name). According to Ezekiel, it will bear the symbolic name *yahweh
shammah* ("The LORD Is There" [48:35]). The absence of the typical
conclusion to a vision report, in which the prophet returns to his point
of origin, is surely significant. The book is truly open-ended, despite
the very specific torah concerning the new Jerusalem.

These three visions accomplish multiple goals. They are consistent
with the prophetic role of the visionary, since they truly provide a cosmic
overview of what the deity is about. One may even speak of an incipient

plot: The deity, who is truly mobile, calls Ezekiel as prophet. Ezekiel, who is privy to the reasons for God's judgment, "sees" the oncoming catastrophe and reports it to the people. Well after the destruction, Ezekiel receives another vision in which the deity reveals to him the "torah" regarding the rebuilt temple and the community that will gather around it. This too becomes the subject of his prophetic proclamation.

Visions are a distinctive form of prophetic discourse. They offer a broad vantage point from which to assay what is happening to humans. Ezekiel's visions offer that vantage point by viewing the history of Judahite Yahwists in the early part of the sixth century B.C.E. from the perspective of God's *kābôd* (glory). One of Ezekiel's great contributions is his ability to interpret that history from a priestly, theological perspective.

As we noted earlier, Ezekiel's three major vision reports occur at the beginning, middle, and end of the book. They function as an organizational foundation for the literary edifice. However, they have another important role, involving movement. The first vision establishes the theological claim that the deity is capable of movement; Yahweh is not inextricably rooted in the temple. The second vision provides the rationale for God's departure from the temple, along with a description of that departure. Finally, in the third vision, we become privy to the deity's return: "And there, the glory of the God of Israel was coming from the east" and "the glory of the LORD entered the temple" (43:2, 4). Together the visions narrate the departure from and return to the temple in Jerusalem. Moreover, the visionary logic makes it clear that the deity, who is able to transcend residence in one temple, is available for worship by those in exile. Accordingly, Ezekiel offers not only a theology but also a theology appropriate for his initial audience, namely, those living in Babylon. Yahweh is available to them where they live.

Symbolic Action Reports

The symbolic action report, in its most basic form, presents the deity commanding the prophet to undertake activity. Such behavior could, apparently, be acted out in silence. Ezekiel was told to take a brick and portray a city on it. Such actions are to be a "sign" for Israel (4:3). One might presume that the people would understand what they are seeing, and such might have been the case for some of the symbolic actions reported in the book.[4] However, in several cases, the symbolic actions are apparently not so clear. When Ezekiel is told to prepare the sort of baggage he would take into exile and then to dig through the city wall with his face covered, we are told again that it is a sign (*môpēt*) for the house of Israel (12:1–6). However, after the act had been performed, the people ask, "What are you doing?" The sign was obviously not self-evident. As a result, the deity presents the prophet with an oracle in which the behavior is explained: "as I have done, so shall it be done to them" (12:11). (See 24:15–24 for another instance in which the prophet acts out a message that the people do not comprehend [cf. 21:1–7].) Whether interpreted (e.g., 12:1–16) or not (4:1–3), the symbolic action presents the people with information about what the deity is doing. Most of the symbolic action reports in the book of Ezekiel emphasize the immediacy of Jerusalem's demise and the exile of its population (4:1–3, 4–8, 9–17; 5:1–4). In only one case (37:15–23) does Ezekiel use a symbolic action report to convey good news. What God is doing has already begun or is soon to happen.

Symbolic Actions: A Sampler

4:1–3	Ezekiel deploying mud bricks
4:4–8	Ezekiel lying on his side
4:9–17	Ezekiel baking unclean bread
5:1–4	Ezekiel cutting his hair
12:1–11	Ezekiel carrying baggage
37:15–23	Ezekiel writing on sticks

If one reads through just the symbolic action reports, or even just reads Ezekiel 4, which contains three such reports, a problem appears. The symbolic action reports emphasize that something terrible is about to happen, but they do not offer an explanation. Such reports are, therefore, very different in their rhetoric from prophetic discourse such as the judgment oracle. The judgment oracle includes both an indictment, which offers a rationale for what the deity will do, and then a brief statement about what the deity will in fact accomplish. The symbolic action report is similar only to the second part of the judgment oracle. As a result, one wonders how even those who understood the symbolic action reports might have responded to them.

The book of Ezekiel does include explanations for that which is happening, but those explanations do not occur early on, apart from the vision of idolatry (chaps. 8–11). The first significant exposition of Jerusalem's sins occurs in chapter 16—"Make known to Jerusalem her abominations" (16:2). A similar phrase appears in chapter 20—"let them know the abominations of their ancestors" (20:4). In each case, the prophet refers to "abominations"; that noun is one his favorite words to describe Israel's malfeasance.[5]

These explanations, however, are remarkably general. The book refers far less frequently to specific misdeeds than it does to general categories of sin such as "violence" (12:19), "your ways" (7:3), "their iniquity" (7:16), "their detestable things" (7:20), and "bloody crimes" (7:23). When the book does become more specific, the infractions seem formulaic. For example, in the lists of sinful behavior in 18:5–8 and 22:6–12, Ezekiel seems to be assaying misbehavior as reflected in Israelite law codes rather than observing behavior in Jerusalem during the early sixth century. And since the indictment in 22:6 is directed against "the princes of Israel," one has the sense that Ezekiel is truly offering an indictment of the royal house of Judah over a long period of time, not simply against royalty in his own time. (The same tonality is present in chapter 18.) Ezekiel is working theoretically on the problem of an individual as related to previous generations. It does not appear that these sins one might commit are in any way specific to his own time or to those with whom he lives. We are left wondering what it is that Ezekiel thinks is uniquely or specifically wrong in his own time. One may point to specific vocabulary, such as idols (*gillûlîm*, literally "pieces of dung" [22:3]). It may be preferable to suggest Ezekiel offers no special indictment of his own generation other than the one offered in the vision of idolatry (chaps. 8–11).

Essays

Ezekiel's great essays (sometimes called discourses) are remarkable. They include chapters 16 (Jerusalem as Yahweh's disloyal wife), 18 (treated later in this chapter), 20 (a historical reprise), and 23 (Oholah and Oholibah). Zimmerli includes chapters 15, 16, 17, 19, 23, 27, 31, and 32 under the general category of figurative or metaphorical discourse.[6] It is not clear that all these chapters share the same basic features. For Zimmerli, the key common denominator is the presence of a metaphor or other figure of speech. In my judgment, the figurative element, though important, is less determinative for the definition than is the notion of the extended essay, in which the prophet works out a position or issue at some length. It is interesting that these prose discourses do not normally employ the metaphors drawn from the natural world. Here, in contrast to his metaphoric poetry, Ezekiel refers either to the "real" world (chap. 20) or the world of human culture (chaps. 16; 18; 23). One is struck by the length: The discourse in chapter 16 runs for fifty-eight verses, in chapter 18 for thirty-two verses, in chapter 20 for thirty-two verses, and in chapter 23 for forty-nine verses. Ezekiel's vision reports are longer than those in other books, and the same is the case with these essay-like discourses. (Some scholars have maintained that, in all four chapters, an original discourse has been expanded by a later hand.) Moreover, these prose discourses tend to be much longer than do the metaphoric poems.

As prose essays, Ezekiel 16, 20, and 23 do not, at first examination, appear similar. Chapter 16 speaks of the history between Yahweh and a personified Jerusalem. This history is addressed to Jerusalem: "make known to Jerusalem her abominations" (16:2). Ezekiel 20:1–3 commences with dialogue between Yahweh and "certain elders" in exile, a dialogue that leads to the deity offering a history between those elders' forbears and the deity. Finally, chapter 23 is a word to the prophet about two sisters, Oholah and Oholibah, whom the deity identifies with Samaria and Jerusalem respectively. In sum, the individuals addressed and the entities described are not coterminous.

Nonetheless, these three chapters share some striking similarities. In all three, the prophet offers an extensive history of the relationship between the deity and the people. This history extends to the perceived beginning of the relationship. According to chapter 16, the deity discovers "Jerusalem" as a newborn infant, abandoned to die in the desert. Moreover, she is of mixed and foreign parentage (16:3: "your father was an Amorite, and your mother a Hittite"). In chapter 20, the deity begins the history by reference to his choice of Israel in Egypt, noting that even before the people had been liberated, they had rebelled against God by continuing to worship idols. Chapter 23 sees the situation in similar terms: "[T]here were two women, the daughters of one mother; they played the whore in Egypt; they played the whore in their youth" (vv. 2–3). Ezekiel is proclaiming a history that was problematic from its conception.

These three chapters also make it clear that Israel was an entity of marginal status—a virtually dead and impure infant or slave. Only as a result of the deity's initiative did the people achieve prominence. Chapter 16 offers a picture of the deity bathing, clothing, and adorning the maturing female: "You grew exceedingly beautiful, fit to be a queen. Your fame spread among the nations on account of your beauty, for it was perfect because of my splendor that I bestowed on you" (16:13–14). The provision for life in chapter 20 is of a different sort, namely, it is religious. Here the deity bestows on Israel "my statutes and ordinances" of a sort that permit and enable life. Chapter 23 is more subtle on this point. There is no overt reference to a relationship between the deity and either of these two sisters (or to their mother). To have a sexual relationship with two sisters would have been taboo. However, verse 35 does suggest that Yahweh is angry because Oholibah has "forgotten" him, implying a time when they "knew" each other.

Moreover, these chapters offer detailed reports about the sins of the indicted parties, using the tropes with which the discourses began. Chapters 16 and 23 involve sexual misconduct, and chapter 20 involves religious disobedience. The prophet seems as caught up in these details of indictment as he was when expounding his experience of the precise quality of the deity's glory. Such attention to detail and to implication seems characteristic of this individual. Ezekiel 16:10–13 enables us to visualize the apparel of a regal woman—her clothing, footwear, jewelry. And in Ezek. 23:20, the prophet depicts the sexual activity in bestial detail.

The results of such wanton behavior are radical. Ezekiel does not move to the world of Neo-Babylonian armies, but remains with the imagery he has created. According to chapters 16 and 23, Jerusalem/ Oholibah will be subjected to punishment by her erstwhile lovers. They will strip her naked and then kill her, either by stoning or by the sword. In this context, Ezekiel's depiction of the deity is clearly embedded in the psychology of the male who feels betrayed by an unfaithful wife. The deity's actions are designed to satisfy his fury, jealousy, and rage (16:23–24). Once the woman has been punished, the deity "will be calm."

Most contemporary readers recoil at this image of the deity. It is one thing for a deity to be holy rather than profane. The death of Uzzah, who touched the ark (2 Sam. 6:7), attests to a deity for whom holiness and violence against human life are linked. Such is typical for deities in many religions. But the case of Ezekiel is different; here the violence is more typically and regrettably human—that of a male against a female. Ezekiel 23:46–49 is, in all likelihood, an addition to the earlier discourse, and it has moved from the language of judgment to the language of admonition. What was originally an oracle against Oholah and Oholibah becomes in the eyes of a later author a warning to all females: "I will put an end to lewdness in the land, so that all women may take warning and not commit lewdness as you have done" (23:48). This later commentary picks up on the gender of Oholibah and yet does not recognize that it is an image designed to depict the religious infidelity of both males and females.

Fortunately these discourses do not always conclude on such a note. Ezekiel 20 began with a dialogue about whether or not the elders in exile might consult the deity, with Ezekiel as an intermediary. The historical reprise is adduced as evidence that Yahweh, not the people, will ask the questions. Though the defeat of Jerusalem still looms, this text concludes with interrogative rather than indicative grammar. Those elders are asked: Will you continue in the way of your ancestors? Will you consult me? The latter question is answered in the negative, which leaves the former question as the more powerful one. The people themselves must offer a response.

Poetry in Ezekiel

Other prophetic books offer no real parallels to Ezekiel's poetry, and this despite the fact that Ezekiel contains less poetry than do other prophetic books. Ezekiel himself was apparently understood to be an accomplished artist: "To them you are like a singer of love songs, one who has a beautiful voice and plays well on an instrument" (Ezek. 33:32). In this regard, it is interesting to compare English translations. The NRSV, for example, deems some verses to be poetry even though the RSV viewed them as prose (e.g., 15:1–5, which is also printed as prose in the MT). Apart from the poetry found in the oracles against the nations, all the rest occurs in chapters 7–24. No literature associated with restoration is set in verse. Moreover, most of the poetry that occurs in those earlier chapters is written in long oracles. Ezekiel will often establish a metaphor and then develop it, though chapter 7 offers more typical prophetic poetry. Sometimes that process seems allegorical, that is, various elements in the extended metaphor can be identified with elements in the real or historical world. In so doing, Ezekiel draws upon images from the worlds of fauna (lion, eagle, dragon) and flora (cedar, grapevine). Ezekiel 19:10–14 offers a case in point. In addressing the princes of Judah, Ezekiel says:

> Your mother was like a vine in a vineyard
>   transplanted by the water,
> fruitful and full of branches
>   from abundant water.
> Its strongest stem became
>   a ruler's scepter;
> it towered aloft
>   among the thick boughs;
> it stood out in its height
>   with its mass of branches.
> But it was plucked up in fury,
>   cast down to the ground;
> the east wind dried it up;
>   its fruit was stripped off,
> its strong stem was withered;
>   the fire consumed it.
> Now it is transplanted into the wilderness,
>   into a dry and thirsty land.

And fire has gone out from its stem,
  has consumed its branches and fruit,
so that there remains in it no strong stem,
  no scepter for ruling.

In an earlier poem, the mother is described metaphorically as a lioness (19:2–9). In that poem, one might identify the lioness and several of her offspring as specific persons. However, the simile in 19:10 moves in a different direction. The mother/vine is more general, referring either to Judah or its royal house (vine imagery is also present in chapters 15 and 17). Also, the referent to planting in verse 10 is not clear. Does it allude to Israel's taking of the land, or to the creation of the Davidic dynasty? In any case, the primary stem of the vine became a scepter, "which towered aloft." Verse 12 appears to refer to the entire vine again and to its destruction by fire. Oddly then, verse 13 refers to the vine as transplanted (again) but in the wilderness, presumably referring to exile in Mesopotamia (v. 13 may be intrusive). Finally, verse 14 returns to the motif of destruction by fire, suggesting the decimation of either Judah or the Davidic house and the end of rule as symbolized by the scepter.

In this poem, characterized in Ezekiel as a lamentation (*qînāh*), the prophet has worked with an image, the vine with its central stem, to demonstrate what has happened to Judah. The verbs present action in the past tense, interpreting and exploring the implications of that which the people have recently experienced. The poem highlights the implications for ruling of the destruction. Some Judahites might think that Jehoiachin, who lived as king in exile, could become the basis for hope in a restored nation. Ezekiel says no. There is no potential scepter, since the entity (vine) that produced it (stem) has been utterly destroyed, removed from its garden-like setting. If there is to be a future, it will not be based on natural growth from this transplanted vine. Ezekiel's poetry often offers a version of events that might be conveyed in more historical terms, but the poetry draws out the implications of those events by depicting them using various images, which lead naturally to new interpretation.

ORACLES CONCERNING THE NATIONS

Scholars often characterize Ezekiel 25–32 as a collection of oracles against the nations, and for the most part that judgment is appropriate. Still, an oracle of promise to Israel occurs here (28:25–26), and oracles against other nations appear outside these chapters (against Edom in chaps. 35–36 and against Magog in chaps. 38–39). The reason for the inclusion of the oracle concerning Israel is clear: Bad news for foreign nations is good news for Israel.

Short Prose Oracles

Ezekiel's oracles against foreign nations commence with four short prose sayings (against Ammon, Moab, Edom, and Philistia), move to a longer section against Tyre (chaps. 26–28), and conclude with four chapters aimed at Egypt (chaps. 29–32). Unlike in Jeremiah 50–51, Babylon receives no invective; probably Ezekiel deems Babylon to be Yahweh's agent of punishment. Interestingly, these oracles offer more poetry as a percentage of the whole than do the oracles against Israel. Moreover, they offer more specific indictments than do the oracles against Israel. One is tempted to say these oracles contain some of Ezekiel's best poetry. These oracles, though uttered at different times (date formulae are prominent and point for the most part to the period just before Jerusalem fell), now belong as one unit. They have been introduced into the book and now separate two chapters (24 and 33) that may have originally belonged together.

There is a stereotypic quality to the first four oracles. The first two speak of punishment by "the people of the east," a phrase that probably refers to desert nomads (Ammon in 25:4; Moab in 25:10). The last two share both indictment and punishment. Both Edom and Philistia are accused of acting with vengeance, and both nations will become the subject of Yahweh's direct action: "I will stretch out my hand against . . ." (25:13, 16).

Tyre

Things change with Tyre. Here one city-state, as opposed to the larger nations just enumerated, receives radical treatment. Tyre, like Judah, was attacked by the Neo-Babylonians. However, unlike Judah, Tyre was able to withstand a siege by Nebuchadnezzar's forces in an attack that took place for over a decade. One senses Ezekiel's (and Judah's) frustration that a neighboring nation could avoid the fate that Judah had suffered. We even hear, within the context of the oracles against Egypt, that Nebuchadnezzar will be permitted victory against that kingdom, since he was unsuccessful in his attack against Tyre (29:17–20).

The oracles against Tyre and Egypt are particularly interesting and explore a range of indictments beyond the typical oracle against the nation. Ezekiel begins his indictment by quoting the reaction of Tyre (here personified) to the defeat of Jerusalem. Defeat by Nebuchadnezzar will result. However, things change in chapter 27. The deity charges Tyre with vanity: "I am perfect in beauty" (27:2). Using the metaphor of the ship (of state?), Ezekiel describes Tyre as a great sailing vessel, one of wonderful beauty. Reference to shipwrights and caulkers make it clear that Ezekiel knows something about the construction of such boats, and his description of Tyre's international trade (27:12–24) reveals his remarkable insight into mercantile matters. One senses that Tyre's economic prosperity may have come, at least in part, at Judah's expense. However, vessel Tyre was rocked by a mighty storm and sank. Remarkably, the deity takes no credit for creating the storm. The final chapter devoted to Tyre, Ezekiel 28, focuses on the anonymous prince of Tyre. A new charge is leveled, that of pride, for this prince has claimed, "I am a god." The basis for this claim was not power but wisdom. God reappears and sentences this ruler to death. As befits the fate of a mortal, Tyre will be cast into "the Pit" (26:20; 28:8). The prince's demise elicits a lament. Ezekiel 28:11–19 is striking because it may allude to a creation tradition different from that attested in Genesis 2–3, though it mentions Eden explicitly. Here again, Ezekiel knows something, here a primordial tradition, that provides the basis for his lament. By the end of these three chapters, we have seen Ezekiel use the rhetoric of indictment, sentence, and lament concerning one small Phoenician city-state. Its ability to withstand Nebuchadnezzar's attack made it a symbol against which this prophet deemed it necessary to inveigh. Whether in nautical or in primordial imagery, Ezekiel wants his audience to know that Tyre may have survived Nebuchadnezzar, but it will not withstand Yahweh.

Egypt

Egypt receives even more attention than does Tyre, although chapters 29–32 are, in some ways, similar to the section concerning Tyre. Egypt is indicted for its pride; it had claimed, "The Nile is mine, and I made it" (29:9). Egypt will receive due punishment—the imagery of being cast onto the ground (29:5; 32:4), that is, not being buried, is prominent—and Ezekiel offers a lament. There are, however, differences. First, there is more history embedded here, such as allusions to Judah's hopes for military assistance from Pharaoh Hophra ("because you were a staff of reed to the house of Israel" [29:6]) and to an attack of Nebuchadnezzar against Egypt, which may have transpired. Second, the primary metaphors differ—Tyre is a ship; Egypt is a crocodile-like dragon—as befits their respective geographic settings. Third, Ezekiel construes the defeat of Egypt using day of the Lord traditions (30:2–3; 32:7), whereas Tyre is understood using primordial imagery. Fourth, in contrast to Tyre, which is to disappear forever, Egypt will perdure; God will "restore the fortunes of Egypt," though it will be a "lowly kingdom" (29:13–16).

The prose speech that occurs at the end of chapter 32 offers a fitting conclusion to the oracles against the nations. It depicts warriors from around the world—the nations—who have fallen in battle and who are now in the Pit. This too will be the fate of Egypt, which will join both major and minor states. Egypt will be buried, not simply left exposed on the land, and will receive decent final rites. Ezekiel's oracles against the nations have less to do with their relationship to Israel and everything to do with the ways of these nations in more universal terms. To be sure, Israel had political and economic relationships with these states. However, their arrogance and self-regard have insulted Yahweh, who in turn will ensure that they will be punished.

LANGUAGE OF HOPE

As we have seen, the book of Ezekiel is often divided into three parts: oracles against Israel, oracles against the nations, and statements of hope. The last section includes individual oracles and sayings (chaps. 33–39) and the vision of temple restoration (chaps. 40–48). It is a commonplace to observe that Ezekiel apparently speaks in a new and different way after the defeat of Jerusalem. The book puts it even more radically, namely, Ezekiel was "dumb," unable to speak prior to Jerusalem's destruction (33:22), but Yahweh enabled him to speak from that point on. Clearly, that moment was a decisive turning point for the prophet. New things could be and were said. And they appear in two ways: in response to the people and through the initiatives of the deity.

Life

In an undated oracle (33:10–20), the people are quoted as saying something that sounds as if it were spoken after the demise of Judah: "Our transgressions and our sins weigh upon us, and we waste away because of them; how then can we live?" Yahweh responds, both in this oracle and in other oracles of promise. The driving issue here is how life can be possible with the temple in ruins and with many of the people (and the temple's priests) in exile. The deity responds in several ways: first, by saying that his response involves his own nature, not that of the people; second, by claiming that the deity will provide the vivifying force. The so-called recognition formula, "they shall know that I am the LORD" (e.g., 39:28), provides the rationale for Yahweh's action of restoration, just as it had for that involving destruction. Yahweh acts for the sake of his name (36:22), not for the sake of the people. Surprisingly, what the deity does will elicit shame from the people, not joy (36:32; 43:10).

The Plain Covered with Bones

Ezekiel offers a very specific idea about how God will enable life. It will come from the divine spirit. The point is made prosaically (39:29). However, the prophet also offers a vision report to illumine his audience in graphic fashion. Ezekiel is taken to a plain covered with bones, a geographic setting located presumably in Mesopotamia, not Israel. The deity asks, "Can these bones live?" (37:3). Though the obvious answer would be "No," Ezekiel demurs. What follows is virtually a new prophetic commission; Ezekiel is supposed to speak God's word to the bones. Through this activity, the bones will become living creatures, in a process similar to the creation of humanity described in Genesis 2. According to the vision report, Ezekiel actually experiences this event. He becomes an agent of revivification, prophesying not only to the bones but also to the wind or "breath" (37:9; cf. Eccl. 11:5 for comparable language about breath and bones). When Ezekiel speaks to this primordial power, the wind enters the lifeless bodies and they live. (In 36:26, Ezekiel makes clear that a new heart will also be provided.)

Lest the ancient (or modern) reader be unclear about the vision report's significance, verses 11–13 confirm that, indeed, the bones symbolize Israel, which has been saying, "Our bones are dried up, and our hope is lost; we are cut off completely." Even this vision is a response to what the people have been saying. The prophet and deity seem intent on addressing the needs of those who have been decimated.

There is a more programmatic side in the oracles and vision of restoration as well, something beyond a response to what the people themselves say. Once the people have been given life, which is a response to their stated concerns, they will return to the land. In a politically charged claim, the book affirms that those in exile will provide the core of the new Israel. Cities will be rebuilt and repopulated

(36:10, 37). The national community will be unified under Davidic leadership (chap. 37). The land will become fertile again (36:30), a virtual Eden (36:35). The vision of temple restoration identifies those structures—both political and religious—that are necessary for restored life in the land.

Gog and Magog

Embedded within these oracles of restoration are chapters 38–39, which also address the future, but a future of cataclysmic phenomena. Ezekiel is commanded to address Gog, a foreign ruler, whom God summons to attack Israel. This is an Israel that has been restored, not the Israel that was to be attacked by the Neo-Babylonians. The name "Gog" may derive from the Lydian ruler Gyges. However, these chapters are transhistorical, with Gog symbolizing any foreign antagonist. Ezekiel 38–39 identifies the attack of Gog and the attending strife with the day of the Lord traditions: "Are you he of whom I spoke in former days by my servants the prophets of Israel?" (38:17); "It has come! . . . This is the day of which I have spoken" (39:8). After Gog's defeat, there will be a sacrificial feast made up of the flesh and blood of those who have been defeated. Carrion and scavengers are overtly invited (39:17). The theological perspective undergirding these chapters is a claim that even such an enemy is ultimately subject to Israel's God, since Yahweh says to Gog, "I will bring you against my land" (38:16).

To be sure, Israel will survive and ultimately be victorious. Still, these chapters attest that those who are to live will continue to experience conflict, and this despite the utopian future conveyed in chapters 40–48. The placement of chapters 38–39 before the vision of temple restoration emphasizes the truly eschatological character of chapters 40–48. That will transpire only after the cosmic conflict attested in the preceding two chapters.

THEOLOGICAL ISSUES

Ezekiel was among the most creative theological thinkers of all Israel's prophets. To be sure, Isaiah was the first to speak about a plan that Yahweh had for the cosmos. Moreover, the book of Isaiah offered lyric poetry about a time beyond punishment. And Jeremiah used the rhetoric of lament in new ways and envisioned a new covenant. But it was the book of Ezekiel that offered the most vigorous attempt to speak about the ways that both Israel and its God would perdure during and beyond the time of disaster. Ezekiel pursues such issues in an innovative manner, by taking a motif or element of tradition and pursuing it to a logical and theological conclusion.

Ezekiel and Priestly Traditions

The book of Ezekiel is related to what might be called priestly traditions, and this quite apart from whether Ezekiel himself was ever ordained as a priest. To be sure, a number of scholars have noted the prominence of so-called priestly vocabulary in the book. This connection has, however, not been explored as thoroughly as one might imagine. For example, von Rad, who was expressly concerned about the ways in which prophets used various of Israel's religious traditions, comments more about Ezekiel's use of Sinai and David traditions than he does Ezekiel's interest in things priestly. In any case, as any number of scholars have demonstrated, there are some very interesting similarities between the Holiness Code of Leviticus 17–26 (a collection of laws that focus on the holiness of both the people and the land they will be entering) and Ezekiel. The same may be said for the relationship between the priestly Tetrateuchal source "P" (a version of Israel's story in Genesis-Numbers that emphasizes purity, genealogy, and the ritual world) and Ezekiel. However, it is important to parse these as discrete relationships. More has been made of similarities between Ezekiel and the Holiness Code, especially Leviticus 26. However, when one compares Leviticus 26 with Ezekiel, one senses both similarities (e.g., the use of the phrase "for I am the LORD your God" in Lev. 26:2) and differences. Zimmerli, following Elliger, has noted some striking family resemblances between Lev. 26:4–13 and Ezek. 34:25–31; both texts use similar imagery to describe the weal that will result from Israel's covenantal obedience.[7] There are also a number of linguistic similarities within the pronouncements of punishment in both books; for example, the phrase "the pride of your power" occurs only in Ezekiel and in the Holiness Code (Ezek. 24:21 and Lev. 26:19). However, there are many differences, and these differences are more significant than the similarities. Key terms in Leviticus, such as "commandment" (*miṣwāh*), are absent from Ezekiel. The notion of progressive punishment (see Lev. 26:14–33) is not significant in Ezekiel. The indictment based on lack of observance of the sabbatical year is not present in Ezekiel, just as the notion of a covenant with the individual patriarchs is absent. Consequently, though Ezekiel and the Holiness Code belong to or use the same stream of ritual tradition, it is inappropriate to speak of one depending on the other.

When one views both Ezekiel and Leviticus from a redaction-critical perspective, one may suggest that portions of each book, perhaps later portions, share similarities. Milgrom has argued convincingly that Leviticus is made up of two primary elements: a priestly code (chaps. 1–16) and the Holiness Code (chaps. 17–26).[8] Each has quite distinct views about sin and holiness. For example, the former deems the temple to constitute the primary zone of holiness whereas the latter deems the entire land to be holy. Ezekiel's restoration vision seems to stake out a position between the two, identifying the city's walls with the temple's walls. However, there are later elements in Ezekiel, such as an emphasis on the Zadokite priests, that seem similar to the priestly code. One has the sense that priestly traditions during Ezekiel's time were in flux and that both Leviticus and Ezekiel—as books—contain disparate elements of these diverse currents in a larger "priestly" river.

The relation of Ezekiel to the priestly source (P) in the Tetrateuch is even more complicated, especially since such arguments have become linked with the relative dating of the P material. One argument runs like this: If Ezekiel shares elements with P, then Ezekiel is probably using P, which would mean that this Tetrateuchal source would be dated to the monarchic period, a view that runs against much thinking about the origins of the Tetrateuchal traditions. In any case, there are some elements in Ezekiel that are similar to elements in P; for example, "they shall increase and be fruitful (Ezek. 36:11 [MT, but not LXX]) sounds like Gen. 1:28: "be fruitful and multiply." Moreover, Ezekiel formulates the language of making a covenant as does P—*qûm* + *bĕrît* (Ezek. 16:60; Genesis 6 and 9). One may, therefore, point to isolated elements that Ezekiel shares with the priestly material. However, the great schema according to which P understands the early history of humankind or the history of God's interaction with the Israelites is not present in Ezekiel. Ezekiel, who was no doubt educated for the priesthood, is proximate to but not identical with later literary ramifications of that priesthood and the documents it produced.

Thus, Ezekiel's relation to the world of ritual and priestly concerns was complex. His was one among many voices within a broad priestly tradition. His training as a priest helps us understand why this tradition was prominent in the book. However, his heterodox location—in exile, away from traditional Zadokite ritual functions—explains why he is different from other exemplars of the priestly enterprise, whether the Holiness Code or P.

Ezekiel as Radical Thinker

Ezekiel was certainly not the first prophet who thought that Israel had offended Israel's God. And he was not the first prophet to use human metaphors, including those involving sexuality, to make this point. Hosea and Jeremiah are his forbears in this regard. However, Ezekiel takes such language and develops it in almost hyperbolic fashion. It is no accident that his rhetoric has been characterized, rightly or wrongly, as "pornoprophetics." Here is a male mind using sexual imagery to convey a radical sense of sin that has permeated Israel's history with Yahweh.

No other prophet—indeed, no other book in the Hebrew Bible—views the relationship between Yahweh and Israel in so negative a light. Ezekiel expresses this judgment using vocabulary and perspectives drawn from his education for the priesthood. One of his favorite terms for Israel's misdeeds is "abominations" (tô'ēbôt), a term regularly, though not exclusively, used to refer to abominable behavior in the religious/ritual realm. He also invokes the typical priestly distinction between the sacred and the profane, when, indicting Israel, he cites them for profaning (ḥll) something, most typically the name of Yahweh (which would have been associated with the temple, where, according to Deuteronomy, the name of Yahweh was made manifest). The language of ḥll (and its obverse, "to sanctify") belongs to classic categories in various religions, and they admit of little ambiguity. Things are normally either sacred or profane. Such vocabulary, along with the conceptual universe behind it, led Ezekiel to think in terms of the total depravity of those (Israelites) who acted so terribly; he uses the phrase "the abominations of the house of Israel" in 6:11.

Ezekiel's Creative Use of Traditions

We have already seen Ezekiel carve out a position about the mobile character of the deity. The book accomplishes this overtly by building upon the initial vision, according to which Ezekiel sees wheels, objects that symbolize God in movement. Such a view builds on earlier motifs (ark, tent of meeting) that had become less prominent due to the notions of God's presence at the temple. The temple was, literally, the bet yhwh, "the house of Yahweh." The deity, as understood according to the tradition of tabernacle and temple, was permanently present. However, there was an alternate understanding symbolized by the tent of meeting, according to which the deity appeared at but was not always at the tent. Ezekiel appeals to this notion, though not explicitly the tent of meeting itself, in order to create theology appropriate for a people in exile. God would be available to them in a foreign land.

Ezekiel 18 offers another instance in which this prophet takes a prior motif and pushes it to the limit. In a number of instances, Ezekiel quotes the people and then launches into a response, even a refutation, of what they are purported to have said. In chapter 18, this pattern of quotation and response occurs three times (the quotations appear in vv. 2, 19, 25). In verse 2, Ezekiel quotes a proverbial saying that utilizes the imagery of eating something sour and of the family: "The parents have eaten sour grapes, and the children's teeth are set on edge." Such a saying must have expressed well the sentiment of those living in exile after the defeat of Jerusalem. The previous generation had acted in a certain way, but those of the ensuing generation were suffering the consequences. Lamentations 5:7 makes a very similar point (and by that same generation of Judahites): "Our ancestors sinned; they are no more, and we bear their iniquities." Moreover, this saying was consistent with the Torah. The Decalogue includes the following statement about the way in which Israel's deity relates to humans: "I the LORD your God am a jealous God, punishing children for the iniquity of parents, to the third and the fourth generation of those who reject me" (Exod. 20:5). Ezekiel's proverb expresses well a basic understanding articulated in the Ten Commandments. However, as elsewhere in the book (i.e., 43:12), Ezekiel offers new torah: "As I live, says the Lord GOD, this proverb shall no more be used by you in Israel" (18:3). Ezekiel's new torah is in fact consistent with another part of the Torah, exemplified in Deut. 24:16—neither children nor parents shall be put to death for the crimes of others. Ezekiel clearly opts for the principle adumbrated in civil law rather than the ideology of treaties (punishment for treaty infractions was disproportionate—if a king violates a treaty, many of his people may be killed) that has made its way into the formulation in the Decalogue.

In order to sustain his new torah, Ezekiel offers three cases that pick up on one part of the imagery in the original proverb—that of the effect of the behavior of one generation on another. He uses the metaphor of the father and his son. If a man is righteous, he shall live (vv. 5–9). If that man's son is unrighteous, he will die, but the father will live. And if the unrighteous son's son is righteous, he will live, but his father—the second generation—will die. Ezekiel offers something like a discursive essay here. Such extended working out of a principle—"know that all lives are mine" (v. 4)—is without parallel in the prophetic corpus.

Some scholars have suggested that this essay is (simply) Ezekiel at work as a priest. But such is hardly the case. To be sure, priests were asked to make judgments about whether someone or something was clean or unclean, righteous or unrighteous. Haggai 2:11–13 offers several examples of this activity. However, Ezekiel the almost priest, and who probably was never able to exercise that role at a temple, uses his education for the priesthood to create an extended discourse on who might be called righteous or unrighteous, rather than offering the priestly pronouncement that a certain person was indeed righteous.

It is important to stress the "almost" priest quality in this essay because of the issues used to grade an individual. The typical priestly judgment involved cleanness versus uncleanness (as the aforementioned case in Haggai demonstrates). One may read through verses 5–9 and identify eleven cases of behavior. (Scholars debate the basis of these lists; some suggest that they reflect criteria for entry into the temple, others that they derive from lists of virtue used in educational contexts.) The three cases that appear in verse 6 seem focused on issues of religious impropriety—something about which a priest might offer a judgment—whereas the eight cases in verses 7–8 stand apart from typical priestly rulings. Again, Ezekiel seems to build on his priestly heritage but in a new and innovative way, expanding and moving beyond the typical topics and principles that guided prior priestly judgments as they are preserved in the Hebrew Bible.

That Ezekiel is working here more as an essayist than as a priestly assessor is made clear by what follows. Ezekiel 18:21–25 might, to the casual reader, sound like more of the same, but the prophet is really doing something quite different. In verses 2–20, the prophet addresses the issue of intergenerational relationships to the deity, and the message is clear: Each generation, each person, stands before the deity. Now Ezekiel focuses on the person, but recognizes that things can change during the course of a human life. Put quite simply, he addresses the cases of a good person gone bad or a bad person who repents.

In this essay, Ezekiel makes three related points. First, the fate of one generation is not fixed by another. Second, an individual's fate is not permanent; it can change based on that person's behavior. Third, even though a person may choose either death or life, life is to be preferred. Instead of talking about doom, Ezekiel says, "I have no pleasure in the death of anyone, says the Lord GOD. Turn, then, and live" (18:32). Here Ezekiel differs in his emphasis from another prophet who cites—and disagrees with—this same proverb, namely, Jeremiah, who notes that "all shall die for their own sins" (Jer. 31:30). Ezekiel, in contrast, emphasizes the possibility of life.

Ezekiel's Vision for the Future

Another distinctive feature of Ezekiel's book is its willingness to offer a specific configuration for a restored Israel. While Second Isaiah's poetry is more rhapsodic than specific, and the ramifications of Jeremiah's new covenant remain inchoate, the book of Ezekiel does not hesitate to identify boundaries, roles, and rules. Ezekiel 40–48 includes distinctive elements. As Blenkinsopp has noted, these chapters offer a calendar distinct from that in the Pentateuch, as well as different offerings and laws of inheritance.[9] Apart from the odd construction of the geography, involving an abstract pattern and even land for the Levites, perhaps the most discernible difference involves the role of human functionaries. The prince (king) has a diminished role, as do the Levites. Instead, the Zadokite priests achieve priority. That group will predominate in restored Jerusalem. Israel is on the way to becoming a theocracy, with rule by God through priests. One may therefore say that this final vision is, or has become, a political document, offering a new polity and emphasizing the power of certain sectors of Judahite society.

Still, Ezekiel 40–48 is profoundly theological. It is rooted in the religious traditions of the ancient Near East. The new Jerusalem described therein draws on the traditions associated with Zion, the dwelling place of Yahweh, and those associated with paradise, the Edenic garden. As for the latter, chapter 47 alludes to a fructifying stream that will flow from the temple. It will be so powerfully sweet that it will turn the Dead Sea into fresh water. Such a flow from Jerusalem reflects, of course, the notion attested in Gen. 2:10–14. This motif becomes powerful in late prophetic literature. Apart from Ezekiel, both Joel 3:18 ("a fountain shall come forth from the house of the LORD and water the Wadi Shittim") and Zech. 14:8 ("on that day living waters shall flow out from Jerusalem") allude to this tradition. This new temple will share qualities with the deity's garden. As for the traditions about Zion as the supreme mountain, when Ezekiel is placed "upon a very high mountain" (Ezek. 40:2), we hear allusions to that mountain from Isaiah ("the mountain of the LORD's house shall be established as the highest of the mountains" [Isa. 2:2]) and from Psalms ("his holy mountain, beautiful in elevation" [Ps. 48:1]). Ezekiel's use of these traditions was ingenious, since they helped authenticate some new elements in his vision of restoration. Just as David (with the ark) and Jeroboam (with the bulls) used archaic traditions to warrant their new cities, so Ezekiel does as well. Ezekiel's vision offers a new torah based in part on a creative use of geography, "territorial rhetoric," to use Stevenson's phrase.[10] The temple overtakes the city; the former's walls become those of the latter. Ezekiel's vision is designed to ensure that the holy and impure do not come in contact with the profane and the impure.

If we take seriously Ezekiel's role as visionary, and the book surely suggests that we do, and if we build upon the remarkable repetition of the formula, "you will know that I am Yahweh," throughout the book one may say that this literature is resolutely theological, more so than most other prophetic literature. The visions explain what Yahweh is doing from the perspective of the deity's "glory," a way of talking about an essential feature of Israel's God. Further, the recognition formulation emphasizes that the purpose of the deity's actions involve "knowledge" about God that Israel (and often the nations) will receive. As Zimmerli suggests, Ezekiel roots his exposition in a fundamental theological affirmation, as expressed at the very outset of the Ten Commandments: "I am Yahweh." The root affirmations are that Israel must know this Yahweh and that this Yahweh is their deity.

THE TEXT AND ITS FORMATION

The Hebrew text of Ezekiel includes a number of expansions. For example, Ezek. 18:32 is shorter in the LXX, which does not include "Turn, then, and live." This situation is generally true for the entire Hebrew manuscript; indeed, it is about 4 to 5 percent longer than the LXX. Emmanuel Tov has argued convincingly that the Greek versions reflect an earlier form of the book that has been supplemented by a layer of additions, some of which are Deuteronomistic (and are therefore similar in thought and vocabulary to the additions present in Jeremiah).[11] He adduces many types of examples (contextually secondary elements, addition of parallel words/phrases, exegetical additions, contextual clarifications, harmonizing pluses, emphasis, new material, and Deuteronomistic formulations). I include two of Tov's cited examples:

1. *New material*. In Ezek. 1:24, the material included here in parentheses is not in the LXX and is, presumably, secondary: "When they moved, I heard the sound of their wings like the sound of mighty waters, like the thunder of the Almighty, (a sound of tumult like the sound of an army)." Here a scribe wanted to offer yet another image to describe the auditory experience of God's presence, an image drawn from the battlefield.

2. *Deuteronomistic formulations*. In Ezek. 8:18, material similar to that found in both Deuteronomy and Jeremiah (the Deuteronomistic prose) appears in the MT (marked by parentheses) but not in LXX: "I will act in wrath;

> my eye will not spare, nor will I have pity; (and though they cry in my hear-
> ing with a loud voice, I will not listen to them)."

For the most part, these and the other additions were designed to help
clarify or reinforce the meaning of the earlier text. Enough such material exists to warrant the judgment that a form of the book of Ezekiel
underwent a redaction, probably in the Greco-Roman period. The
LXX preserves in Greek a form of the book prior to that redaction,
whereas the MT includes the literature in that latest edition.

Ezekiel's original words were, however, probably supplemented even
before the form of the book attested in LXX was created. Scholars disagree vigorously about the extent to which one may identify later additions to the book or, for that matter, Ezekiel's own words. Greenberg
represents one pole, arguing that most of the book may be attributed to
the prophet himself. His is essentially an argument from design. He discerns what he takes to be intricate literary devices and patterns that
one should attribute to the product of "an individual mind of powerful
and passionate proclivities."[12] Zimmerli, and more recently, Pohlmann,
argue on behalf of a different position, namely, that much in the book
was added by later editors.[13] In what Zimmerli describes as a process of
reinterpretation or continuing interpretation (*Nachinterpretation*), the
original words of Ezekiel have been embellished and updated for new
audiences. He attributes some of this activity to a school or disciples associated with Ezekiel. However, he also maintains that Ezekiel himself may
have embellished or developed his own earlier writings and/or sayings.

Zimmerli's redaction-critical work undergirds his magisterial commentary on Ezekiel. He thinks that a complex process of "literary
editing" resulted in this book. It occurred in several ways. Narrative
introductions or summaries grew up around earlier proclamations,
such as 21:25, which reports that Ezekiel recounted this vision to those
in exile. Certain sections of the book emerged as units in which an original element was developed in a new direction. For example, Zimmerli
deems Ezek. 16:1–43 to be the original core of this long chapter, with
verses 44–58 and 59–63 offering expansions beyond the original message. Further, earlier units have been reworked on the basis of subsequent events; Zimmerli maintains that Ezek. 12:1–6 has been
"reworked" based on what actually happened to Zedekiah. All these
developments can be construed as changes that took place when originally oral proclamation was written and revised.

However, Zimmerli identifies a different kind of process, one in
which material that was originally written was subjected to further

modification, such as the introduction of material from Zeph. 1:18 ("Neither their silver nor their gold will be able to save them on the day of the LORD's wrath") into Ezek. 7:19. On occasion, such reworking was thoroughgoing, such as the introduction of wheel imagery into the call vision in order to cast Yahweh's throne as a chariot.

More generally, Zimmerli thinks that originally distinct sections of the book (e.g., the oracles against Tyre [26:1–28:19], which themselves were integrated into another larger unit, the oracles against the nations [chaps. 25–32]) were composed, edited, and then fitted together to create the final product. He deems the chronologically defined sections (1:1–3:15; 8–11; 20:1–44; 24:1–14; 33:21–22) to lie at the original core of the composition. For him, chapters 40–48 make up one of the latest such additions. Still, from our perspective this section is constitutive of the book, since it is one of the three primary vision reports. Put another way, what may have developed late in the redaction process remains of fundamental importance for the book in its current form.

Zimmerli was neither the first nor the last to offer a thoroughgoing redaction-critical analysis of Ezekiel. Nonetheless, his view is probably the most nuanced. The most recent redactional-critical anlaysis is that of Pohlmann, who, in first a monograph and now a commentary, focuses on the compositional history of the book. Unlike Zimmerli, Pohlmann has attempted to identify discrete redactional strata in the book. According to Pohlmann, one may identify *"das ältere Prophetenbuch,"* the original book, to which two important redactional strata have been added—the *golah* and the diaspora redactions. *Golah* means "to go into exile," and he uses this term to refer to the group of Judahites that was taken into exile in 597—the first exile, as it were. Similar to Jer. 24:1–10, these texts place hope for restoration with this group, and with neither those who will be exiled in 587 (Ezek. 14:21–23) nor those who remain in the land (33:21–29). In contrast, there are several authorial hands concerned with the diaspora, namely, all those Yahwists who have been taken from the land. Pohlmann thinks the primary book was in Palestine in the sixth century, that the *golah* redaction was added in the fifth century, and that the diaspora strands derive from the fourth century. Pohlmann is chary about identifying the contents of that older book because of the thoroughgoing character of the later redactions. Still, he looks especially to Ezekiel 15, 19, and 31 as resources. These are poetic texts, all of which Pohlmann characterizes as laments (*Klagetexte*). They stem from the period of 587 and focus on the downfall of the royal house, though without much language of indictment. Moreover, they have been reinterpreted (e.g., in Ezekiel 17 by the prose in vv. 11–19).

Though Pohlmann has offered the most recent, comprehensive redaction-critical analysis, many readers will find Clements's position more appealing, namely, that most of the book would have been completed by 516, when the issues about the administration of ritual in the just completed Second Temple would need to have been decided.[14] Even this view, however, would permit for a substantial period, during which the book of Ezekiel would have grown through the process known as *Nachinterpretation*.

Bibliography

Allen, L. *Ezekiel 1–19*. WBC. Dallas: Word, 1994.

———. *Ezekiel 20–48*. WBC. Dallas: Word, 1990.

Blenkinsopp, J. *Ezekiel*. IBC. Louisville, Ky.: John Knox, 1990.

Bloch, D. *The Book of Ezekiel*. 2 vols. NICOT. Grand Rapids: Eerdmans, 1997, 1998.

Darr, K. "Ezekiel." In *The New Interpreter's Bible*, edited by L. Keck et al., 6:1073–607. Nashville: Abingdon, 2001.

Davis, E. *Swallowing the Scroll: Textuality and the Dynamics of Discourse in Ezekiel's Prophecy*. BLS 21. Sheffield: Almond, 1989.

Greenberg, M. *Ezekiel 1–20*. AB 22. Garden City, N.Y.: New York: Doubleday, 1983.

Lust, Johann, ed. *Ezekiel and His Book: Textual and Literary Criticism and Their Interrelation*. BETL 74. Leuven: Leuven University Press, 1986.

McKeating, H. *Ezekiel*. OTG. Sheffield: JSOT Press, 1993.

Pohlmann, K.-F. *Das Buch des Prophet-en Hesekiel*. ATD 22. 2 vols. Göttingen: Vandenhoeck & Ruprecht, 1996, 2001.

Renz, T. *The Rhetorical Function of the Book of Ezekiel*. VTSup 76. Leiden: Brill, 1999.

Stevenson, K. *The Vision of Transformation: The Territorial Rhetoric of Ezekiel 40–48*. SBLDS 154. Atlanta: Society of Biblical Literature, 1996.

Zimmerli, W. *Ezekiel: A Commentary on the Book of the Prophet Ezekiel*. Hermeneia. 2 vols. Philadelphia: Fortress, 1979, 1983.

5

The Book of the Twelve

Names and labels are powerful symbols. The title of this chapter is a perfect example. The final portion of the "latter prophets" had routinely been known by a previous generation of biblical interpreters as "the Minor Prophets," a phrase that bore a slightly derogatory tone, when compared to "the Major Prophets." By contrast, the label "the Book of the Twelve" places these documents in a position comparable to their prophetic kin—Isaiah, Jeremiah, and Ezekiel. Jeremiah is the longest of these three prophetic books, occupying 116 pages in one edition of the Hebrew Bible, whereas Ezekiel is the shortest, occupying ninety-five pages. The Book of the Twelve stands in between, with ninety-six pages; Isaiah runs 105 pages. Simply in terms of mass, the Book of the Twelve, considered as a unit, belongs in the same league as the other exemplars of prophetic literature.

THE BOOK OF THE TWELVE AS A UNIT

The notion that these twelve books cohere is an ancient one. The phrase "twelve prophets" dates to the pre-Christian era. For example, Sir. 49:10 reads, "May the bones of the Twelve Prophets send forth new life from where they lie." Hence, as early as circa 200 B.C.E., we know that these twelve figures were viewed as a group. Moreover, there is overwhelming evidence that these twelve biblical books were viewed as a scribal unit. The rabbis probably thought that they belonged inextricably together or, at the very least, as one rabbi put it, that they should all be copied on one scroll so that the small books, such as Malachi, would not be lost (*Baba Batra* 13b). Jewish scribal practice—as stated in the Babylonian Talmud—normally required that four empty lines be left between biblical books. Three lines were, however, permitted between the Minor Prophets, suggesting that the scribes understood them to comprise one entity. Finally, the Qumran caves have yielded a fragmentary leather scroll upon which the Minor Prophets were apparently written. One may thus say conclusively that the Book of the Twelve was, as early as the Greco-Roman period, viewed as an assemblage of prophetic literature that was to be written and read together.

Still, the title, "the Book of the Twelve" bears no such antiquity, even though ancient scribes clearly placed these works on the same scroll. No Hebrew scroll with a title like "the Book of the Twelve" has been discovered. There are two Hebrew words that might readily be translated as book or scroll (i.e., *měgillāh* and *sēper*). However, neither term is associated with the Twelve in the era we have been discussing.

There is an obvious point of contrast between the Twelve and the other prophetic books: the presence of a sole author to whom each of the other "latter prophets" may be attributed. There is neither an Ezekiel nor an Isaiah to hold the Twelve together. The case for "the Book of the Twelve" will have to rest elsewhere: either in the search for a theme or plot that unifies this literature, or in a claim that these books were edited in a way that enabled readers to read them together.

One motif that occurs with striking prominence in the Twelve is the phrase "the day of the LORD." It is explicitly present in all but Jonah and Nahum, and it is implicit in the latter (Nah. 1:7). Moreover, "the day of the LORD" is relatively infrequent in the other three prophetic books. In Isaiah it appears primarily in oracles against foreign nations (13:6; 22:5) and in later texts (e.g., 34:8). Some of the important representative exemplars in the Twelve are Hos. 9:5; Joel 2:31; Amos 5:18–20; Obadiah 15; Mic. 2:4; Hab. 3:16; Zeph. 1:7–16; Hag. 2:23; Zech. 14:1; and Mal. 4:1, 5. As we will have occasion to note below, "the day of the LORD" is more than just a phrase. Those words draw upon an Israelite tradition about a dramatic moment when Yahweh will establish himself as true king, often in a military manner. If Isaiah focuses on Zion, Jeremiah on the rhetoric of lament, and Ezekiel on "the glory of the LORD," then the Twelve highlights Yahweh's day. The vocabulary of temporality is a key to this prophetic collection.

Historical Perspectives

The Book of the Twelve contains some of the earliest as well as latest exemplars of prophetic literature. At one end of the spectrum, Amos reflects conditions of the mid-eighth century. On the other hand,

Zechariah 9–14 dates from well into the Persian period (ca. 550–330). The Twelve thus covers a period of roughly four hundred years, including the period of two kingdoms, the time of Judahite statehood (721–587), exile, and restoration. These centuries were times of international upheaval. With Amos, the earliest prophet attested in the Twelve, Israel and Judah lay on the western perimeter of the Neo-Assyrian Empire. Late in the seventh century, that Mesopotamian power fell to another, the Neo-Babylonians. Then, midway through the sixth century, Persia, an empire with its roots to the east of Mesopotamia, decimated the Babylonians.

Each of these empires at one time or another placed troops in Syria-Palestine. Life in both Israel and Judah was thus, in considerable measure, a function of foreign imperial activity. The Neo-Assyrian empire destroyed Israel in 721, the Neo-Babylonian Empire destroyed Judah in 587, and the Persian Empire allowed for and funded partially the rebuilding of Judah as a province within the empire. Each of these three nodal moments receives attention in the Twelve. In some sense, each could be called "the day of the LORD"; yet, that "day" also always remained as a future event.

The other three major prophetic books (Isaiah, Jeremiah, and Ezekiel) provide interesting points of comparison concerning the issue of historical breadth. Isaiah's inaugural vision dates to 743. If one may conclude that Isaiah 56–66 dates to the period immediately after the completion of the Second Temple, then that book represents a period of roughly 240 years. The chronological issue for Jeremiah is complicated because of the various ways in which Jer. 1:2 may be understood—as either the date of Jeremiah's birth or the date at which his work as prophet began. But the date itself is secure, namely, 627. Apart from the so-called historical appendix (Jeremiah 52), the book appears to conclude with activity attested early in the exilic period (Jer. 43:8–44:30). Here the chronological sweep is decidedly shorter than Isaiah—more like forty years. Ezekiel presents the most compressed time frame, beginning in 593 and concluding in about 571 (see Ezek. 29:17), just a little less than a quarter century. In sum, none of the "major" prophets can compare with the historical sweep offered by the Book of the Twelve.

Order of the Literature

Assessing the order of biblical books might seem to be an entirely mechanical matter. Such is not the case, however. One may reflect about the various orderings within the Book of the Twelve.

The Order within the Book of the Twelve

During most of the twentieth century, it had been a commonplace to assume that the Minor Prophets were written and edited as individual books, then collected and finally ordered. And such may have been the case. But the real question turns on the principles for their ordering.

One principle appears to have been chronological. Hosea and Amos are early books, and they appear early on in the collection, whereas Haggai and Zechariah are late and appear near the end of the collection. But there are troubling exceptions. Joel, the second book of the Twelve and one without any explicit historical allusions, is routinely dated to the Persian period. Yet this book appears as the second in the collection. Moreover, immediately before Micah, whose superscription anchors it firmly to the eighth century, comes Obadiah, which dates to circa 587, and Jonah, which, though mentioning Nineveh, is almost certainly postexilic in origin. Were Jonah to appear as the final book in the Twelve—and it may well have been the last book to have been written—this collection would end with a question: "And should I not be concerned about Nineveh, that great city, in which there are more than a hundred and twenty thousand persons who do not know their right hand from their left, and also many animals?" (Jonah 4:11). The tone of the Book of the Twelve is very different, concluding with the final verse of Malachi: "He [Elijah] will turn the hearts of parents to their children and the hearts of children to their parents, so that I [Yahweh] will not come and strike the land with a curse" (Mal. 4:6).

Two charts display the difficulties we have been discussing. Chart 1 orders the books according to their canonical arrangement. Chart 2 indicates the probable moments of origin for the books, though the dating of the final two books—Joel and Jonah—remains difficult. (Zechariah involves at least two different moments: ca. 520 for chaps. 1–8 and later in the Persian period for chaps. 9–14.)

Evidence of an alternative canonical ordering exists. The major LXX manuscripts present an order different from the Hebrew text for the first six books: Hosea, Amos, Micah, Joel, Obadiah, and Jonah. This order, at least in the first three books, reflects more nearly the moments of historical origin, as shown in chart 2. However, that principle breaks down with the next three books. Thus, both the Hebrew and Greek textual evidence allows one to infer that the principle of chronological arrangement does not offer a comprehensive explanation for the ordering of the books. Other dynamics must have been at work.

by Canon

CHART 1	CHART 2
Hosea	Amos
Joel	Hosea
Amos	Micah
Obadiah	Zephaniah
Jonah	Nahum
Micah	Habakkuk
Nahum	Obadiah
Habakkuk	Haggai
Zephaniah	Zechariah
Haggai	Malachi
Zechariah	Joel
Malachi	Jonah *last written*

Another principle involves the actual language of the books. Similar phraseology at the end of one book and the beginning of another may have made it seem appropriate for the two books to be placed together. For example, the following lines occur near the end of Joel (3:16) and near the beginning of Amos (1:2): "The LORD roars from Zion and utters his voice from Jerusalem." Such similarity in poetic diction may have influenced a scribe to juxtapose these two books. Similarly, one may point to the end of Haggai, with its references to "horses" (Hag. 2:22), and the first chapter of Zechariah, with its vision of steeds of many colors (Zech. 1:7–17), as another place in which similar vocabulary may have influenced the placement of these books.

Further, the very notion of "the Twelve" requires brief comment. Why not eleven or thirteen prophets? To answer that there were twelve books waiting to be included is not self-evident. The final book, known as Malachi in English, probably does not reflect a named prophet; the word *mal'ākî* in Hebrew means "my messenger." It is not a typical Hebrew name. Moreover, the title of the book, "An oracle. The word of the LORD . . . ," is similar to the introductions that occur at Zech. 9:1 and 12:1. As a result, one may theorize that the four chapters of Malachi were split off from Zechariah 9–14 to create a separate book that would then make a total of twelve such books. The number twelve was symbolically significant for ancient Israel, as the notion of the twelve tribes readily suggests. In sum, it is likely that the final portion of the Twelve was configured in such a way as to yield twelve prophets, not eleven and not thirteen.

The Placement of the Book of the Twelve

There is a final and related issue concerning the order of these books: the placement of the Twelve in the various canonical traditions. The Christian Bible concludes the Old Testament with the Twelve since it places the Prophets at the end. The Jewish Scriptures place the Twelve at the end of the second section, the Prophets (*nĕbî'îm*), and just before the beginning of the Writings, with its lead book, Psalms. As a result, the two canons conclude in different forms and with different tones. The Jewish canon ends with a challenge to live in Judah and worship at the temple in Jerusalem (2 Chr. 36:23), whereas the Christian Old Testament concludes with the affirmation that Elijah will return to effect familial harmony. The one focuses on place, the other on person and relationships. Hence, the very placement of the Twelve at one or another point in the canon affects our perceptions of the way in which the Bible concludes.

Formation of the Individual Books and of the Twelve

One may raise two different questions about literary formation when discussing the Twelve. On the one hand, it is appropriate to ask about the process according to which an individual book was created. For example, how did Hosea come to exist? There are some biographical and autobiographical sections at the beginning of the book, which are then followed by various poetic speeches. Did someone organize the speeches, and, if so, according to what principles? Were the prose pieces in chapters 1 and 3 put in their current order for some particular purpose? Answers to such questions usually result from redaction criticism. In sketches about each prophetic book, I will comment, when appropriate, about such issues important for the interpretation of that book.

On the other hand, one may raise questions about the formation of the Twelve itself.[1] In effect, we have already done this when discussing the order of these twelve books. However, that discussion presupposes a model according to which there were twelve books ready to be ordered. Other models do exist. For example, some scholars have maintained that there was an early collection of minor prophets made up of three or four books, and that it grew to eight or nine, and then to twelve.[2] Another model involves the notion of several discrete collections. For example, Jeremias has recently argued that Amos and Hosea exerted mutual formative influence and must have been part of an early collection.[3] In a comparable vein, Nogalski posits two such entities, a

Deuteronomistic collection (Hosea, Amos, Micah, Zephaniah) and the Haggai-Zechariah corpus.[4] These collections were combined and supplemented at a later time. One element that appears with increasing frequency in these discussions is the claim that there was a Deuteronomistic collection of minor prophets, a claim based in part on the conviction that a number of these books include Deuteronomistic elements (i.e., Amos, Micah, and Hosea).[5] Some scholars, such as Nogalski, have suggested that as the collection grew, the beginnings and endings of books were refined and revised so as to provide linkages with contiguous prophetic books. Such observations, if sustained, would weigh heavily toward conceiving of the Twelve as a single book, since the material in the books, not just their order, was designed with the larger whole in view. At the moment, however, there is no scholarly consensus about these matters.

Two other matters deserve some mention within the context of the formation of this prophetic literature. First, some of the books in the Twelve appear to have been updated, particularly with reference to the defeat of Judah in 587 and the experience of exile, the demise of nationhood, and the end of the Davidic kingship. It is difficult to read Amos 9:11–15 and not imagine that these verses were written to express hope for Israel after it had suffered the aforementioned catastrophes. Second, similar updatings can also be seen clearly in the book of Isaiah (24–27; 34–35; 40–55; 56–66). It may be that comparable forces were at work with the Twelve.[6] Questions about the formation of the Twelve are not easily isolated from questions about the formation of other biblical prophetic literature.

All such concerns about the ways in which the Twelve came to exist involve a topic inherent to the study of all prophetic literature. During the monarchic period, both leather and papyrus were probably used for the inscription of longer texts. All of the "major" prophets—Isaiah (8:1–4; 30:8), Jeremiah (32:9–15; 36), Ezekiel (2:9–3:3)—mention in one way or another the creation or use of texts as part of the prophetic enterprise. Moreover, such practice is attested in several of the Twelve (Hab. 2:2–3 and Mal. 3:16). Writing in the performance of the prophetic role would have been one important generator for prophetic literature. But there must have been at least one other impulse, namely, the desire to see whether that which the prophets anticipated would work itself out. The classic formulation of Deut. 18:22 virtually requires the archival preservation of prophetic utterance: "If a prophet speaks in the name of the LORD but the thing does not take place or prove true, it is a word that the LORD has not spoken." One can imagine that the words of Amos 2:13–16, when preserved and remembered after the destruction of Israel in 721, would have gained even greater authority than they might originally have borne. Such would have been the case with other prophets attested in the Book of the Twelve.

Even though there are significant ways in which these twelve books may be read together, the simple fact that they occur as individually titled books also enables them to be treated separately. Moreover, each of these books elicits its own interpretive strategies. For example, the rich poetry of Hosea has regularly generated literary studies. By contrast, Amos's hard-hitting rhetoric has led to analysis of the social world that he addresses. As one moves through these twelve books, one or another method, or combination of methods, will be appropriate. In this chapter, we have chosen to highlight the methods appropriate to the study of each book along with the interpretive results they help generate.

HOSEA

Hosea is unique in the Hebrew Bible. It is the only book that reflects the activity of a native of the northern kingdom, Israel, who assesses the life of that nation. This national rootage helps us understand why the book of Hosea is so different from Amos, which dates to roughly the same period—the mid-eighth century B.C.E. Amos saw Israel with Judahite eyes, whereas Hosea perceived life there from the perspective of a native.

Unlike Amos, Hosea refers in quite specific terms to the political world of Israel. To be sure, the superscription (1:1) identifies a general period (the reigns of the southern kings involve almost one century) during which Hosea was active. The rest of the book focuses on a much shorter time span, namely, the final decades in the life of the northern kingdom. Moreover, the book highlights two features of that world. First, we find a number of references to improper behavior in the international realm. In particular, Hosea indicts Israel for entangling and conflicting alliances involving the Egyptians and the Neo-Assyrians. Israel had apparently agreed to be a vassal of the Neo-Assyrian Empire but then revolted, probably because of a promise of help from Egypt (2 Kgs. 17:3–4).

> Ephraim has become like a dove,
> silly and without sense;
> they call upon Egypt, they go to Assyria.
> (Hos. 7:11; see also 5:13; 7:8; 14:3)

For Hosea, such illicit activity is linked to religious improprieties, as this confession of the people indicts:

> Assyria shall not save us;
> we will not ride upon horses;
> we will say no more, "Our God,"
> to the work of our hands.
> (Hos. 14:3)

The second feature of the last decades of Israel's existence found in the book of Hosea is the internal political intrigue that Israel experienced during this time. There was radical royal instability; between 746 and 721 (the year in which Israel was destroyed) seven kings ruled in the northern kingdom. Of that number, at least half were assassinated. The book uses graphic images to depict this situation:

> All of them are hot as an oven,
> and they devour their rulers.
> All their kings have fallen;
> none of them calls upon me.
> (Hos. 7:7)

Hosea even refers to specific murders. Reference to Gilead as "a city of evildoers, tracked with blood" (Hos. 6:8) probably alludes to the assassination of Pekahiah by Pekah, who was aided by fifty persons from Gilead (2 Kgs. 15:25). Hosea knows and is interested in this political world in a way that Amos is not.

Study of Hosea has been driven by the peculiarities of the book. This is especially true for the first three chapters, which focus on a marriage that God commands Hosea to enter. Early on debate swirled around the question of historicity: Did Hosea actually engage in such a marriage? Moreover, what is the relationship of Hosea 1 to Hosea 3? Do they provide two versions of the same command? Did Hosea marry the same woman twice?

After years of reflecting on these questions, many scholars have now decided that the texts in Hosea simply do not allow for ready answers, especially to the first question. Moreover, the immediate drive to answer historical questions has preempted some more obvious—and answerable—questions. For example, a standard feature of biblical interpretation is the posing of a question about literary type: What kind of literature does the text present?

Hosea 1:2–8 and 3:1–4 are both prose reports of a prophetic symbolic action, the first written in the third person, the second written in the first person. Some symbolic actions are easy to perform, such as the buying and breaking of a ceramic pot (Jeremiah 19). Other prophetic actions, however, require the prophet to involve his whole being. Isaiah fathered a child with a prophetess (Isa. 8:1–4), Jeremiah was called to a life of celibacy (Jer. 16:1–4), and Ezekiel was forbidden to mourn the death of his wife (Ezek. 24:15–24). Hosea 1 and 3 belong in this world of lived prophetic symbolic actions.

By placing Hosea's "marriage" in this context, we are able to discern that the marriage itself is not the message. Hosea 1:1–8 makes it clear that the children born to Hosea and Gomer, and even more the names given to them—"I am not yours," "Not pitied," and "Not my people"—are the message that the deity intended Hosea to convey to the people. (The same is true in Isa. 8:1–4—the child's name provides the key.) Similarly, the ownership and sexual isolation of the unnamed woman in Hosea 3 symbolizes a message about Israel's isolation from necessary political and social structures. The key to understanding Hosea 1 and 3 is asking the right questions, initially literary ones.

Scholars continue to approach Hosea 4–14 with the full arsenal of biblical studies methods. Form-critical perspectives help us discern the smaller speeches that make up the book. Divine oracles clearly outnumber prophetic speeches. However, form criticism of Hosea is far more difficult than form criticism of Amos since there are so few introductory and concluding formulae in this first book of the Twelve. Still, even without such formulae, as one reads Hosea 4, it is difficult not to discern a boundary between speeches as one moves from verse 3 to verse 4. (The boundaries are less apparent when one moves through the poetry in chap. 2.) In addition, the presence of a metaphor (Israel as a cake [7:8–10]) or a simile (Israel like a dove [7:11–13]) aids the reader in discerning distinct poems.

Redaction criticism helps us understand the formation of the book. First, the book has been configured into three primary parts: chapters 1–3, 4–11, and 12–14. The second and third parts each move from language of judgment to discourse about salvation. Such a thematization probably derives from an editing of the book after the demise of the northern kingdom (721) and, quite possibly, after the defeat of the southern kingdom (587). Certain elements, such as David as king (3:5) and the people of Judah (1:11; 8:14; 12:1) do not reflect concerns of Hosea in eighth-century Israel, since those elements deal primarily with Judah. Hosea 1:7; 2:1–2; and 3:5, among others, reflect an interest in restoration after destruction. Moreover, Hos. 14:9 appears to be a late attempt to integrate Hosea with the wisdom tradition in a way comparable to the way in which Psalm 1 relates the Psalter to wisdom literature.

> Those who are wise understand these things;
>   those who are discerning know them.
> For the ways of the LORD are right,
>   and the upright walk in them,
>   but transgressors stumble in them.
>
> (Hos. 14:9)

Quite simply, Hosea is a book that emerged over time.

Tradition history is more important than either form criticism or redaction criticism for the study of Hosea, in part because Hosea represents an area in which the traditions were different than they were for all other prophets. Zion as the seat of Yahweh's reign and David as the quintessential king played no role in the northern kingdom. Rather, the tradition about God's covenant with Israel that was made at Sinai had pride of place in Israel. Hence, we should not be surprised to read Hos. 4:1–3 and discover an indictment that reflects the classic summary of the Sinai covenant, namely, the Ten Commandments: "Swearing, lying, and murder, and stealing and adultery break out."

The Ten Commandments (or Decalogue) offer a comprehensive, though distilled, version of covenantal obligations. Both religious and ethical issues are in view. One might say that if Amos focuses on ethical issues (though religious issues are mentioned [e.g., Amos 5:21–23]), then Hosea focuses on religious issues (though ethical issues are mentioned [e.g., Hos. 4:8; 7:1]). Proper and sole veneration of Yahweh is the primary issue in this book.

Also significant is Hosea's interest in earlier Israelite history. On numerous occasions, Hosea reviews how Yahweh acted on behalf of Israel and then how Israel, once it was in the land, rebelled (Hos. 9:10). Or, using different vocabulary, what Israel once "knew" they have since "forgotten" (see 4:6).

Finally, both literary and social-world analysis may assist in the study of Hosea. Hosea's poetry is rich and complex. We have mentioned earlier the importance of attending to the diverse figures of speech. Further, attention to gender issues—for example, reading the book from a feminist perspective—casts new light on the abuse of the woman in chapters 2 and 3. The gendered social world conveyed in the text may be the subject of fruitful research.

Theological issues loom large in the book of Hosea, which is part of Israel's literature that engages and polemicizes the veneration of Baal. The stories of Elijah are also part of that story, as is the Deuteronomistic History. But Hosea is the book where the challenge of Baalism is taken most creatively and dangerously.

As early in the book as Hos. 2:8, 13, we learn that worship of Baal stands as one of Hosea's signal indictments. Though scholars debate vigorously the nature of religion in Israel, one important point is whether Yahwism included elements of Canaanite religion. There is little doubt that many of the indictments of the book, such as the worship at high places (4:13) and veneration of figurines (4:12, 17), are part of this larger critique of Baal worship.

Hosea responds to these indictments by offering images of punishment. Sometimes these images are ambiguous (9:7–9). At other times, they are vicious (13:7–8). The "day of the LORD" will appear (9:5–6), but precisely what will happen is unclear, even though an attack by Assyria is on the horizon (10:6).

Hosea repeatedly expresses the conviction that God loves Israel like a parent (or like a spouse); yet, unlike a human, punishment will be more instructive than destructive.

> When Israel was a child, I loved him,
>   and out of Egypt I called my son.
> (11:1)

> How can I give you up, Ephraim?
>   How can I hand you over, O Israel?
> (11:8)

> I am God and no mortal,
>   the Holy One in your midst,
>   and I will not come in wrath.
> (11:9)

Comparable is the marital metaphor:

> Therefore I will now allure her,
>   and bring her into the wilderness,
>   and speak tenderly to her.
> . . . .
> There she shall respond as in the days of her youth.
> (2:14–15)

It remains difficult to reconcile the language of punishment with this poetry that expresses hope for reconciliation or restoration. Some scholars have argued that the latter should not be attributed to Hosea but to a later hand. However, one of the primary motifs in the book, namely, love, with all its ambiguity in both Yahwism and Baalism, could, even in Hosea's time, cut against the notion of an absolute end to a relationship between Yahweh and Israel. That is, Yahweh's love for Israel surpasses his desire to react solely to Israel's sin.

Hosea remains one of the most challenging of prophetic books. No other book so inextricably intertwines the world of human love with the discourse of religious polemic, often in metaphoric language as ambiguous as it is elegant.

JOEL

In one sense, reading the book of Joel is straightforward. It describes an attack on Judah (Joel 1:6). The prophet admonishes the people to respond with fasting and other ritual behavior. His admonitions are successful. Yahweh then becomes "jealous" for the people (2:18) and answers their calls for help. Thereafter (2:28–3:21) the book moves from the present to the future, focusing on the good things—often in hyperbolic terms—to which Judahites can look forward (e.g., "the mountains shall drip sweet wine, the hills shall flow with milk" [3:18]).

However, the book of Joel also presents the reader with several problems. The most serious one involves the nature of the catastrophe that the book describes. Is it a locust plague described as if it were a military attack (1:4), or is it a military attack described as if it were a locust plague (1:6)? The difficulty of providing an answer to these questions is related to another difficulty, namely, identifying the historical setting in which Joel was composed. Unlike the prophetic books on either side—Hosea and Amos—there are no kings listed in the book's superscription. Without allusions to a Jeroboam or to an Ahaz, we are left with little data about the book's temporal setting.

There is language about a physical setting that provides an important key to the book's interpretation. The place is "Zion" (2:1), and the temple (1:13; 2:17) is situated on it. At a minimum, the book of Joel dates to a time when the temple existed in Jerusalem. Many scholars think that this temple was the one rebuilt in 515 B.C.E., since significant portions of the book (e.g., Joel 3:1) expressly allude to the restoration of Judah's fortunes after its defeat in 587.

We are not accustomed to thinking about prophets and temple (see chapter 1). Some popular definitions of prophets define them over against priests. However, such a judgment would fall wide of the mark in ancient Israel. Jeremiah, Ezekiel, and Zechariah were members of priestly lineages; they were individuals who could be both priest and prophet. Though we are told nothing about Joel's family, apart from his father's name (Pethuel), much in the book suggests that he functioned in a priestly capacity as well.

The language in Joel provides evidence of that priestly ability. It is instructive to compare the imperative verbs in Joel 1–2 with comparable grammar in Amos. Whereas Amos tells the people, "Let justice roll down like waters, and righteousness like an everflowing stream" (Amos 5:24), Joel admonishes the people and especially the priests, "Sanctify a fast, call a solemn assembly" (1:14), and "Sanctify the congregation; assemble the aged" (2:16). One searches through Joel in vain for language of ethical admonition. Instead, throughout the early portion of the book, Joel challenges the people to undertake appropriate forms of lamentation at the temple by way of a response to the momentous crisis they face.

The major theological issue at work in the book is embedded in this language of lament. Joel uses traditional language: "the day of the LORD is near" (1:15; cf. 2:1). One could read that proclamation and infer that Joel thinks Yahweh will respond to the current crisis. Indeed, such is the case. However, Joel also claims that Yahweh is already at work during the present moment. After describing again the troops arrayed against the land (2:4–10), the prophet interprets this army as none other than the one belonging to Israel's God: "The LORD utters his voice at the head of his army; how vast is his host!" (2:11). The implication of this theological claim is clear. Israel should turn to Yahweh since that deity is the one responsible for the suffering they are enduring.

Such consistent appeal to ritual language should elicit a way of reading the book that is sensitive to general religious issues (e.g., how did lamentation work and function in ancient Israel?). Scholars who have addressed religious practices in ancient Israel have discovered that lamentation could be a communal as well as an individual practice. Laments are the most frequent form of psalm. (For an individual lament, see Ps. 28; for a communal lament, see Ps. 44 or the book of Lamentations.) Communal lamentation—the chanting of a lament, fasting, wearing sackcloth, and weeping—was almost certainly the practice for which Joel was calling. Such practices of lamentation were often undertaken at the temple. Within the context of such lamentation, a priest could offer a word on behalf of the deity, indicating that God had responded to the community's plight. Joel reflects just such temple-based worship in ancient Israel (see the reference to a specific place in the temple precinct, "between the vestibule and the altar" [2:17]).

Joel 1:1–2:17 focuses on the need for lamentation as a response to the incredible destruction the land had been suffering. The poet uses various images to convey this plight: military ("For a nation has invaded my land, powerful and innumerable" [1:6]); conflagration ("For the fire has devoured the pastures of the wilderness, and flames have burned all the trees of the field" [1:19]); locust plague ("What the cutting locust left, the swarming locust has eaten; what the swarming locust left, the hopping locust has eaten; and what the hopping locust left, the destroying locust has eaten" [1:4]). Joel 2:18 reports that "the LORD became jealous for his land and had pity on his people." Joel writes as if the lamentation had actually occurred and that God is now responding to the people. From this perspective, Joel was a successful prophet!

Much of the remainder of the book is written in the form of divine speech. Prior to 2:18, the only "I" from whom we hear is the prophet (1:19). Beginning with 2:19, Yahweh speaks repeatedly about what will happen as a result of his taking pity on "his people" (2:19), the "children of Zion" (2:23). Most immediately, the army/locusts will be removed. However, the scale of the deity's activity enlarges: "I will show portents in the heavens and on earth, blood and fire and columns of smoke. The sun shall be turned to darkness, and the moon to blood" (2:30–31). To be sure, the deity responds to Israel's agricultural crisis. Whereas earlier there was drought and dessication (e.g., 1:10, 12, 17), after God acts there will be such marvelous fertility that "the mountains shall drip sweet wine and the hills shall flow with milk" (3:18).

But just as Israel receives weal, Israel's enemies suffer the deity's wrath. Whereas earlier Israel was becoming a wasteland, now Israel's enemies—Egypt and Edom—incur such a fate (3:19). Such rhetoric of international violence is of a piece with oracles against the nations found in all three of the "major" prophets. But Joel seems to highlight this element, particularly in its variation on a theme struck in both Isa. 2:2–4 and Mic. 4:1–4. Whereas those prophets anticipated a time of peace and pilgrimage—a time when swords would be beaten into plowshares—Joel challenges the nations to sanctify themselves for war with God's warriors. These nations are commanded, "Beat your plowshares into swords, and your pruning hooks into spears" (3:10).

Such cosmic and violent images resonate with later prophetic texts (e.g., Isaiah 24–27; Ezekiel 38–39; Zechariah 9–14). As a result, some scholars have maintained that much of Joel 2:28–3:21 may date to a later time, when intensely eschatological imagery was becoming prominent in Syria-Palestine. That some of these verses are apparently written in prose (e.g., Joel 2:30–3:8) has been viewed by some as a warrant for this position.

After having finished reading Joel, the inquisitive reader may well pose the following question: In what way is the author of this book acting as a prophet? The answer depends in considerable measure on one's definition of a prophet. If a prophet is an intermediary who conveys the words and plans of the deity to humans, then Joel does indeed fit the bill. Moreover, as we stated earlier, the first portion of the book portrays Joel as a speaker who was able to convince both priests and the larger populace to participate in the lamentation practices that provided their only hope.

AMOS

The book of Amos offers a vigorous collection of oracles and speeches along with a series of vision reports. They reflect the activity of a Judahite farmer who worked as a prophet in the northern kingdom. Despite the brevity of this collection, the book of Amos and the scholarship devoted to it offer a microcosm of work on prophetic literature. Virtually every method or perspective available has been exercised on these nine chapters. As a result, no prophetic book has a bibliography comparable in size to that in Amos.

As with Hosea, the book of Amos commences with a superscription that relates the prophet's activities to the reigns of Israelite (Jeroboam) and Judahite (Uzziah, also known as Azariah) kings. Both kings exercised long reigns during the middle part of the eighth century B.C.E. The longer of the two reigns was that of Uzziah, the Judahite king (786–746). Unlike Hosea, Amos does not discuss the political world but rather the social and economic conditions of the northern kingdom. For example, when Amos refers to other nations (e.g., Ashdod and Egypt in 3:9–11), they are summoned to witness the "oppression" in Israel.

Form-critical analysis of prophetic literature works particularly well on the poetry in Amos. Because of the prominence of both introductory and concluding formulae in this book, it is relatively easy to determine where short oracles or prophetic speeches begin and end. Moreover, rhetorical changes assist the reader when such formulae are absent. For example, even though a formula occurs neither at the end of Amos 3:2 nor at the beginning of 3:3, the shift from language of judgment to a series of questions makes it clear that we are dealing with two separate speeches.

Form-critical inventories of Amos reveal essentially three different kinds of speech. First, there are five first-person vision reports (7:1–3, 4–6, 7–9; 8:1–3; 9:1–4). Second, the book includes a number of prophetic speeches, instances in which the prophet speaks in his own voice and talks about the deity in third person language (e.g., 5:18–20). Third, and most prominent, Amos utters divine oracles, in which he quotes the deity directly, conveying Yahweh in first person language (e.g., 5:21–24). The first form is essentially prose, whereas the last two appear typically as poetry. The vision reports focus primarily on the inescapability of the judgment that will befall Israel, whereas the oracles and sayings also include a justification for that judgment.

A form-critical examination of Amos virtually demands that redaction-critical work ensue in order to answer the question of the significance, if any, of the ordering of the discrete speeches. Put another way, how do the rhetorical questions in 3:3–8 work well after 3:1–2? One might argue that the principle at work in the questions, namely, things happen for a reason (a snare does not spring unless something trips it [v. 5]), helps the reader understand what has been said in a far more cryptic way in verses 1–2. There is a connection between God's having chosen Israel and what will happen to Israel. Such a connection is embedded in the natural order of things. It is not due to a whimsical act of a deity. Such is the logic of redaction criticism.

There are, however, other redaction-critical issues present in the book. First, some sort of collecting of materials based on similarity in genre is present. All the oracles against the nations appear in the first two chapters. The vision reports have been put into a meaningful sequence. All the woe oracles appear in chapters 5–6. Intentional collection and ordering are well attested in this book.

In addition, it appears that new literature was created to accompany Amos's original sayings. Scholars have identified diverse elements that entered the Amos tradition over time. For example, it is unlikely that Amos would have been concerned with Beersheba, a city in the far south of Judah, when he was talking to the citizens of the northern kingdom. Hence, one may postulate that those texts which mention Beersheba (5:5; 8:14) derive from a time when Amos's words were being re-presented in a Judahite setting. Second, some texts may date to the late seventh- and early sixth-century traditions associated with the Deuteronomic reform of Josiah as well as to the continuing Deuteronomistic tradition. As for the former, the condemnation of the altar at

Bethel (Amos 5:5) seems to be of a piece with the polemic against that ritual site in Josiah's time (2 Kgs. 23:15). As for the latter, the oracle against Judah (Amos 2:4–5) offers the sort of indictment about violation of torah that is a hallmark of the Deuteronomistic History. Finally, Amos 9:11–15 probably reflects the defeat of Judah and Jerusalem in 587. The oracle is clearly concerned about the southern kingdom, as specific allusion to "the booth of David" demonstrates (9:11). There are strong similarities between this oracle and other Persian period prophetic texts (cf. Amos 9:13 with Joel 3:18, which has a Jerusalemite focus). In addition, 9:15 alludes to exile from which Judahites would return (unlike the exile that the northern kingdom suffered, from which none would return). In sum, the words of Amos elicited other words that enabled the Amos collection to speak to ensuing generations of Israelites in different places and conditions.

In recent decades, there has been something of a counterreaction. Some scholars have become dissatisfied with attempts to discern so many redaction-critical refinements. Instead, they propose to read the book in its final form, often with the presupposition that the book was created as one large work or composed in several major sections. The work of Shalom Paul (see bibliography) represents this approach. However, some of the most recent and impressive redaction-critical research on Amos is pointing to the formation of that literature as it may have been influenced by another prophetic book, namely, that of Hosea (see Jeremias). These claims are pushing redaction-critical study of Amos in an entirely new direction, linking it with analysis of other books that make up the Book of the Twelve.

Tradition history has also informed analysis of Amos. The very fact that there are rhetorical questions (e.g., 3:3–8) has led some scholars to look throughout the Hebrew Bible for other exemplars of rhetorical questions. They have found them in Wisdom literature (see e.g., Job 6:22–28). Consequently, Hans Walter Wolff has argued that Amos was influenced by wisdom traditions, particularly so-called clan wisdom, wisdom that would have developed in family circles rather than at the royal court.

Finally, scholars have been interested to know what social and economic circumstances lay behind various biblical books. Such social-world concerns are especially germane for a book that overtly addresses economic (5:11) and social (5:12) issues.

The book of Amos allows for no easy summary. However, if one attends to the vision reports and the judgment oracles, at least three of the book's major thematic elements become clearer: (1) an end is com-

ing, (2) there are good reasons for that end, and (3) Yahweh will cause
the demise of Israel. The book constructs a theology of judgment.

The initial vision reports cluster in chapter 7. Twice, Amos sees
destructive acts—the first apparently a locust plague, the second a cosmic fire that devoured the salt water deep (truly a mythic image). On
both occasions, Amos speaks out:

> O Lord GOD, forgive, I beg you!
> How can Jacob stand?
> He is so small!
>
> (7:2b)

Such intercession apparently worked, as had also been the case with
Joel. Amos apparently had a prophetic role of more than divine herald.
He could "talk back" to the deity on behalf of the people. One could
imagine as well that he could talk to the people from the same perspective, namely, as one interested in their welfare. Several sayings in
chapter 5 reflect this concern (e.g., "Seek good and not evil, that you
may live" [5:14]). Amos's prophetic message was not always one of negative pronouncement, in part because of the diverse prophetic roles that
he could exercise.

Still, the last three visions reports (7:7–9; 8:1–3; 9:1–4) do not convey
Amos in an intercessory mode. In the penultimate report, he is precluded
from such action because of a word trick that the deity plays. Amos sees
a basket of summer fruit (Hebrew *qāyiṣ*; 8:1), which the deity interprets
to mean the end (Hebrew *qēṣ*; 8:2). Amos does not have the opportunity
to intercede before Yahweh offers the word of decisive judgment, which
is intensified in the final vision report. By the end of the visionary
sequence, Amos has learned that Israel cannot escape God's destruction.

This conclusion to the visions cries out for an explanation. Why will
the deity act in such a punitive fashion? The judgment oracles answer
this question. With their classic two-part form made up of an indictment and a sentence, these oracles both explain and offer a judicial decision. When one surveys 2:6–7; 4:1; and 5:10–12, it becomes clear that
one major reason for the coming destruction is violation of social and
economic norms, particularly the oppression of the least powerful and
the poor in the society. Moreover, it appears that economic developments in the northern kingdom were dispossessing Israelites from their
traditional position as independent land owners and creating a wealthy
group who had been securing land through illicit use of the court system. Amos seems to say that there is a level of economic consumption
that violates Israel's covenant norms of justice and righteousness

(6:4–6). Therefore, those in the land should know that Yahweh's day will be coming as a direct response to the social and economic conditions that they have created.

The second element of the judgment oracle, the sentence, typically spells out what will happen. One might expect to hear Amos speak about the destruction that the Neo-Assyrian armies would wreak on the northern kingdom. Indeed, there are some allusions to destruction within the context of warfare (e.g., 5:3–6; 6:14). However, most of the judgments in Amos occur in divine oracles. The deity will act against Israel. The first person language predominates in this rhetoric:

> On that day, says the Lord GOD,
>   I will make the sun go down at noon,
>   and darken the earth in broad daylight.
> I will turn your feasts into mourning,
>   and all your songs into lamentation;
> I will bring sackcloth on all loins,
>   and baldness on every head;
> I will make it like the mourning for an only son,
>   and the end of it like a bitter day.
>
>   (8:9–10)

The one who had chosen Israel for a special relationship (3:2) will now act definitely against that nation.

Texts such as this one are both frightening and baffling. They frighten because the language is so negative, and they are baffling because one cannot be sure exactly what it is that Yahweh would do. In these two verses, it initially sounds as if there might be an eclipse of the sun. But then the imagery shifts in the middle of the poem to that of funeral lamentation. Then, in the final two lines, the prophet uses two similes, the last one of which is remarkably vague: "I will make it like the mourning for an only son, and the end of it like a bitter day" (8:10b). The similes do not translate quickly into the language of everyday events. But we know that whatever happens involves death and/or an end. In such judgment oracles, we learn far more about specific indictments than we do about concrete forms of destruction. Such rhetoric would have been particularly effective in communicating the fearful future Israel faced.

The book of Amos includes three so-called hymnic fragments (4:13; 5:8–9; 9:5–6). Scholars have debated the reasons for these locations as well as whether, together, they form one coherent psalm. There is no consensus on either issue. For the final form of the book, however, these small poems, each of which share a refrain—"the LORD is his name"—demonstrate that traditional language of praise, as attested in the book of Psalms, was held to be consistent with what Amos proclaimed. The God who destroys (5:8; 9:5) is also the God who creates (4:13) and who provides for continuity in the natural order (5:8; 9:6).

The book of Amos also includes a prose account of the prophet's activity in the northern kingdom (7:10–17). He was accused of treason and commanded to exercise his prophetic role in Judah. To that challenge, he offered an uncompromisingly negative judgment on Amaziah, the priest of Bethel. The oracle to this Israelite priest concludes with the essentially negative judgment that Amos proclaims elsewhere in the book: "Israel shall surely go into exile away from its land" (7:17). Such was to be the fate of all those who ignored Yahweh's covenantal demands to "let justice roll down like waters, and righteousness like an everflowing stream" (5:24).

OBADIAH

Both because of its brevity and subject matter, Obadiah has received little concerted scholarly attention. No other book in the Hebrew Bible is so brief, comprising only one chapter. Form-critical and general historical issues have provided the most prominent topics for the book's analysis. As for the first, Obadiah is, quite simply, one oracle against a nation. Whereas other prophetic books may include a series of such oracles, devoted to the great empires and/or to the smaller Syro-Palestinian states, Obadiah is directed at only one foreign nation (cf. Nahum, which is directed against Nineveh). Though focusing essentially on Edom, the book may in fact be divided into two different pronouncements. Verses 1–14 do indeed castigate Edom, but verses 15–21, though including negative judgments about Edom, offer positive language about Israel. It is almost as if woe for Edom means weal for Judah. Finally, the literary seam between these two blocks stipulates that "the day of the LORD is near against all the nations" (v. 15). Even little Obadiah at this point adheres to the central motif of the Twelve, namely, "the day of the LORD."

Readers may wonder why Edom elicits such enmity. It is easy to explain why the Neo-Assyrians would be subject to such fulminations (see Nahum). But what is the rationale for such rhetoric directed against this state to the southeast of Judah?

Most scholars have answered this question by scouring the pages of Syro-Palestinian history to provide a context for the accusations in verses 1–14. To be sure, there are some generic judgments (i.e., Edom was proud [v. 3]). But this sort of statement could be—and was—made about a number of other nations. However, the prophet does become far more specific, condemning Edom for standing aside when Judah was under attack (v. 11), for gloating over Judah's misfortune (vv. 12–13), and for handing over Judahites to the enemy.

> You should not have stood at the crossings
>   to cut off his fugitives;
> you should not have handed over his survivors
>   on the day of distress.
>
> (v. 14)

Obadiah seems to have one moment in mind: when Judah was under attack by the Neo-Babylonians in the period 597–587, a time when some Judahites were taken into exile. Moreover, other texts in the Hebrew Bible attest a tradition about Edom acting improperly when Judah was defeated, most notably Ezekiel 15 and Ps. 137:7.

However, not all particularities are historical. Some are structural in the society. A sociological approach to Obadiah would do more than look simply at the events surrounding 587. It would highlight other language, most particularly that of kinship. Edom and Judah are brothers (vv. 10, 12), and the names of those eponymous brothers are used: "Esau" (vv. 6, 9) and "Jacob" (v. 10). Ancient enmities are at work in this oracle. This is strife that Judah places in its family stories (Gen. 25:23–30). Moreover, it is embedded in the family, a place where conflict can be especially proximate and intense. Neither Moab nor Ammon, other small Syro-Palestinian states, bear such a close kinship relationship to Judah/Israel. This specific kinship relationship helps explain why Edom, and no other state, stands in such a relationship of potential hatred with Israel: "I will surely make you the least among the nations; you shall be utterly despised" (v. 2).

Just as Zephaniah anticipates that a remnant will survive the great destruction on Yahweh's day, so too does Obadiah: "For the day of the LORD is near against all the nations. . . . But on Mount Zion there shall be those that escape" (vv. 15, 17). But unlike Zephaniah, there is no hope that the nation(s) will share in the blessings of Yahweh's imperium. Using the language of geography, the poet avows that Mount Zion will dominate Mount Esau (v. 21).

Obadiah belongs to that body of literature—oracles concerning the nations—attested elsewhere in prophetic literature (Zephaniah; Isaiah 13–27; Jeremiah 46–51; Ezekiel 25–32). As such, it is concerned with issues that extend beyond borders of Israel and Judah. So too does the next prophetic book, Jonah, though in a vastly different way.

JONAH

Jonah is truly the odd book out in the Book of the Twelve. It is a short story, not a collection of sayings/oracles, vision reports, or accounts as we find in all eleven other books. Yet the very first verse of the book identifies Jonah implicitly as a prophet, that is, as someone who receives God's words directly. Moreover, 2 Kgs. 14:25 identifies Jonah, son of Amittai, explicitly as a prophet. Both by dint of its canonical placement and of the narrative identity of its protagonist, the book of Jonah is to be read as part of the prophetic literature in the Hebrew Bible.

Though popular readings focus on the "large fish" scene (1:17–2:10), many scholars had heretofore focused on the question of historical setting. To what period is this story to be dated? Though the question is interesting, the text provides no data that allow for a precise answer. Most scholars do agree that the story postdates the destruction of Jerusalem in 587, primarily because the issues in the story are similar to those in other texts that postdate that event. One such issue is whether or not those outside the kinship structure of Israel can be true Yahwists (cf. Isa. 56:3–8, a text that derives from the early Persian period). Another is the prominence of prayer as a religious rite in the Persian period (cf. Ezra 9:5–15; Neh. 9:6–37). Still, little can be said in response to the question about the book's historical origins.

One other critical question has been prominent in the scholarly literature about Jonah: Is the poem in chapter 2 an original part of the story? Many interpreters now understand this psalm of thanksgiving to be an important part of the book. The hymn is appropriate, since it celebrates Jonah's rescue from his attempted suicide of death by drowning. Jonah thanks Yahweh for saving his life.

> I called to the LORD out of my distress,
>   and he answered me;
> out of the belly of Sheol I cried,
>   and you heard my voice.
>   (2:2)

> You brought up my life from the Pit,
>   O LORD my God.
>   (2:6b)

Most recently, scholars have probed the book primarily from a literary perspective. Two questions have driven research: What kind of short story is this, and what is its theme or meaning? As for the former, the list of possible subtypes is daunting: parable, lampoon, and satire are only among the most prominent. In the final analysis, the choice of generic label depends upon the answer to the latter question. What is the theme or essential topic of this short story? Since scholars have established no consensus by way of an answer to this question, readers are encouraged to undertake a responsible literary reading of their own.

At a minimum, Jonah is a story about a reticent but ultimately successful prophet. When first charged to go to Nineveh and to "cry out against it" (1:2), Jonah heads in the other direction. His detour on shipboard and in the big fish are well-known. When he arrives in Nineveh, he offers the briefest of prophetic sayings: "Forty days more and Nineveh shall be overthrown!" (3:4). Nineveh's king responds in remarkable fashion by proclaiming that all living beings—including animals!—should put on sackcloth and pray to God. When God observes that all Ninevites respond in this way to Jonah, the deity decides not to punish Nineveh as had earlier been the plan. Jonah's rhetoric has worked marvels.

The remainder of the book focuses on Jonah's reaction to his "success." Only here do we find out why the prophet had initially fled from undertaking his mission. He feared that God would be "gracious, merciful, slow to anger, and abounding in steadfast love" (4:2). Jonah's hunch about God's character was well grounded; such descriptions of the deity reflect traditional theological language (Exod. 20:5–6; 34:6–7; Ps. 103:8). As it turns out, Jonah's premonitions were correct. God's decision not to punish Nineveh "was very displeasing to Jonah, and he became angry" (4:1).

God offers Jonah a symbolic action involving a bush, but Jonah remains upset. He declares that "it is better for me to die than to live," the second time in the story he has been willing to give up his life. Thereafter God poses a question to Jonah: "And should I [Yahweh] not be concerned about Nineveh, that great city, in which there are more than one hundred and twenty thousand persons who do not know their right hand from their left, and also many animals?" (4:11). In short, the book of Jonah conveys a God who is merciful, not only to Nineveh but to pagan mariners, and even to Jonah when he is about to drown. The notion of a God who is merciful to Israelite and non-Israelite alike provides a key to understanding this short story.

The book is oriented around theological issues. One might say that the author has created a satiric version of prophetic performance—Jonah is in some ways the most "orthodox" of Israelite theologians—to make a theological point. The book is full of satire and irony; even Jonah's name works in this way. Jonah, who is by our reckoning a hawk, has a name that means "dove," even in the ancient world a symbol of purity and peace. By using such irony, the author challenges some fairly common theological notions in ancient Israel, such as the idea that those who do not comply with the deity's will must die and that foreign and sinful cities, like Nineveh, will be destroyed.

Jonah is, like Jeremiah, someone who functions as "a prophet to the nations" (Jer. 1:5). Jonah's words are overtly directed to non-Israelites, but Israelites themselves are surely part of the implied audience. The words end up affecting weal rather than woe for Nineveh. Even the foreign mariners in chapter 1 survive the storm after they pray and sacrifice to Jonah's God (1:14–16). To that extent, the book of Jonah stands at odds with some other prophetic rhetoric about foreign nations, which regularly conveys language of indictment and destruction. Instead, Jonah seems open to the beneficent ways in which Yahweh might interact in the international realm (see the introduction and Gen. 12:3).

MICAH

The book of Micah begins with a superscription rather like the ones that introduce Hosea and Amos. All three books relate the activity of a prophet to several kings. However, Mic. 1:1 refers only to Judahite kings, a sign that the book's primary concern is with Judah, not Israel, though the book does refer to the destruction of the northern capital (1:5).

The oracles in Micah often sound like those in other prophetic books, especially Amos and Isaiah. This similarity should not surprise readers, since Micah, like both Amos and Isaiah, was a Judahite, and, like Isaiah, was active during the latter half of the eighth century. Moreover, some of the critical problems posed by the book are similar to those of Isaiah in terms of the ways in which the book grew over time. Both Micah and Isaiah achieved their final form in the Persian period.

Form-critical and redaction-critical work were a hallmark of Micah scholarship during much of the twentieth century. Form-critical analysis has focused on lawsuit (1:2–7; 6:1–8) and wisdom-style (7:5–6) rhetoric prevalent in the book, as well as the absence of typical introductory and

concluding formulae. Redaction critics have proposed an almost dizzy-
ing number of hypotheses about the way in which the prophet's words
evolved over time. Earlier consensuses—for example, that much of chapters 1–3 could be attributed to Micah whereas much of chapters 4–7
stemmed from later hands—are no longer uniformly held. Still, poems
such as 5:2–5a; 4:6–13; and 7:8–20—the latter two of which contain the
personification of Zion, which is so prominent in exilic texts—appear to
reflect a period after the defeat of Jerusalem in 587.

The results of traditio-historical and sociological analysis seem more
secure. As for the former, the results are both positive and negative.
Though a Judahite, Micah does not seem to hold Jerusalem or Zion in
the same high theological regard as did his contemporary Isaiah. Unlike
Isaiah, he anticipates the decimation of the capital and the temple:

> Zion shall be plowed like a field,
> Jerusalem shall become a heap of ruins,
>   and the mountain of the house a wooded height.
>   (3:12)

(This judgment must have been well remembered, since it is quoted in
Jer. 26:18.)

Such antipathy can be explained partly by the rootage of the prophet.
Not a Jerusalemite, he came from the small town of Moresheth. He
holds the country's leadership in the capital—"heads of Jacob," "rulers
of the house of Israel," "chiefs of the house of Israel" (3:1, 9)—culpable for what is wrong. Some have maintained that he was a person who
held local authority (i.e., an elder) in the village, one who would have
held out for traditional values in the face of the imperial power of the
Davidic house. The norms that undergird the indictments are clear:

> He has told you, O mortal, what is good;
>   and what does the LORD require of you
> but to do justice, and to love kindness,
>   and to walk humbly with your God?
>   (6:8)

Such a statement and question affirm traditional covenant norms, as do
other explicit statements about justice and equity (3:9).

Amos and Micah come from comparable social worlds, namely, small
towns in Judah. Amos, however, was a herald to Israel. By contrast,
Micah speaks to his own capital and nation. Micah 1:2–9 redirects the
rhetoric of an Amos, who originally addressed Samaria and Israel, to
Jerusalem and Judah, the new object of Yahweh's indictment and sen-

tence (see especially 6:9–16, which is clearly directed to "the city" [v. 9]). Even the hopeful sections of the book look to a small town— Bethlehem of Ephrathah, "one of the little clans of Judah"—as the source for a new ruler (5:2). The implicit critique of Jerusalem continues, since the capital will not produce the anticipated ruler.

As one in a small farm town, Micah is particularly concerned about land ownership, especially the ways in which people improperly lose ownership of their land:

> They covet fields, and seize them;
>   houses, and take them away;
> they oppress householder and house,
>   people and their inheritance.
>
> (2:2)

His other primary polemic is aimed at the improper official disposition of duties by the nation's leaders (3:1–3, 11). Like other prophets, Micah uses graphic imagery to indict his audience—here, the vocabulary of cannibalism:

> You who hate the good and love the evil,
>   who tear the skin off my people,
>   and the flesh off their bones;
> who eat the flesh of my people,
>   flay their skin off them,
> break their bones in pieces,
>   and chop them up like meat in a kettle,
>   like flesh in a caldron.
>
> (3:2–3)

Like many prophets, Micah envisions a time of judgment. The language of physical destruction is present in Micah (e.g., 1:7), as is that of exile (1:16; 4:10) and loss of land (2:4). But there is surprisingly little talk of physical violence against the people who are to be punished; they will lament (2:4), be dismayed and ashamed (3:6), but they apparently will remain alive. Hence, over time the book could speak about a return from exile; the people continued to live, either impoverished in the land or in exile. But they could be gathered together, they could return (4:6; 5:7; 7:12).

There were certainly additions to Micah's original sayings. Virtually all of chapter 7 provides an elaborate interplay of traditional psalmic and wisdom discourse concerning the fate of Jerusalem and the people. Scholars as early as Gunkel viewed it as a liturgy. This addition to the book clearly envisions a time of restoration for Israel. But there is also evidence of revision, not simply addition. For example, the first five verses of an oracle (5:10–15) offer words of judgment upon Judah, apparently for inappropriate religious practice. However, the final verse of the oracle extends such destruction to "the nations," Israel's enemies and destroyers, a view consistent with later prophetic rhetoric. The sense of an earlier oracle has been revised to meet a new situation.

Such dynamics in the additions and revisions seem to be in accord with portions of the book of Isaiah. Micah 4:6–7; 4:8; or 4:13 could as easily be found in the later chapters of Isaiah. Indeed, Mic. 4:1–3 is found in Isa. 2:2–4. Still, there is a difference between the later material in these books. The prominence of good news for Zion as promulgated in Isaiah is not present in Micah. Rather, it is the people—"the remnant of Jacob" in Mic. 5:7–8 or the "us" in the concluding poem of the book— who are the primary concern of this prophetic tradition. Even at the end of the book, Micah's origins outside Jerusalem inform his hopes—and the hopes of those who preserved his words—for the future.

Micah focuses on life in Judah. Still, there is concern for the international sphere (e.g., 5:15; 7:16). The next prophetic book, Nahum, highlights one city, Nineveh, which had been of pivotal importance in Jonah.

NAHUM

Nahum resembles Obadiah to the extent that it focuses on a nation other than Israel. Whereas Obadiah was concerned with Edom, Nahum deals with a city, Nineveh. These books (along with Jonah) attest to the international side of the prophet's task, which is confirmed by "oracles concerning the nations" in the Major Prophets (Isaiah 13–27; Jeremiah 46–51; Ezekiel 25–32).

Study of Nahum has tended to dwell on the historical particulars of the Neo-Assyrian Empire's demise, on the graphic depictions of warfare in a city, and the spectacular poetry that conveys it in this book:

> The chariots race madly through the streets,
>   they rush to and fro through the squares;
> their appearance is like torches,
>   they dart like lightning.
>
> (2:4)

> Horsemen charging,
>   flashing sword and glittering spear,

piles of dead,
  heaps of corpses,
dead bodies without end—
  they stumble over the bodies!
(3:3)

Nowhere else in the Hebrew Bible is human warfare so artfully depicted. Within the ambit of ancient Near Eastern art, Neo-Assyrian wall reliefs offer the best analogies.

Nineveh, the subject of this attack, was the capital of the Neo-Assyrian Empire. It had achieved this status under Sennacherib and remained important until its defeat in 621 at the hands of the Neo-Babylonians. Though the book's superscription does not refer to a Judahite king, one might infer that Josiah (who reigned from 640 to 609) was on the throne while Nahum was active.

One perspective that has not been utilized as fully as possible is tradition history. What was it about Nineveh that captured this prophet's imagination and literary gifts? Part of the answer to that question hinges on an assessment of other prophetic literature concerning Nineveh. Probably the earliest texts are those in Isaiah. Early on, the king of Assyria was understood to be an instrument of God against Judah (see Isa. 7:17–18). However, a number of other texts (Isa. 10:5–19; 14:24–27; 30:27–33; 31:8–9) attest that Assyria itself would become the subject of God's punitive wrath. The reason? Assyria had overstepped its role as God's agent. The Assyrian emperor had said:

As my hand has reached to the kingdoms of the idols
  whose images were greater than those of Jerusalem and Samaria,
shall I not do to Jerusalem and her idols
  what I have done to Samaria and her images?
(Isa. 10:10–11)

From Yahweh's perspective, the answer is "No," though Isaiah puts it in the form of a question: "Shall the ax vaunt itself over the one who wields it, or the saw magnify itself against the one who handles it?" (Isa. 10:15). Again the answer is "No."

The book of Zephaniah also attests to this tradition about Assyria. Zephaniah 2:13–15 refers to Assyrian pride, again quoting the personified city: "I am, and there is no one else." These texts from Isaiah and Zephaniah help provide some of the warrant for the ferocious language in Nahum. Moreover, this prophetic backdrop offers the reasons for Yahweh's anger at Assyria, reasons that are, for the most part, implicit

in the book of Nahum. In that book there is more language of judgment than there is language of indictment.

Nahum offers some unusual literary features. Whereas Habakkuk
concludes with a hymn and Amos has hymnic passages scattered
throughout the book, Nahum begins with a hymn. Verses 2–8 comprise
the first portion of an alphabetic acrostic poem ('*alep* through *kap*, the
first eleven letters of the Hebrew alphabet). Using the imagery of theophany, a prominent feature of day of the Lord sections throughout the
Twelve, the psalm emphasizes two features of that day. It will signal the
end for Yahweh's adversaries and protection for those who seek refuge
with the deity.

The hymn serves as a theological prolegomenon to the book. In fact,
the entire first chapter functions this way. If one were to read Nah.
1:2–15 without the book's superscription, there is no way that Assyria
would come to mind. The prophet focuses initially on the great god
Yahweh and then on the interaction between Yahweh and those who
plot against him (v. 9). Here, the psalmic resonances are strong (cf. Ps.
2:1). One may infer that Jerusalem is being addressed in 1:12–13, but
the identity of the adversary (v. 11 or 14), remains unclear until the
defining moments of chapters 2 and 3.

Nahum 1:15 resonates with other prophetic literature, both earlier
and later.

> Look! On the mountains the feet of one
>   who brings good tidings,
>   who proclaims peace!
> Celebrate your festivals, O Judah,
>   fulfill your vows,
> for never again shall the wicked invade you;
>   they are utterly cut off.

Amos 4:13 attests the conviction that Yahweh walks on the heights of
the earth. Zechariah 14:4 reports that the deity steps on the heights of
Jerusalem and with cosmic effect. The remarkably similar Isa. 52:7
affirms that the deity's messenger can do the same. Whether Zeph. 1:15
refers to the deity or the deity's herald is uncertain. But the concluding
portions of that verse demonstrate that Judah may resume its religious
life because Yahweh is about to act on its behalf.

Apart from the sparkling descriptions of the attack against Nineveh,
chapters 2–3 are characterized by direct discourse—speech directed
either to the city, Nineveh, or its king (2:1, 13; 3:5–19). It is divine ora-

cle (the deity speaks in first person language) rather than prophetic speech. Chapter 3 commences with the classic particle, "woe," indicating that the context is dire. The language is full of sarcasm, as if any such action would really help:

> Draw water for the siege,
> strengthen your forts;
> trample the clay
> tread the mortar.
> . . . .
> Multiply yourselves like the locust,
> multiply like the grasshopper!
> (3:14–15)

The threats are scatological and pornographic:

> I am against you,
> says the LORD of hosts,
> and will lift up your skirts over your face.
> . . . .
> I will throw filth at you
> and treat you with contempt,
> and make you a spectacle.
> (3:5–6)

Nahum includes the discourse of humiliation and violence, written from the perspective of a humbled province of the Neo-Assyrian Empire. Just as Israel has been destroyed and Judah subjugated by the Neo-Assyrian war machine, now, with the demise of Nineveh imminent, this Judahite prophet offers poetry that, in effect, is an answer to prayers of lament such as Psalm 83, which mentions Assyria (v. 8) explicitly. To say this is to suggest that Nahum's activity, as is the case with other prophets (e.g., Joel), is bound up with the worship life of ancient Israel (see Nah. 1:15, "festivals," "vows").

No assessment of Nahum can stop without mention of the other book devoted to Nineveh, namely, Jonah. Both books are highly theological and both end with questions: "For who has ever escaped your endless cruelty?" (Nah. 3:19). The answer to that rhetorical question is, of course, no one. Jonah raises a different issue: If those in Nineveh repent, can they escape punishment for that endless cruelty? The two books should be read together in order to gain the fullest prophetic commentary on the fate of this city.

HABAKKUK

Within the book of Habakkuk, the reader encounters three distinct forms of literature: dialogue, woe oracle, and victory psalm. Scholars have focused on clarifying the integrity of these three elements and also positing contexts, both historical and cultural, for them. For example, many have argued that chapter 3 is an ancient poem, far older than the rest of the book and replete with mythic depictions of the deity.

Despite such diversity of literary style, the person who composed the book has provided salutary transitions between the three sections and, in so doing, has offered a response to the powerful theological challenge posed at the outset of the book. When we hear the prophet say:

> O LORD, how long shall I cry for help,
>   and you will not listen?
> Or cry to you, "Violence!"
>   and you will not save?
>
> (Hab. 1:2)

> So the law becomes slack
>   and justice never prevails.
> The wicked surround the righteous.
>
> (1:4)

we immediately hear resonances with Jeremiah:

> Why does the way of the guilty prosper,
>   Why do all who are treacherous thrive?
>
> (Jer. 12:1)

> How long will the land mourn?
>
> (12:4)

> I must shout, "Violence and destruction!"
>
> (20:8)

and with Job:

> Even when I cry out, "Violence!" I am not answered;
>   I call aloud, but there is no justice.
>
> (Job 19:7)

> Why do the wicked live on?
>
> (21:7)

The Hebrew Bible includes a substratum of complaint language that has its origins in human experience but that in Israel was refined and included in worship through the psalms of individual and communal lament. As we shall see, Habakkuk 3 makes clear that this prophet is willing to use those liturgical resources in carving out a response to these questions that appear in Habakkuk, Jeremiah, and Job.

Habakkuk complains twice (1:2–4, 1:12–2:1), and God responds twice (1:5–11; 2:2–5). Of these two sets, what the deity says is the more surprising. Habakkuk laments injustice in his world, presumably within the context of Judahite society. Yahweh responds, "I am rousing the Chaldeans," as if to say that what is wrong inside Judah must be dealt with by an international force. Habakkuk has cried out "Violence!" (1:2), which is exactly what the Babylonians will bring (1:9). Then Habakkuk counters by claiming that such international intervention will result in the decimation of all people, not just the wicked: "The enemy brings all of them up with a hook. . . . destroying nations without mercy" (1:15, 17). The deity responds by challenging Habakkuk to write "the vision." But what is this vision? The answer is not immediately clear, but it becomes so in chapter 3. Initially, God admits that the wicked do in fact triumph (2:4–5). Then the deity cites five woe oracles (2:6b–19), which inveigh explicitly against the Babylonians but also implicitly against the evil ones whom Habakkuk identifies at the beginning of the book.

In Hab. 2:20, the prophet speaks again, moving deeper into the rhetoric of lament. Lamentation involves more than complaint. In a lament, a worshiper would routinely affirm confidence in God who is a reliable source of help. Habakkuk does exactly that: "But the LORD is in his holy temple; let all the earth keep silence before him!" (2:20).

With that affirmation, the book moves to even more overt liturgical language, so especially in 3:1 and 3:19. In between those verses, we hear the voice of the prophet in verses 2 and 16–18. Within that testimony, we find the (old) vision (vv. 3–15), which has sustained Israel from its earliest days. The vision conveys a God who appears in and disturbs the natural order:

> He stopped and shook the earth;
> he looked and made the nations tremble.
> The eternal mountains were shattered.
> (3:6)

This poetry depicting theophany moves to a description of the deity as divine warrior, with weapons affecting the cosmic order:

> The sun raised high its hands;
> the moon stood still in its exalted place,
> at the light of your arrows speeding by,
> at the gleam of your flashing spear.
>   (3:10b–11)

and with warfare that defeated Israel's enemies:

> You pierced with his own arrows the head of his warriors,
> who came like a whirlwind to scatter us.
>   (3:14)

One might have thought that this poem could serve as straightforward evidence that God would save his people from the Babylonians. The prophet does not seem to have read it that way. Instead, he trembles and waits for calamity (3:16).

Habakkuk is often viewed as an unusual exemplar of prophetic literature. The people of Israel are never directly addressed. Habakkuk seems as much a priest as a prophet. Yet, Habakkuk, by making the vision plain (2:2)—so plain that someone running by may read it—is doing exactly what intermediaries are supposed to do. The book enables people to understand what the deity is and will be doing with the people. The vision was clear, but the prophet would sit, waiting to see precisely what would happen, as had Jonah before him.

> I will wait quietly for the day of calamity
> to come upon the people who attack us.
>   (3:16)

Such quietude does not, however, prevent this same person from being active:

> GOD, the Lord is my strength;
> he makes my feet like the feet of a deer,
> and makes me tread upon the heights.
>   (3:19)

The book of Habakkuk wrestles with the world of theodicy. In so doing, it admonishes the earth to "keep silence before [the LORD]" (2:20). In a less cosmic vein, the next prophet continues with that motif of silence: "Be silent before the Lord GOD! For the day of the LORD is at hand" (Zeph. 1:7).

ZEPHANIAH

Zephaniah's genealogy (1:1) has routinely caught the attention of biblical scholars. Is it possible that this prophet was a prince ("son of Hezekiah") and/or someone of African descent ("son of Cushi")? No easy answers are possible, but this book does seem uniquely focused on the king's house (e.g., 1:8). Moreover, the time of Zephaniah's work is reasonably clear. It dates to the reign of Josiah (640–609). And since it inveighs against many of the improprieties addressed by that king's reform activities—which took place circa 621 and involved such things as attacking the veneration of deities other than Yahweh (1:4–5)—it is likely that the prophet uttered these oracles earlier rather than later in Josiah's reign. (See 2 Kings 22–23 and 2 Chronicles 34–35 for descriptions of Josiah's reforms.)

The book of Zephaniah commences with an introit (1:2–6) that announces God's judgment against all life and, more particularly, against Judah. Thereafter, we find both prophetic speeches and divine oracles uttered against Jerusalem (1:7–18), sayings that conclude with references to a "full, terrible end" (1:18). The prophet then turns to oracles against other nations (2:4–15) before focusing on a "soiled, defiled, oppressing city" (3:1) and its inhabitants' fate (3:1–20).

Scholars have used diverse methods in assessing Zephaniah. Tradition history has provided an important perspective by attending to the hallmark tradition in the Twelve—"the day of the LORD"—which receives pride of place here (see especially 1:14–18). Redaction critics have suggested that the book has been updated with the addition of 3:9–20, which seems to address the people of Israel after the time of punishment has occurred (e.g., 3:20 presupposes the exile). The motifs present in those verses seem consistent with postexilic prophetic literature, e.g., cosmic catastrophe (v. 8). Finally, literary critics have drawn attention to the intertextual resonances between Zephaniah and other portions of the Hebrew Bible (e.g., the relation of 1:2–3 to Genesis 1).

The book commences with a remarkable inventory of destructive acts. Just as the deity acted and spoke to create in Genesis 1, here Yahweh will cut off all life: "I will utterly sweep away everything from the face of the earth" (Zeph. 1:2). Are we to understand such an asseveration as hyperbole, an overexaggerated pronouncement, or does God really intend to kill all life—as the reference to fish and birds as well as humans suggests? Verse 4 claims the attack will fall primarily on those who live in Jerusalem, especially those guilty of religious malpractice. But there is elsewhere in the book the notion that far more than Jerusalem will suffer (cf. 3:8: "all the earth shall be consumed"). Zephaniah seems to be living out of the theo-logic of covenant curses, that is, the notion that the punishment will not be proportionate to the crime. This idea is consistent both with covenant traditions as well as with human experience with warfare.

One of the Ten Commandments states clearly the idea of disproportionate covenant punishment. If Israelites venerate an image, God will punish children for the iniquity of the parents to the third and fourth generation (Exod. 20:5). Likewise, a proverb cited in Ezek. 18:2 says, "The parents have eaten sour grapes, and the children's teeth are set on edge." It is precisely such religious violations that Zephaniah seems to have in mind. Perhaps one could say that Zephaniah thinks all in Israel could be, but may not be, destroyed.

Zephaniah portrays the ominous fate for Israel using a staccato description of Yahweh's day:

> That day will be a day of wrath,
>   a day of distress and anguish,
> a day of ruin and devastation,
>   a day of darkness and gloom,
> a day of clouds and thick darkness,
>   a day of trumpet blast and battle cry.
>   (1:15)

Such language reflects both theophany and holy war traditions—God is present in the natural order and is portrayed as a holy warrior. One should expect cosmic devastation, and indeed, "the whole earth shall be consumed" (1:18).

Still, Zephaniah expresses the conviction that some will survive the "day of the LORD." He allows for this possibility in the admonitions that appear in 2:1–3; it is just possible that "the humble" in Israel may be hidden on the day of Yahweh's wrath. They are admonished to seek Yahweh (2:3), that is, to use proper forms for divination, which some have not done (1:6). Although Zephaniah understands fully the punitive nature of Yahweh's day (1:15–18), involving destruction of both Judah and other nations, some will survive, namely, "the remnant of the house of Judah" (2:7) and "the remnant of my people" (2:9). The fate of the foreign nations is ambiguous—as is Israel's. On the one hand, we are told that no inhabitant will be left (2:5). On the other hand, those of Ammon will be subject to Israel (2:9). As earlier in the book, Zephaniah utilizes traditional language to make his point. Zephaniah 2:14 presents a classical example of covenant curses, depicting what was once a city as a ruin inhabited only by wild animals.

The most subtle rhetorical move in the book occurs at the transition between chapters 2 and 3. We reach the conclusion of an oracle directed at Nineveh, the Neo-Assyrian capital, in 2:15. Then in 3:1, in a woe oracle against an unnamed city, the prophet offers a withering indictment. (Such language of woe had occurred earlier, in 2:5.) Early on, one might assume that he was still addressing Nineveh, but by verse 5, it is very clear that he is now talking about another capital, namely, Jerusalem. The fate of Israelite and non-Israelite cities will be shared—they will both incur devastation.

Zephaniah 3:9–20 tempers the hard language of punishment. The prophet clearly anticipates that Yahweh will act again on Israel's behalf. The perspective is international, resonating with other prophetic literature (e.g., cf. Zeph. 3:9 with Mic. 4:5). Moreover, Jerusalem is still addressed, but in ways totally different from earlier in the book. For the first time we hear about Zion, which is now personified (cf. the many personifications of Zion in Isaiah: 40:9; 49:14; 52:1): "Sing aloud, O daughter Zion" (3:14). Most striking is the notion of a group inside Israel: "For I will leave in the midst of you a people humble and lowly" (3:12). This may well refer to a sect within postexilic Israel, perhaps a perfectionist one, but almost certainly a group that preserved the earlier words of the prophets and lived in the hopes for radical restoration of Yahweh's kingship (3:15).

In sum, the book of Zephaniah deploys many Israelite images and traditions in formulating its speeches. Day of the Lord, creation, Zion, and covenant traditions are only the most prominent of such rhetoric. Moreover, Zephaniah provides a comprehensive picture of Yahweh's interactions with Israel by offering indictments of Israel, judgments on foreign nations, and a vision of the time beyond punishment—a rather remarkable package for so brief a book.

HAGGAI

Many books that make up the Twelve commence with a chronological formula. Hosea and Amos refer to rulers on the throne in both Israel and Judah. Micah, at a later time, specifies only Judahite kings. Haggai continues this precedent of referring to someone on the throne, but now the ruler is the Persian emperor, Darius! With this book (and Zechariah), we explicitly enter the Persian period (ca. 550–330), a time when a non-Semitic civilization to the east of the classical Mesopotamian cultures (Assyria and Babylonia) exercised dominion throughout the ancient Near East, including Syria-Palestine. It was no longer possible to refer to a Davidic king, since that form of political leadership had effectively ended with the defeat in 587. Attention to the political reality of the Persian Empire has informed recent efforts to understand this small book, which dates to a three-month period in 520. In addition, some scholars have addressed the ways in which Haggai's sayings have been incorporated into a chronological scheme rather like that present in Zechariah but also with similarities to Chronicles.

During Darius's reign, the Persians consolidated conquests by his predecessors (especially those of Cyrus, whom the book of Isaiah viewed as a messiah [Isa. 45:1]). Although Cyrus was remembered as having permitted those in exile to return to Judah (Ezra 1:1–11) and having authorized the reconstruction of the temple in Jerusalem (Ezra 6:3–5), such restoration efforts had apparently languished. Darius's reign, in part because of his administrative reorganization of the empire, provided a more productive context for such work.

Though the historical context of the book is relatively clear, its literary features are less so. Readers of the book in most English translations will discover a book set out entirely in prose. However, *Biblia Hebraica Stuttgartensia* construes Haggai's speeches (1:3–11; 1:15b; 2:3–9; 2:14–19; 2:20–23) as poetry. As is often the case, it is difficult to know where to draw the line between prose and poetry. Clearly, Haggai is not a story, as is the prose narrative of Jonah.

The book's form is unique, at least for prophetic books. Following the lead of Lohfink, one may view Haggai as a "brief historical account."[7] This book has a distinct purpose, which is consistent with its form. The book of Haggai intends to explain how it was that the temple was rebuilt and what role the prophet, as well as Joshua and Zerubbabel, had in that construction program.

Just as there is a chronological focus, so too there is a geographical and theological focus, namely, the temple. Haggai interprets meager crop yields and generally unsatisfactory economic conditions (1:6, 9) as Yahweh's response to "his house" (1:9), which still lays in ruins. Even though those living in Judah had built houses for themselves, they had not rebuilt the house, the temple. Hence, Yahweh has called forth drought and dessication (1:10–11). However, once Haggai presents this interpretation, the people, with the high priest and governor at the lead, begin to rebuild the temple. Haggai, along with Jonah, is a successful prophet! Moreover, Haggai promises that the so-called Second Temple will be as glorious as the one built by Solomon (2:1–9). Moreover, it will allow for purification of what is now ritually unclean (2:10–14).

The twenty-fourth day of the ninth month in 520 was to be of signal importance ("from this day on" [2:15]). Scholars have interpreted references to a stone being placed upon another stone in the Lord's temple (2:15) as a reference to the ceremony, attested in other ancient Near Eastern cultures, in which a temple that had been profaned was ritually rededicated. That day signals the end of drought and the rebirth of fertility. In addition, Yahweh will begin "shaking the heavens and the earth" (2:6). This shaking will allow wealth to flow into the temple, but it will also, apparently, shake up the current political order. This day in 520 symbolizes some aspects of Yahweh's day.

In the final oracle of the book, Haggai turns to a member of the Davidic line, Zerubbabel, who now holds the office of governor. Using language that highlights the Davidic house's special place in Yahweh's polity, Haggai appears to tempt Zerubbabel to think about reviving the role of the Davidic line: "I will take you . . . and make you like a signet ring; for I have chosen you, says the LORD of hosts" (2:23). The signet ring was worn by a king as a symbol of his royal power. Moreover, earlier biblical texts speak of God "choosing" David.

In the years when Judah was reconstructing not only buildings but also its social, political and religious life, Haggai seems to be advocating a re-creation of the older order—oriented around temple, king, and prophet. Haggai is very much a conservative, affirming many of the traditions attested in earlier prophetic and historical books. Such perspectives have resulted from reading Haggai with an eye both to sociological and political-religious perspectives.

ZECHARIAH

Zechariah, like Haggai, explicitly reflects Persian period realities. Darius's reign remains the frame of reference, but now the time period is a bit broader (520–518)—still relatively early in Darius's reign and before the rededication of the temple (515).

The latter chapters of Zechariah constitute a problem comparable to that posed by the book of Isaiah. Zechariah 9–14 presents a different literary style and reflects a later historical time period from that of chapters 1–8. For that reason, scholars regularly talk about First and Second (or Deutero-) Zechariah. During the past two decades, given the interest in reading the "final form" of biblical books, readings that attempt to integrate these two sections have been attempted.

Zechariah 1–8 offers an adroit blend of visionary and oracular material. Both types of material are set in prose. The relationship between the two has been explored, with some scholars suggesting that the oracles are a later addition—even a challenge to the visions—while others maintaining that the oracles are integral to an understanding of the visions. In either case, the visions do capture the reader's attention because they are so vivid—even colorful—and bizarre.

The eight visions embedded in Zechariah 1–6 describe a universe that is initially at peace (1:7–17), that moves through action (second and third visions), identifies pivotal roles for the high priest and governor (fourth and fifth visions), articulates the new world at work (sixth and seventh visions), and then returns to the world depicted in the first vision, which is now far more energized (eighth vision). The symbolism is rich and diverse, reflecting at one point the cosmic deep (1:8) and at another point an oil lamp (4:2).

Those who work from the perspectives of form criticism and tradition history can place these visions within the larger context of vision reports in other prophetic books. Though vision reports appear in earlier prophetic books (e.g., Amos and Isaiah), they become more prominent in latter times, most notably in Ezekiel and Zechariah. Those who study even later biblical and related literature (e.g., Daniel) have observed that Zechariah's visions appear to pave the road from prophetic vision to apocalyptic vision. Unlike earlier prophetic visions, those of Zechariah include an angelic interlocutor and interpreter (e.g., 1:9; cf. Dan. 7:16), a feature present in much apocalyptic literature.

Still, Zechariah deserves to be understood as prophetic literature. Like Haggai, Zechariah's visions and oracles address the concrete issues of life in Judah circa 520. What sort of life should Yahwists envision? Zechariah's perspective is less pragmatic than Haggai's. Rather than call for the rebuilding of the temple, Zechariah's visions put matters in a cosmic perspective. The deity is acting on Judah's behalf. Moreover, as with Haggai, the Davidic heir, Zerubbabel, will have an important role, more so than the high priest The oracles tend to treat more mundane matters (e.g., fundraising [6:9–15]) and the appropriateness of various religious practices (7:1–5; 8:18–19).

All such attention to the concrete problems of restoration circa 520 is absent from Zechariah 9–14. This prophetic literature offers challenges unlike virtually any other exemplar of the genre. There is no clear historical background, and boundaries between poetic sections are unclear.

At a fairly late date in the formation of the text, an editor configured these chapters into two primary entities—Zechariah 9–11 and 12–14—both of which are introduced as "An Oracle. The word of the LORD. . . ." Military activity predominates in the first oracle, with the deity often portrayed as divine warrior. Both those inside and outside "Israel" will suffer the effects of warfare. Much of this first oracle is composed as poetry. In contrast, and written primarily in prose (13:7–9 is the exception), chapters 12–14, and particularly chapter 14, focus on a day, the ominous "day of the LORD." On that day, Yahweh will appear to violent effect. A new era, with new light and time (14:7), will result from Yahweh's rule as king. That Yahweh would rule as king is not a new theme in Israel (cf. the so-called kingship psalms). However, the radical impact of that kingship (e.g., with mountains crumbling [14:4]) is expressed in a new and intense way in these Persian period texts. It is possible to understand Zechariah 9–14 as a continuation of the cosmic perspective introduced in Zechariah's visions. But that cosmic perspective is no longer expressly related to Zechariah, the years of 520–518, or Darius's reign. However, Judah, and even more Jerusalem, remain as the primary focus of God's activity. This entire book implicitly argues on behalf of the restoration occurring in Judah and even on behalf of other nations (14:16).

MALACHI

The final book of the Twelve may not originally have been a separate book. As suggested earlier, the formulae with which the book begins, "An oracle. The word of the LORD . . ." is very similar to the formulae at the beginning of Zechariah 12 and 14. That is to say, the Twelve may at one point have concluded with three oracles, not with a book attributed to Malachi. This case can be strengthened by observing that the Hebrew word *mal'ākî*, regularly translated as a proper name, "Malachi," could as well be translated by the phrase "my messenger." Put another way, there may be no individually named prophet with which to associate what we have traditionally known as the book of Malachi.

Unlike the two penultimate prophetic books, Haggai and Zechariah, Malachi offers no clear information about its point of origin. There is reference neither to a Persian emperor nor to a Judahite official or high priest. However, a number of scholars have agreed that the issues addressed in the book—such as the need for a purified priesthood, the importance of paying tithes, and concern for the Levites—are strikingly similar to those addressed in the fifth century by Ezra and Nehemiah. Following this logic, Malachi probably has its origins in the first half of the fifth century B.C.E., making it yet another prophetic book dating to the Persian period.

Malachi is made up of six rhetorical units (1:2–5; 1:6–2:9; 2:10–16; 2:17–3:5; 3:6–12; 3:13–4:3) devoted to diverse topics such as proper sacrifice (1:6–2:9) and tithing (3:6–12). The units are framed by an introduction and an epilogue. These discourses, though not sharing comparable structure, often convey a strident tone in which the opponents of Yahweh's prophet are quoted—at least words are put in their mouths (it is hard to imagine someone saying "All who do evil are good in the sight of the Lord" [2:17])—and their causes challenged. Those approaching this literature from a form-critical perspective do not agree on its nature. Some have characterized these units as disputations, others as akin to Greek diatribes. (Diatribes often included questions, imputing speeches to one's opponents, hyperbolic claims, and stylized dialogue—all elements present in Malachi.) The texts do attest to a remarkably aggressive engagement within the Yahwistic community. Even 1:2–5, which has as its goal the affirmation of God's love for Israelites, inveighs against the Edomites ("I have loved Jacob, but I have hated Esau" [1:2–3]).

From a sociological perspective, the book of Malachi addresses or refers to specific groups in Israel. It attacks the priests who conduct sacrifices at the temple. It seems particularly sympathetic to the cause of the Levites, other priests who, in the Persian period, were becoming marginalized. In addition, and after the conclusion of the interchanges, the book refers to "those who revered the LORD" (3:16). Within the community, some are righteous and some are wicked, and the fate of the righteous now becomes the concern of this Persian period prophetic text. To use the imagery of Malachi 4, the wicked will be consumed by fire, whereas the righteous will "go out leaping like calves from the stall." Such an attempt to distinguish between what will happen to the righteous and the wicked is shared by Zechariah as well, and it appears in later biblical texts (i.e., Daniel). Moreover, such concerns are absent from earlier books in the Twelve, wherein prophets routinely speak about all Israel sharing the same fate.

Just as the first book of the Twelve, Hosea, has been appended with a wisdom-style final verse (Hos. 14:9), so too Malachi concludes with two additions. The first (Mal. 4:4) integrates Malachi, and probably the Twelve, with the Torah. The latter addition (Mal. 4:5–6) anticipates the return of Elijah, now an eschatological prophet, who will enable the people to prepare for the day of Yahweh—a motif present throughout the Twelve. These two verses build a link between the Twelve and the former prophets (Joshua–Kings) in which Elijah appears, and they imply that though the Twelve constitute a concluded prophetic "canon," the work of prophets will continue in the person of Elijah.

THE DAY OF THE LORD

In the introduction to this chapter as well as in the individual discussions, we have noted the prominent place of "day of the Lord" traditions in the Book of the Twelve. Its literal sense involves both deity (Yahweh) and temporality (day). But it includes much more. The Book of the Twelve attests to an expectation that Yahweh's day is a day for worship (Hos. 9:5; Zeph. 1:7) but that it is also a day of doom (Amos 5:18–20), of destruction—both of Israel (Mic. 2:4; Hab. 3:16; Zeph. 1:9; Mal. 4:1) and other nations (Obad. 15)—and of cosmic disorder (Joel 2:31). Nonetheless, as with all days, the hours move onward; new things appear. The final three parts of the Book of the Twelve point to that future. The book of Haggai attests to the expectation of a new political leader "on that day" (Hag. 2:23). The book of Zechariah, particularly in chapter 14, imagines a thoroughly new set of experiences: "On that day there shall be neither cold nor frost. And there shall be continuous day" (Zech. 14:6–7, RSV). Finally, the book of Malachi anticipates "the great and terrible day of the LORD" (Mal. 4:5). But before it comes, Elijah will reappear and reconcile families. This motif of day and temporality is particularly appropriate for the Book of the Twelve, which encompasses so much of Israel's experience with Yahweh. The Book of the Twelve witnesses to the destruction of both Israel and Judah, but anticipates renewed life for Yahwists "on that day."

Bibliography

The Book of the Twelve
Collins, T. "The Scroll of the Twelve." In *The Mantle of Elijah: The Redaction Criticism of the Prophetic Books*, 59–87. BS 20. Sheffield: Sheffield Academic Press, 1993.
House, P. *The Unity of the Twelve.* BLS 27. Sheffield: Sheffield Academic Press, 1990.
Jeremias, J. *Hosea und Amos: Studien zu den Anfängen des Dodekapropheton.* FAT. Tübingen: Mohr, 1996.

Jones, B. *The Formation of the Book of the Twelve: A Study in Text and Canon.* SBLDS 149. Atlanta: Scholars Press, 1995.

Nogalski, J. *Literary Precursors to the Book of the Twelve.* BZAW 217. Berlin: de Gruyter, 1993.

———. *Redactional Processes in the Book of the Twelve.* BZAW 218. Berlin: de Gruyter, 1993.

Nogalski, J., and M. Sweeney, eds. *Reading and Hearing the Book of the Twelve.* Symposium. Atlanta: Society of Biblical Literature, 2000.

Schart, A. *Die Entstehung des Zwölfprophetenbuchs: Neubearbeitungen von Amos im Rahmen schriftenübergreifender Redaktionsprozesse.* BZAW 260. Berlin: de Gruyter, 1998.

Steck, O. *Der Abschluss der Prophetie im Alten Testament: Ein Versuch zur Frage der Vorgeschichte des Kanons.* BThSt 17. Neukirchen-Vluyn: Neukirchener, 1991.

The Twelve Prophetic Books[8]

Hosea

Davies, G. *Hosea.* OTG. Sheffield: JSOT Press, 1993.

Macintosh, A. *Hosea: A Critical and Exegetical Commentary on Hosea.* ICC. Edinburgh: T. & T. Clark, 1997.

Mays, J. *Hosea: A Commentary.* OTL. Philadelphia: Westminster, 1969.

Wolff, H. *Hosea: A Commentary on the Book of the Prophet Hosea.* Hermeneia. Philadelphia: Fortress, 1974.

Yee, G. "The Book of Hosea." In *The New Interpreter's Bible,* edited by L. Keck et al., 7:195–297. Nashville: Abingdon, 1996.

Joel

Barton, J. *Joel and Obadiah.* OTL. Louisville, Ky.: Westminster John Knox, 2001.

Coggins, R. *Joel and Amos.* OTG. Sheffield: Sheffield Academic Press, 2000.

Crenshaw, J. *Joel: A New Translation with Introduction and Commentary.* AB 24C. New York: Doubleday, 1995.

O'Connor, K. "Joel." In *HarperCollins Bible Commentary,* edited by J. Mays et al., 643–47. San Francisco: HarperSanFrancisco, 2000.

Wolff, H. *Joel and Amos: A Commentary on the Books of Joel and Amos.* Hermeneia. Philadelphia: Fortress, 1977.

Amos

Auld, A. *Amos.* OTG. Sheffield: JSOT Press, 1986.

Jeremias, J. *The Book of Amos: A Commentary.* OTL. Louisville, Ky.: Westminster John Knox, 1998.

Mays, J. *Amos: A Commentary.* OTL. Philadelphia: Westminster, 1969.

Paul, S. *Amos: A Commentary on the Book of Amos.* Hermeneia. Minneapolis: Fortress, 1991.

Wolff, H. *Joel and Amos* (see above).

Obadiah

Barton, J. *Joel and Obadiah* (see above).

Mason, R. *Micah, Nahum, Obadiah.* OTG. Sheffield: JSOT Press, 1991.

Raabe, P. *Obadiah: A New Translation with Introduction and Commentary.* AB 24D. New York: Doubleday, 1996.

Wolff, H. *Obadiah and Jonah.* Minneapolis: Augsburg, 1986.

Jonah

Limburg, J. *Jonah*. OTL. Louisville, Ky.: Westminster John Knox, 1993.
Trible, P. "The Book of Jonah." In *The New Interpreter's Bible* (see above), 7:461–529.
Sasson, J. *Jonah: A New Translation with Introduction, Commentary, and Interpretation*. AB 24B. New York: Doubleday, 1990.
Wolff, H. *Obadiah and Jonah* (see above).

Micah

Hillers, D. *Micah: A Commentary on the Book of the Prophet Micah*. Hermeneia. Philadelphia: Fortress, 1984.
McKane, W. *The Book of Micah: Introduction and Commentary*. Edinburgh: T. & T. Clark, 1998.
Mason, R. *Micah, Nahum, Obadiah* (see above).
Mays, J. *Micah: A Commentary*. OTL. Philadelphia: Westminster, 1976.
Wolff, H. *Micah: A Commentary*. Minneapolis: Augsburg, 1990.

Nahum

Garcia-Treto, F. "The Book of Nahum." In *The New Interpreter's Bible* (see above), 7:591–619.
Machinist, P. "Nahum." In *HarperCollins Bible Commentary* (see above), 665–67.
Mason, R. *Micah, Nahum, Obadiah* (see above).
Roberts, J. *Nahum, Habakkuk, and Zephaniah*. OTL. Louisville, Ky.: Westminster John Knox, 1991.

Habakkuk

Hiebert, T. "The Book of Habakkuk." In *The New Interpreter's Bible* (see above), 7:621–55.
Roberts, J. *Nahum, Habakkuk, and Zephaniah* (see above).
Sweeney, M. "Habakkuk." In *HarperCollins Bible Commentary* (see above), 668–70.

Zephaniah

Ben Zvi, E. *A Historical Critical Study of the Prophet Zephaniah*. BZAW 198. Berlin: de Gruyter, 1991.
Berlin, A. *Zephaniah: A New Translation with Introduction and Commentary*. AB 25A. New York: Doubleday, 1994.
Roberts, J. *Nahum, Habakkuk, and Zephaniah* (see above).

Haggai

Coggins, R. *Haggai, Zechariah, Malachi*. OTG. Sheffield: JSOT Press, 1987.
Meyers, C., and E. Meyers. *Haggai, Zechariah 1–8: A New Translation with Introduction and Commentary*. AB 25B. Garden City, N.Y.: Doubleday, 1987.
Petersen, D. *Haggai and Zechariah 1–8: A Commentary*. Philadelphia: Westminster, 1984.
Wolff, H. *Haggai: A Commentary*. Minneapolis: Augsburg, 1988.

Zechariah

Coggins, R. *Haggai, Zechariah, Malachi* (see above).
Meyers, C., and E. Meyers. *Haggai, Zechariah 1–8* (see above).

————. *Zechariah 9–14: A New Translation with Introduction and Commentary*. AB 25C. New York: Doubleday, 1993.

Petersen, D. *Zechariah 9–14 and Malachi: A Commentary*. OTL. Louisville, Ky.: Westminster John Knox, 1995.

Malachi

Coggins, R. *Haggai, Zechariah, Malachi* (see above).

Hill, A. *Malachi: A New Translation with Introduction and Commentary*. 25D. New York: Doubleday, 1998.

Petersen, D. *Zechariah 9–14 and Malachi* (see above).

Schuller, E. "The Book of Malachi." In *The New Interpreter's Bible* (see above), 7:841–77.

6

Prophetic Literature outside
Prophetic Books

In this final chapter, we turn to prophetic literature and traditions that appear outside the boundaries of prophetic books but still inside the Old Testament canon. Though there is a natural tendency to think that prophetic literature is coterminous with books associated with a named prophet, the Hebrew Bible presents clear instances of literature associated with the behavior of other intermediaries (e.g., Balaam and Elijah) that lie beyond the boundaries of prophetic books. Less overt are instances in which scholars have identified traces of prophetic literature, such as, a so-called prophetic source (or redactional layer) in the Deuteronomistic History or prophetic elements in the Psalter. Finally, prophetic literature has eventuated in reflection about prophecy. Those in ancient Israel wondered if there were a paradigmatic prophet, or if there were limits on who could be a prophet. Various stories and statements that address these issues comprise what one might call traditions about prophecy. In this chapter, we will consider both prophetic literature outside prophetic books and traditions about prophets. In so doing, we will address all three sections of the canon: Pentateuch, Prophets, and Writings.

PROPHETIC LITERATURE AND TRADITIONS
IN THE PENTATEUCH

Prophets and prophetic traditions appear in surprising ways in the Pentateuch. One may use four categories as a guide to thinking about prophecy in the first five books of the Hebrew Bible: First, certain individuals—Abraham, Miriam, and Aaron—are given prophetic role labels. Second, the Pentateuch includes narratives in which certain Israelites act as prophets. Third, the Pentateuch introduces a non-Israelite—Balaam—who works as a prophet. Fourth, several texts depict Moses as a prophetic figure. Much of our attention will focus on Moses.

Prophetic Appellations: Abraham, Aaron, and Miriam

The Tetrateuch uses the most prominent prophetic role label, *nābî'* ("prophet") or *nĕbî'āh* ("prophetess") to describe three individuals apart from Moses: Abraham, Miriam, and Aaron. However, in all three cases, the use of the role label does not describe features that one might normally expect of someone known as a prophet. Each case works differently and, therefore, requires brief comment.

Abraham (Gen. 20:7). In this second of the wife-sister narratives, God tells Pharaoh: "Now then, return the man's wife; for he is a prophet, and he will pray for you and you shall live." What are we to make of such a characterization of Abraham? He did, of course, intercede on behalf of Sodom (Gen. 18:22–33), but he did not "pray" on their behalf. Other prophets interceded on behalf of Israel, but again the language of prayer is not used (see, e.g., Amos 7:1–6). The only person other than Abraham who prays "for" (*ba'ad*) someone is Moses. He does such in Num. 21:7, when he prays on behalf of the people. Hence, one may say that in Gen. 20:7, Abraham is defined as a prophet since he exercises an intercessory role of a sort otherwise attested by Moses.[1]

Aaron (Exod. 7:1). Immediately after Yahweh has engaged Moses in dialogue about his task, the deity tells him: "See, I have made you like God to Pharaoh, and your brother Aaron shall be your prophet." Their relationship is to be verbal: Moses is to speak what God commands, and then Aaron is to communicate these words to Pharaoh. Aaron's task as prophet is to work as a vocal intermediary between Moses and Pharaoh.

Exodus 7 (and for that matter Exod. 4:30) presupposes one notion of prophetic activity: God communicates through the prophet to an audience. It is a paradigm of prophecy based on linguistic performance, on the conveying of divine speech. Such a paradigm is nowhere clearer than in Deuteronomy 18, where the role of a prophet like Moses is adumbrated. According to Deut. 18:18, that individual shall "speak to them everything I command." With considerable irony, Aaron receives a task—serving as a prophet—that elsewhere has been identified as ideally accomplished by his younger brother, Moses.

Miriam (Exod. 15:20). The narrator labels Miriam as a *nĕbî'āh* ("prophetess") and as Aaron's sister. Kinship language helps frame the larger tale, just as such language did in Exod 7:1. Some scholars have suggested that Miriam's designation as a "prophetess" depends upon the musical activity and dancing that follow immediately in the narrative. Instead, the key for understanding her as a "prophetess" probably derives from her association with Aaron, her brother. As we will see when examining Numbers 12, there is a tradition of both Aaron and Miriam challenging the prophetic-like authority of Moses. Both claim, implicitly, to have prophetic powers. The author of Exod. 15:20 almost certainly knew that tradition. Hence, when narrating the events surrounding Israel's liberation at the Reed Sea, the author presumed Miriam was a prophet. But she is no more a prophet in the classical mold than is Aaron (or Moses).

In sum, the description of Abraham, Aaron, and Miriam as prophets reflects unusual understandings of what it means to be a prophet. They do not reflect what was typical for Israelite prophecy. Rather, these descriptions of Abraham, Aaron, and Miriam appear to reflect other Pentateuchal traditions. Moreover, all three individuals are in some way related to literature in which Moses stands as an archetypal figure.

Israelite Prophetic Activity (Numbers 11)

Numbers 11 narrates incidents that depict the prophetic behavior of several individuals. The chapter includes several episodes, set in the wilderness era, that attest prophetic activity.[2] A number of diverse traditions swirl in this chapter: murmuring in the wilderness, Moses as intercessor, provision of food, itinerary citations, the diversification of leadership in Israel (seventy elders), and the Eldad/Medad incident.[3] In the final two sections of the chapter (vv. 10–25, 26–30), explicit language of prophetic behavior appears.

In verses 10–25 (excepting vv. 18–23/24, which belong to the provision of food tradition), Moses complains about the burden the people create for him (cf. Exod. 18:13–27; Deut. 1:9–18). Yahweh responds by telling Moses to select seventy elders, who are to receive a portion of the "spirit" (*ruaḥ*) that Moses possesses. In order to be so enfranchised, these individuals have to leave the camp and appear at the tent of meeting. Once there, they receive this spirit; the text reports that "they prophesied. But they did not do so again" (v. 25).

What are we to make of this statement? If the seventy elders prophesied, why did they do it only once? The singularity of that event may well mean that it was a kind of initiation rite, but not something that the elders did routinely. These elders were now supposed to undertake judicial activity, since the burden that they were to address involved settling disputes (cf. Exod. 18:16 and Deut. 1:12; Judg. 4:4 may also be related). One may surmise that the author was not advancing the claim that these elders were to be understood as prophets any more than other spirit-empowered leaders—such as the judges—were prophets (e.g., Judg. 3:10). The role label "prophet" is not included in these verses. Rather, the presence of the spirit enables these elders to take on a new task, namely, helping to administer the burden that the people present for Moses. For this author, the activity of prophecy is linked essentially to the divine spirit.[4] If there was "spirit," prophecy occurred, even though we might be hard pressed to view the seventy elders as undertaking typical prophetic roles. Perhaps the author of these verses was attempting to legitimate a new role for these elders by appealing to the already existing and respected role of prophet.

Numbers 11:26–30 follows hard on the seventy elders' episode. If the prior text presents a picture in which spirit-inspired "prophecy" derives from Mosaic authority, this episode concerning Eldad and Medad involves empowerment by the "spirit" quite apart from Moses: "Two men remained in the camp, one named Eldad, and the other named Medad, and the spirit rested on them; they were among those registered, but they had not gone out to the tent, and so they prophesied in the camp" (11:26). Eldad and Medad acquire the spirit in the camp, not at the tent, and without having been included among the seventy chosen elders. Although both "a young man" and Joshua appear to disapprove of such activity, Moses accommodates it, saying, "Would that all the LORD's people were prophets, and that the LORD would put his spirit on them!" (11:29).

Both episodes in Numbers 11 associate prophetic behavior, "prophesying," with the presence of "the spirit." In the first, the seventy elders receive a portion of the spirit that had been allocated to Moses. He is with them when they receive it. But in the second case, we have no reason to think that Eldad and Medad partake of Moses' spirit. It may be precisely for this reason that Joshua shouts, "Stop them!" They were empowered by a spirit that apparently worked outside the "official" authority structures.

This apparently positive view of the installation of the elders should, however, now be read in a negative light. Robert Wilson has made this case clearly: "By weaving the appointment story into the account of Israel's illegitimate request [for meat] and the punishment that resulted from it, the editor implies that the appointment of the elders was necessary only because of Israel's sin. The appointment and the prophetic behavior that accompanied it are now interpreted negatively."[5] Hence, one may say that the final form of Numbers 11 cuts in a direction different from the ingredient traditions. Prophecy has become associated with Israel's apostate behavior rather than with Yahweh's beneficence.

The Pentateuch, therefore, knows about various individuals who were prophets—either figures such as Abraham, Miriam, or Aaron, who are labeled as prophets in Genesis or Exodus, or individuals who have been empowered by "the spirit" and who engage in "prophecy." All these figures are in some way either similar to or related to Moses. And the latter—those individuals in Numbers who possess quasi-prophetic authority—are finally cast in a negative light.

Non-Israelite Prophetic Activity (Numbers 22–24)

The mysterious world of Balaam, son of Beor, could detain us (see the introduction). However, for the purposes of this chapter, we will be brief. Israel's authors knew a tradition, also attested in Transjordanian Iron Age epigraphic materials, about a seer who was able to utter blessings and cursings. Like Israel's prophets, Balaam was capable of uttering a *māšāl* or a *nĕ'um*, both of which might be translated as "oracle" or "saying." More to the point, Balaam, a non-Israelite, possessed Yahweh's word. This element occurs in both the prose and poetic versions of his activity. In the prose material, we are told that "the LORD met Balaam [and] put a word into his mouth" (Num. 23:16). In the poetry, we learn about "the oracle of one who hears the words of God" (Num. 24:4, 16). As we shall soon see, such a focus on possession of the divine word constitutes a major element in Deuteronomy 18, in which an important notion of prophecy is articulated. Thus, one might expect this Balaam to be an unsullied prophet, even if not an Israelite.

Such, however, was not to be Balaam's fate in Israelite tradition. By the end of the book of Numbers, this foreign prophet is the subject of negative judgment because of the counsel he provides to Israel at Baal Peor (Num. 31:16). Moreover, Josh. 13:22 reports Balaam's execution and remembers him as a (foreign) diviner. Strikingly, a prophet who spoke powerful and positive words concerning Israel receives a sentence of death. Even the utterance of apparently "true" prophecy could not save Balaam from the fate proclaimed for all non-Yahwistic prophets.[6] As a seer-prophet, Balaam was thought to give a bad name to the entire prophetic enterprise.

Moses as Prophet

Both the Tetrateuch and the book of Deuteronomy include texts that
have led some to think that Moses was a prophet. Morover, there is a
considerable body of scholarly literature that talks about either Moses
as a prophet or about a tradition of Mosaic prophecy.[7] As for the former, some identify Moses with a particular kind of activity, such as
working within the context of a ritual of covenant renewal. This theory involves a particular understanding of the prophet as a covenant
mediator. As for the latter, other scholars argue that there was an understanding of prophecy specific to the northern kingdom. A number of
texts—Hosea, Deuteronomy, Jeremiah—reflect an understanding of
"Mosaic prophecy" as it was passed on over time and moved from the
northern to the southern kingdom. Robert Carroll holds that "the
model of Moses for the prophetic figure was a seminal idea in Israel."[8]

Although such understandings of Mosaic prophecy have been influential, they are also fundamentally problematic. Lothar Perlitt
addressed this matter incisively in 1971.[9] He concluded that Moses
played no role in prophetic literature and that the prophets played a
minimal role in the Pentateuch. It is important to explore both of these
claims. Hence, we must make a detour away from the Pentateuch and
into the latter prophets.

If Moses were a seminal figure in prophetic traditions, one might
expect him to cast a major shadow over the latter prophets. One strug-
gles, however, to find such a shadow. The name "Moses" appears in only
four texts within the entire corpus of the latter prophets. In none of those
cases is Moses either labeled as a prophet or described as undertaking
any sort of activity that one might reasonably describe as prophetic. In
what I take to be their order of composition, these texts are:

1. Micah 6:4: "I sent before you Moses, Aaron, and Miriam." Here
the prophetic text alludes to Yahweh's acts on behalf of Israel and identifies three leaders associated with the exodus and wilderness periods.
But this text offers no reason to think that Micah understands Moses,
Aaron, and Miriam to be prophets (in opposition to the Tetrateuchal
traditions that do identify each of these individuals as prophets).

2. Jeremiah 15:1: "Though Moses and Samuel stand before me, yet
my heart would not turn toward this people." Again, Moses is associated with someone else, this time the enigmatic Samuel. Jeremiah's
logic seems clear, however. It is like that of Ezekiel when he refers to
some ancient worthies: Noah, Job, and Daniel (Ezek. 14:14). Even
though these preternaturally righteous individuals might appear, their

righteousness would not dissuade God from punishing the people. In any case, neither Moses nor Samuel is viewed as a prophet.

3. Isaiah 63:11–12: "Then they [the people] remembered the days of old, of Moses his servant.[10] Where is the one who brought them up out of the sea with the shepherds of his flock? Where is the one who put within them his holy spirit, who caused his glorious arm to march at the right hand of Moses?" With these questions, a prophet of the early Persian period alludes to those hoary moments when Moses acted at God's behest. But this poet does not remember Moses as a prophet.

4. Malachi 4:4: "Remember the teaching of my servant Moses, the statutes and ordinances that I commanded him at Horeb for all Israel." This verse, along with Mal. 4:5–6, comprises an epilogue to Malachi, and to the entire corpus of the latter prophets as well. In this verse, redactors have identified Moses as the one who provides torah for Israel. Moreover, they distinguish Moses in this role from the quintessential prophet, who is yet to come, namely, Elijah (Mal. 4:5–6). These prophetic traditionists do not view Moses as a prophet.

The only text in the latter prophets that might attest to Moses as prophet occurs in Hos. 12:13: "By a prophet the LORD brought Israel up from Egypt, and by a prophet he was guarded." The first line surely refers to Moses, but the second line is ambiguous. Do these two lines refer to Moses alone, or do they allude to two individuals, such as Moses and Joshua? In my judgment, Moses and Joshua is the more likely answer. In any case, Hos. 12:13: provides no unambiguous evidence for a tradition about Mosaic prophecy, since another individual may be present in the allusion.

This brief overview of texts in the latter prophets suggests that a tradition of Moses as prophet was neither known nor influential in prophetic circles. That there is no explicit reference to Moses in the book of Jeremiah is truly striking, since some scholars have argued that the book of Jeremiah has been influenced by the Deuteronomic school and/or so-called northern or Ephraimitic traditions. To be sure, some in ancient Israel maintained that Moses was like a prophet. But this conviction was shared neither by prophets nor by those who preserved and edited the literature attributed to them. This is for good reason, if—as I contend—the idea of a Mosaic prophet was designed to curtail the power and authority of those whom we know as prophets.

Now we may leave our detour into the latter prophets and return to the Pentateuch, which provides diverse testimony about Moses as prophet. Deuteronomy 18:15–22 appears to establish Moses as a paradigm for prophecy. The first thing that should be said about

Deuteronomy 18, however, is that it does not state explicitly that Moses was a prophet (as was also the case with Numbers 11). Verse 15 reads simply, "The LORD your God will raise up for you a prophet like me." Many interpreters have presumed that the "like me" means "like Moses who is a prophet." Though such might be implied, the text could well mean something else, namely, that the prophet whom Yahweh will raise up will be like Moses, that is, someone whom the people are to heed. In this view, Moses might not be a prophet, but someone who as a prophet would have authority comparable to that of Moses. Verse 18 emphasizes another aspect of the prophet to come: Yahweh will put his words in the mouth of the prophet. Here too, even though the prophet may have God's word, and even though Moses may have God's word, that does not necessarily mean that Moses was a prophet.

Further, Deut. 18:9–22 is not clear about how many such prophets there will be. Many scholars have argued that the text means there will be a succession of prophets, not a sole prophet.[11] But, as Blenkinsopp has insisted, to allude to a succession of prophets beginning with Moses means that one must enlarge the notion of prophet to include, at a minimum, Joshua and all the judges.[12] One could read Deut. 18:9 as parallel to Deut. 17:14. Both texts refer to roles—king and prophet—that will commence only after Israel is in the land. In that case, one would expect the succession of prophets to begin with Samuel, Nathan, or the like.

In sum, the primary text in discussions about a tradition of prophets like Moses, Deuteronomy 18, presents no unambiguous claim that Moses was a prophet. Further, the Deuteronomistic History attests no such succession of prophets. Finally, the notion of Moses as a paradigm for prophetic behavior is noticeably absent from the latter prophets. It would appear therefore that Moses was not a model for prophets in ancient Israel. At a minimum, Moses was in some consequential way like a prophet.

Two other Tetrateuchal texts allude to Moses as a prophet and yet adumbrate a quite different notion than that presumed in Deuteronomy 18. These texts help explain the real connection between Moses and prophecy. We will look at them now in depth.

Numbers 12:6–8

Immediately after the composite text (Numbers 11) that we examined earlier comes a more coherent narrative involving three siblings: Aaron, Miriam, and Moses (all of whom at one place or another are labeled "prophet" or "prophetess").[13] Since Aaron and Miriam initially complain about Moses' marriage to a Cushite woman, this narrative undoubtedly involves a subtext of kinship issues. This text is also about authority—who can challenge whom and why (the issue of authority obviously could manifest itself in a kinship relation). Miriam and Aaron have spoken against Moses, a situation that elicits an oracle in which the deity asks them, "Why then were you not afraid to speak against my servant Moses?" (v. 12:8). Then, as if to underline the danger inherent in such boldness, the deity strikes Miriam with leprosy. (Aaron apparently could not be so afflicted since he functions in Israelite traditions as a progenitor of priests, someone who perforce must be ritually clean.)

The oracle (vv. 6–8) embedded in the narrative is not altogether clear. Verse 6 appears to be corrupt. One may translate, "If there is a prophet among you, I, Yahweh, will make myself known to him in a vision, in a dream I will speak to him. Not so with my servant Moses, he is entrusted with all my house. With him I speak mouth to mouth, visibly,[14] not in riddles. He can see the image of Yahweh."

Though at points obscure, the significance of this oracle within the context of the surrounding narrative must be something like this. First, the oracle does not claim that Moses is a prophet. Second, Yahweh communicates with Moses in a distinctive—one might even say "non-prophetic"—way. As a result, Moses holds a status different from prophets, with whom Yahweh communicates via visions and dreams (cf. Jer. 23:16). Such modes of communication seem perfectly acceptable. With Moses, however, Yahweh speaks "mouth to mouth." Moses communicates with the deity in a uniquely direct manner, so much so that, according to this oracle, Moses is, contra Exod. 33:17–23, able to gaze upon Yahweh's form or image (*pānîm*). Third, the phrase "my house" refers regularly to the temple, not to all the people of Israel.[15] Hence, as one responsible for that house, Moses apparently assumes priestly responsibilities.

References to the physical presence of Yahweh and to the house/temple reflect priestly traditions in this oracle.[16] Moses here becomes a paradigmatic priest (and not a prophet), someone who has charge of the temple. This oracle presents such a role as involving a more direct, one might say "better," form of communication with the deity than that of the prophets.

Numbers 12, therefore, sets the controversy between Moses, Aaron, and Miriam within the context of a priestly authority that Moses possesses—a form of authority that was superior to that of the prophets, with whom Aaron and Miriam are implicitly likened. Prophecy comes off second best, the more so since Moses as the ultimate authority figure is not deemed to be a prophet.

At the outset of the narrative, Aaron and Miriam had asked, "Has the LORD spoken only through Moses? Has he not spoken through us also?" (v. 12:2). Although the text provides no explicit answer, the implicit answers are "yes" and "no," respectively. If we understand Aaron and Miriam as prophets, as do other Tetrateuchal texts, then we can perceive the radical challenge that Numbers 12 presents to those who claim that Yahweh might speak through them as prophets. Numbers 12 is designed to subordinate prophets to a Moses who is characterized as a priest.

Deuteronomy 34:10–12

This Pentateuchal text has often been cited as a classic example for the notion that Moses was a paradigmatic prophet. However, such a judgment takes seriously neither the tradition history reflected in this verse nor its canonical function.[17]

These three verses appear to be a paean out of place. Moses is already dead, Joshua has been enfranchised, and the people's response to him has already been described. Still, the author writes, "Never since has there arisen a prophet in Israel like Moses, whom the LORD knew face to face" (v. 10). Even this initial verse of this coda to the book of Deuteronomy presents problems. First, the singularity of Moses that was present in Numbers 12 is again affirmed. He is unlike prophets. Second, Yahweh knew or communicated to Moses in a distinctive way, "face to face," which is comparable to the "mouth to mouth" diction in Num. 12:8. Similar language occurs in Exod. 33:11: "The LORD used to speak to Moses face to face." In this verse, as in Numbers 12, there is a priestly connotation, since Moses' "conversations" with Yahweh take place at the tent, the forerunner of the temple. Third, no one was "like Moses." Here Deut. 34:10 seems to challenge the expectation established in Deuteronomy 18. The same verb (*qûm*), along with the comparative *k*, appears in both Deuteronomy 18 and 34. However, what one might have expected to happen on the basis of Deuteronomy 18 has not been the case, according to Deuteronomy 34. There has been no sequence or succession of Mosaic-like prophets. Prophets there may have been, but they were not cast in a distinctive Mosaic mold.

Deuteronomy 34 goes on to articulate another way in which Moses was distinctive—he worked signs and wonders. One might think that this is an odd way to describe prophetic activity. Yet that very vocabulary is associated in Deuteronomy with a prophet who might arise (*qûm*) in Israel (Deut. 13:1): "If prophets or those who divine by dreams appear [*qûm*] among you and promise you omens or portents, and the omens or the portents declared by them take place . . ." Deuteronomy 13 goes on to define the case in which such a prophet or diviner might advocate veneration of other deities. But the text does suggest that an Israelite prophet might refer to omens or portents.

Deuteronomy 34 defines the paradigm for such omens and portents, namely, the miracles associated with the plague traditions and the wilderness wandering. These were part of the standard tradition, and they were also firmly part of the past. The language of signs and wonders inheres in Deuteronomy.[18] When one looks at such texts, one discovers that without exception it is Yahweh, not Moses, who performed those portents. Hence, the author of Deut. 34:11–12 has turned Moses into a demigod, attributing to him acts that elsewhere only Yahweh has accomplished. It is no surprise then that, for the writer of Deut. 34:10–12, Moses was "unequaled" in his ability to act in so wondrous a fashion. Whether as known by the deity face to face or as a performer of wonders, Moses had no competitors or imitators, either before him or after him. There were no Mosaic prophets from the perspective of the epilogue to Deuteronomy.

At the outset of this section, one might have had the impression that things prophetic in the Pentateuch were utterly diverse. Such has proven not to be the case. With the exception of the Balaam material, all the texts that we have examined reflect or point in some way to Moses. This Mosaic focal point does not, however, provide evidence of a tradition involving Mosaic prophecy or prophets. If anything, the figure of Moses has been used to challenge the authority of other prophets, to put prophets in their place. In this regard, the very inclusion of literature about Balaam, the Transjordanian prophet/diviner who becomes a palpably negative figure in Israelite tradition, emphasizes the singularity of Moses.[19]

Apart from the labeling of Abraham, Miriam, and Moses as prophets, one may discern in the Pentateuch a somewhat negative view of prophecy. It is something that foreigners do or might do. It is something that those on the margins—like Eldad and Medad—might do. And when standard leaders are initiated into their roles as elders by dint of the spirit, the narrative about them has been cast into a negative light. Moreover, prophecy is associated with those who revolt against Moses' proper authority. Prophecy is something that was never done again as well as Moses might, in theory, have done it. The most explicit claims concerning Moses and prophecy (Numbers 12; Deuteronomy 34) offer a nonprophetic understanding of his authority, namely, that of Moses seeing God "face to face" or communicating with him "mouth to mouth." If seeing God "face to face" or "mouth to mouth" is a hallmark of prophecy, Israel had only one prophet, and none thereafter.

In the Pentateuch, Moses was depicted in such a way that he could hardly be replicated. He was a wonder-worker on the scale of the deity, and he had priestly prerogatives, such as the ability to be in the immediate presence of the deity and the responsibility for Yahweh's house. No other prophet, not even those who, like Ezekiel, Jeremiah, and Zechariah, were also priests, could emulate this ultimate prophet/priest/hero.

This once-for-all quality of discourse concerning Moses hints at the role of such a figure and the theological claim it implies. Mosaic authority stems from an unrepeatable event that authorizes the unique status of Mosaic torah within the Yahwistic community. Other torahs, whether that of Ezekiel (Ezek. 43:12) or someone else, were to be eschewed. To be sure, there were prophets who spoke God's words, but their words paled in comparison to the constitutional words—perhaps one should say "word"—uttered by Moses. The tradition of Moses as prophet, therefore, has more of a polemical rather than an authorizing tone vis-à-vis prophecy. To claim that Moses was a prophet is, finally, to maintain that Israel witnessed only one individual who spoke the constitutive word from Yahweh. For the authors and the editors of the Pentateuch, the books of Isaiah, Jeremiah, Ezekiel, and the Twelve pale as literature in comparison. This view highlights Torah and tends to diminish the authority of the more historically contingent oracles and sayings of the prophets.

PROPHETIC LITERATURE AND TRADITIONS IN THE FORMER PROPHETS

At the outset, it is appropriate to observe that the literature that scholars today term the Deuteronomistic History had been for many years known as the former prophets. (The Deuteronomistic History includes Deuteronomy, Joshua, Judges, 1–2 Samuel, and 1–2 Kings; the former prophets do not include Deuteronomy.) Put another way, and for reasons discussed in the first chapter, many readers have associated things prophetic with six historiographic books. Our task at this point is to assay the extent to which portions of these books might be properly construed as prophetic literature. If prophetic literature is literature that derives from the exercise of the prophetic role, then some elements in these books fit the definition, such as the narratives about Elisha.

Martin Noth, who developed the notion of a Deuteronomistic History, theorized that the author/editor who created it used some source materials. Among those were cycles or collections associated with prophetic figures such as Elijah, Elisha, Ahijah, Isaiah, and Micaiah.[20] This judgment works especially well for Elijah and Elisha, since there is an abundant literature about both figures. We begin with Elisha.

Elisha

The prose accounts about Elisha are found primarily in the book of 2 Kings, though he first appears as a character in 1 Kgs. 19:19–21. His death is reported in 2 Kings 13. Amid these chapters, we hear about a prophet, often referred to as a "man of God " (2 Kgs. 4:16). In the introduction, we labeled narratives about such prophets as legends, stories that celebrate the power, activity, and life of a holy person. Elisha is presented to us as a peripatetic, or someone who moves from place to place; in Elisha's case, the locale is the northern kingdom. In fact, the general notices of itinerary—such as "one day Elisha was passing through Shunem" (2 Kgs. 4:8) and "when Elisha returned to Gilgal" (2 Kgs. 4:38)—are about all that link these legends. As Elisha is on the road, he interacts with kings and the wealthy but more typically with commoners and the poor. In addition, he supports and is supported by a group known as "the sons of the prophets."

Elisha was apparently active during the reigns of four Israelite kings: Jehoram (849–843), Jehu (843–815), Jehoahaz (815–802), and Jehoash/Joash (802–786). Although many of the legends are unrelated to the world of nations and wars, some are. For example, the narratives construe Elisha as integrally involved in the revolt that ended in the assassination of Jehoram and the accession of Jehu (2 Kings 9–10). Elisha sent "a member of the company of prophets" (2 Kgs. 9:1) to anoint the general Jehu as the king of Israel. That action sparked the rebellion. According to this account, Elisha is both a kingmaker and a king breaker. On the military scene, Elisha was remembered—when on his deathbed—as consulting with the king about his future wars with the Arameans (2 Kgs. 13:14–19).

Important though these historiographic legends are, the majority involve the lives of ordinary Israelites and the ways in which the power of this holy person affects them. Rofé has offered a useful typology of such legends. At the core, he discerns the simple legend, a relatively short account that celebrates the power of such a prophet, often in response to a dire situation. Second Kings 2:23–25 is a classic exemplar.

Young boys jeer at Elisha, whereupon he curses them and forty-two are killed. Though some readers are offended at such violence, it is useful to remember that holiness, the power of the sacred, is dangerous, as the story about the death of Uzzah after he touches the ark so clearly demonstrates (2 Sam. 6:6–7). Holiness does not—at least in these legends—necessarily involve goodness. Perhaps more typical is the legend preserved in 2 Kgs. 4:1–7. Here Elisha provides a miraculous supply of olive oil to a widow (the deceased husband had been one of "the sons of the prophets") so that she can sell it to create an endowment upon which she can live.

A number of the legends about Elisha seem to have been elaborated, and with a distinct ethical or theological flavor. Second Kings 4:8–37 offers a compelling example. In this narrative, Elisha wants to repay a wealthy woman for supporting him, even after she says that no recompense is necessary. At his helper Gehazi's suggestion, Elisha declares that she will have a child. The rest of the story raises serious questions about whether this action of Elisha constitutes an appropriate use of his power. The narrative humanizes this preternaturally powerful person and, at the same time, conveys this woman as an exceedingly strong character who strives to preserve the life of her child, who had died. One senses that this was originally a short tale about a miraculous birth that then served as an occasion for literary (the characters) and theological (wise use of the sacral power) elaboration. Other sorts of elaboration of legends also ensued, such as the life of a prophet, an account that expressed an interest in the birth, inception into the prophetic role, or death of a prophet.

These legends about Elisha are, for the most part, not integral to the flow of the Deuteronomistic History. Scholars have accounted for this in at least two ways. First, some deem the stories to be an independent source that was inserted into the Deuteronomistic History. Some of these accounts may have been revised at a later time; for example, the international flavor of 2 Kgs. 5:1–19 could reflect Israel's experience in exile. Second, other scholars have suggested that the legends were added to the Deuteronomistic History well after it had been composed.[21] In either case, it is possible to read the narratives about Elisha as prophetic literature that sits rather loosely in its larger literary context.

These legends depict Elisha as a holy man. He is not so much known for what he said, but for what he did. The tales that attest his deeds expand the boundaries of prophetic literature, which is often construed as interested primarily with ethical concerns. The legends about Elisha move beyond the moral to focus on the holy.

Elijah

Many readers of the Old Testament confuse Elijah and Elisha. Both are prophets, they appear both together and sequentially, both act with great power, both are labeled as men of God. In fact, similar stories were told about both prophets. (Compare 1 Kgs. 17:8–16 [Elijah and a widow] with 2 Kgs. 4:1–7 [Elisha and a widow], or 1 Kgs. 17:17–24 [Elijah revives a son] with 2 Kgs. 4:18–37 [Elisha revives a son].) Nonetheless, the picture of Elijah as prophet and his legends are very different from the picture of Elisha and his legends.

The literature concerning Elijah is set in the period immediately preceding that of Elisha. Elijah was active during the reigns of Ahab (869–850), Ahaziah (850–849), and Jehoram (849–843). This middle part of the ninth century was a time when the Omride dynasty flourished. They created alliances with Tyre, established détente with Judah, and often stood at odds with the Arameans, though Israel and Syria did cooperate in opposing the newly resurgent Neo-Assyrians. Elijah is introduced in 1 Kings 17, immediately after the Deuteronomistic History reports that Ahab married Jezebel, the daughter of the king of Sidon. This marriage no doubt was part of a political alliance between these two nations. However, the Deuteronomist—and Elijah—focus on its religious ramifications, namely, the veneration of Baal in Israel. Though the Deuteronomistic History narrates the wars that Ahab fought with the Arameans (1 Kings 20) and even refers to a prophet (20:13), Elijah plays no role in this political world (in contrast to the role that Elisha played in later military activity).

One may hypothesize that the stories about Elijah were originally rather like those told about Elisha. But they have been integrated—particularly those in 1 Kings 17–19—around the motif of drought, oriented around a polemic against the veneration of Baal, and fleshed out with great theological sophistication. The literary style is sufficiently different from that of the Deuteronomist that it makes sense to think that the Elijah material was probably a source that was incorporated into this larger work. Though different in literary style from the Deuteronomist, the Elijah material is more consistent with it, particularly with regard to the polemic against the veneration of foreign deities, than are the legends about Elisha.

First Kings 17 introduces Elijah, declaring to Ahab that drought will rule the land. Then "the word of the LORD" (v. 8), a classic prophetic idiom, comes to Elijah, commanding him to reside in a wadi where the natural world will provide for him. This announcement of drought represents an implied theological polemic, since Canaanite religion (of which Jezebel and Ahab are presented as advocates) involved the veneration of Baal, who was understood to be capable of providing rain and, more generally, fertility for the land and people. Hence, what might appear to be an abrupt beginning to the Elijah material is, in fact, directly related to the verses that immediately precede it, since they report that a temple of Baal had been built in Samaria.

As the stories proceed, Ahab and Elijah are brought into a direct encounter, which results in the contest between Elijah and the four hundred fifty prophets of Baal. The scene is redolent with irony, such as the drenching of an altar with buckets of water during a time of drought and a fire so vicious that it consumed stones and dust (1 Kgs. 18:33–35, 38). This contest on Mount Carmel is won by Elijah and Yahweh, the more so since after the fire of Yahweh had devoured the sacrifice and the altar, the drought was broken by heavy rain. According to 1 Kings 18, the role of Elijah as prophet is clearly one of religious zealot.

The author of this chapter implicitly declares that Yahweh, not Baal, should be Israel's God because Yahweh can do what Baal might have done had he won the contest. That claim, however, raises an implied question: How is Yahweh different from Baal? The next scene, on Mount Horeb (another name for Mount Sinai), addresses this issue.

According to 1 Kings 19, the victorious Elijah flees for his life. He goes far to the south, beyond Beersheba (v. 3), to the mountain at which Yahweh had appeared to Moses. That traditional background is very important for this writer. The earlier theophany, described in Exodus 19–20, involved wind, earthquake, and fire. According to Exodus 19–20, as well as other classic theophanies, Yahweh was present in and through these elements of the natural order. However, this Israelite writer was sensitive to the fact that Baal was also understood to appear in this way. Hence, in order to distinguish Yahweh from Baal, this reprise at Mount Horeb challenges the expectations of the standard Yahweh or Baal theophany and depicts Yahweh as a deity who can appear through "a sound of sheer silence" (1 Kgs. 19:12). Moreover, this scene also suggests that for Elijah, the time of titanic contests is over and that it is now time to go about the routine business of being a prophet—anointing kings and securing Elisha as a successor (vv. 15–18). Elijah no longer functions as a religious zealot. Instead, he appears at Horeb, as did Moses, but Elijah experiences the deity in an entirely new way. Hence, the theological claims of this "drought" narrative are at least twofold: Yahweh is more powerful than Baal, and Yahweh is different from Baal.

Readers need to compare Elijah's response to Baalism with the one that we charted when looking at the book of Hosea. These two northern prophets—Elijah and Hosea—take quite different positions in response to the challenge presented by Baal. Hosea seems much less willing to think about Yahweh as fundamentally different from Baal.

The narratives concerning Elijah include more than the drought story. First Kings 21 offers a scene in which Elijah confronts Ahab. Though Baalism is not overtly at stake, the presence and values of Jezebel, the Sidonian queen, are. Ahab desired a vineyard owned by Naboth but was unwilling to acquire it. Jezebel conspired to have Naboth killed, whereupon Ahab was able to acquire the property. Such action not only involved premeditated murder but also violated the norm of preserving a family's land holdings, as Naboth had told Ahab earlier in the story: "The LORD forbid that I should give you my ancestral inheritance" (21:3).

In 1 Kings 21, Elijah functions rather like Nathan had when he confronted David after the king had had Bathsheba's husband, Uriah, killed. In 1 Kings 21, however, the situation is even more dire since, though a king had demurred from violating the norm concerning family land, a foreign queen had flaunted this value.

The Elijah stories portray a prophet who challenges the legitimacy of the cultural symbiosis represented by the marriage of Ahab and Jezebel. The narratives challenge both the religious (the veneration of Baal) and the ethical (loss of ancestral land) feature of this alliance. The prophetic literature associated with Elijah—clearly a holy man—is quite different from that involving Elisha. Whereas the latter is primarily a collection of unrelated legends, the literature about Elijah is more integrated and has a more overt theological and ethical agenda. Moreover, the texts portray distinct social locations for the two protagonists—the sole prophetic voice of Elijah versus Elisha with his "sons of the prophets."

Other Narratives about Prophets

The Deuteronomistic History includes other narratives about prophets. The collection about Isaiah is the next longest (2 Kgs. 18:13; 18:17–20:19 // Isaiah 36–39), on which see above in the chapter devoted to the book of Isaiah. Then there are accounts involving individuals such as Nathan (2 Samuel 12), Gad (2 Samuel 24), Ahijah, the Shilonite (1 Kgs. 11:29–39; 14:1–18), Micaiah ben Imlah (1 Kings 22) and Huldah (2 Kgs. 22:14–20). One even encounters narratives alluding to unnamed prophets (e.g., 1 Kings 13; 20:35–43). In most cases, these accounts present the prophet as one who interacts with kings, often in a scene of confrontation. These accounts (with the exception of 1 Kings 13) do not bear the legendary cast of those associated with Elijah and Elisha. Instead, they present the prophet as one who conveys the word or perspective from the divine king to the earthly ruler. Scholars have often used the phrase "court prophet" to refer to some of these individuals. The phrase seems apt, especially for Nathan and Gad, though it remains unclear whether either individual was actually subvented by the court. Nathan was certainly at court for a long period of time—he was active before Solomon was born and he participated in the palace intrigues concerning which of David's sons would rule after him (1 Kings 1). Gad was known as "David's seer" (2 Sam. 24:11).

Some of these accounts are fairly straightforward and consistent with other elements of the Deuteronomistic History. For example, 1 Kgs. 11:29–39 depicts Ahijah speaking an oracle to Jeroboam and performing a symbolic action, both of which confer kingship upon this individual. The account is spare, offering little by characterization or the like. Other accounts have a more complicated agenda or offer a more nuanced narration. The narrative of Nathan offering a parable to David, after which the king traps himself, is replete with psychological insight (2 Sam. 12:1–6). The narrative in 1 Kings 13 about two prophets—one from Judah and one from Israel—provides profound theological reflection about the authority of a prophet and the words that he speaks.

Prophetic Perspectives in the Former Prophets

Even beyond these various narratives and accounts, the former prophets contain phraseology and perspectives that betray the presence of some writers/editors who valued highly the work of Israel's prophets. In fact, such work became part of the historiographic claims in the Deuteronomistic History. One may discern this feature in various ways. First, one finds instances in which a prophet speaks an oracle presaging some future event, such as the demise of Jeroboam's lineage (1 Kgs. 14:6–11). Then when the event takes place—in this case the killing of Jeroboam's descendants (1 Kings 15:29)—the editor reports that it happened "according to the word of the LORD that he spoke by his servant Ahijah the Shilonite." Prophetic words affect the fate of various individuals in a pattern that could be described as "prophecy and fulfillment."

Second, the great reprise about the destruction of the northern king-dom (2 Kgs. 17:7–23) likewise builds the prophets into this momentous history:

> Yet the LORD warned Israel and Judah by every prophet and every seer, saying, "Turn from your evil ways and keep my commandments and my statutes, in accordance with all the law that I commanded your ancestors and that I sent to you by my servants the prophets." . . . The people of Israel continued in all the sins that Jeroboam committed; they did not depart from them until the LORD removed Israel out of his sight, as he had foretold through all his servants the prophets.
>
> (vv. 13, 22–23)

What could be said about one prophet and one king has now been gen-eralized to "every prophet and seer." Moreover, the author refers to the entire nation (even Judah is mentioned) and the demise of the north-ern kingdom, not just to one or another king.

Third, prophets occur at pivotal moments in Israel's history, and they are usually associated with a king. As O'Brien has observed, this can occur in a positive way: Nathan with David, Isaiah with Hezekiah, and Huldah with Josiah. Thereafter, prophets are able to judge other kings when they deviate from the paradigm established, particularly, by David.[22] Prophets thus appear to have been used as a structuring device in the Deuteronomistic History.

In sum, much in the former prophets seems to have been influenced by a perspective that took with utmost seriousness the power of the prophets and their words. The texts we have just discussed do not emphasize individuals like Elisha, a holy person who exemplified the power of the deity. Rather, the paradigm that lies behind the Deuteron-omistic History is that of the prophet as speaker—one who conveys the history-making words of the deity.

Prophetic Source or Redactional Stratum?

How then should one explain the presence of prophetic literature and perspectives in the former prophets? Scholars have answered this ques-tion in essentially two ways. Some, following Noth's lead, think that the Deuteronomist drew on sources that narrated things prophetic (see above). Campbell has offered a variant on this position, claiming that there is one basic source that the Deuteronomist incorporated, which he calls "the prophetic record."[23] Others (often defined as the "Göt-tingen school") argue that the Deuteronomistic History was written during the exilic period and then was subsequently revised. One such revision—labeled DtrP—involved the addition of both prophetic accounts and the historiographic perspectives we have just discussed.[24] Those who advocate this position point to a number of texts that share both formal and philological features such as the threats against northern dynasties (1 Kgs. 14:7–11; 16:1–4; 21:20b–24; and 2 Kgs. 9:7–10a). They maintain that the similarities between these texts, along with their relationship to other material in the Deuteronomistic History (e.g., the notices about prophecy and fulfillment, threats against Jerusalem and Judah, and threats against Jezebel and Ahab) can best be explained by appeal to a revision of the Deuteronomistic History after it was first composed. Moreover, they identify certain phrases, such as "the word of the LORD came to me," that were used primarily by prophets during the late monarchic period, especially Jeremiah. These phrases have made their way into accounts of prophets from a much earlier time (see the appearance of that phrase in 1 Kgs. 18:1, 31). Hence, one may infer that the Deuteronomistic History has presented a prophet such as Elijah using much later idioms. Again, this can best be explained by appeal to a late, prophetic redaction of that history.

The conflict between the notions of prophetic source versus prophetic redaction is clear. One may, however, attempt to bridge this chasm in two ways. First, both positions affirm that prophetic material in the former prophets stands out as something distinctive. For the purposes of this book, it is possible to claim that one may discern prophetic literature embedded in a larger historiographic corpus. Second, one may accept elements from both positions. It is possible to maintain that the Deuteronomistic Historian incorporated earlier accounts about an Elijah or an Elisha, different though they are. Then, at a later period, the history was edited with an eye to prophecy as it was understood in the exilic or early postexilic context. Such a synthetic view permits one to affirm that the Deuteronomist fashioned the Elijah story to fit his purpose or that the Deuteronomist simply included a series of legends about Elisha. However, it also permits the reader to understand that certain features—phrases such as "the word of the LORD"—entered the former prophets at a later period, as was also the case with latter prophets.

PROPHETIC LITERATURE AND TRADITIONS IN THE WRITINGS

This final section of the chapter might seem to strain credulity. Why should one speak about things prophetic in the final section of the

Hebrew Bible? The answer lies in a close relationship between prophets and the world of ritual. A number of prophets were members of priestly houses; the clearest cases are Jeremiah, Ezekiel, and Zechariah. Others were active in ways related to the temple, such as Joel calling the people to fast and lament. Still others knew well the world of sacral practice, as seen in Isaiah's commissioning vision in the temple. If the world of worship made its way into prophetic literature, one might expect the world of prophetic activity to have influenced the literature of worship. Such appears to be the case.

The search for things prophetic in the Psalter has regularly been associated with the work of Sigmund Mowinckel, though it was pre-saged in important work by Hermann Gunkel, who observed that Psalms contained a number of oracles. Mowinckel's multivolume *Psalmenstudien*, which includes a section on cultic prophecy and prophetic psalms, proved to be a seminal work.[25] In it, Mowinckel argues that Psalms contains a number of oracles that represent the work of "cultic prophets" at the temple. These cultic prophets would speak oracles of promise to those who had uttered laments, e.g., Psalm 35:3, "I am your salvation," or 27:14. They also spoke promises to the king (e.g., Ps. 2 or 110). Such discourse also could involve ethical admonition (see Ps. 50:7–15; cf. also Ps. 81; 91) of a sort we normally associate with prophetic discourse.

Mowinckel's notion of a cultic prophet has since been challenged. Some scholars think that a priest without any prophetic role might speak in first person language on behalf of the deity. Nonetheless, scholars have attempted to develop one or another element of Mowinckel's overarching hypothesis. Bellinger has focused on psalms of lamentation and has discerned "prophetic elements," which he defines as "predictive and seeking repentance from God's people."[26] He maintains that one element in the laments, namely, statements expressing the people's conviction that they would be heard, is consistent with this prophetic element. In addition, he follows Mowinckel's lead by investigating the books of Joel and Habakkuk as prophetic books that are related to psalms, though he argues that the psalmic language has been historicized and that neither Habakkuk nor Joel were to be understood as cultic prophets.

More recently, Tournay has offered a far-reaching theory.[27] He too identifies many connections between psalms and prophetic writings. He conceptualized the connections through two primary elements in both literatures: theophanies and oracles. These, Tournay thinks, are evidence that prophets of some sort were introducing the discourse of prophecy into the worship world of the Second Temple. Tournay's judgment about both the date and the author of these prophetic psalms points to another part of the Writings, namely, the books of Chronicles.

Prior to Tournay's work, several scholars had noted that a group in Chronicles, the Levitical singers, had been viewed as prophets. Tournay builds on this observation, claiming that the Levitical singers are to be understood as "cultic prophets." However, given Chronicles' character as a book that often reflects the realities of the postexilic period even though it is narrating premonarchic history, the singers/prophets represented the incorporation of things prophetic into the world of worship at a fairly late period. Tournay, along with others, contends that as prophets in the traditional mode became less and less visible, the activity of prophetic intermediation moved into the world of the temple. It is no accident that certain psalms are attributed to some of these singers (e.g., the psalms of Asaph [50; 73–83]). Moreover, Asaphites—Asaph, Heman, and Jeduthun—are depicted in Chronicles as engaging in prophetic behavior. They are even described as "prophesying" (e.g., 1 Chr. 25:1: "David and the officers of the army also set apart for the service the sons of Asaph, and of Heman, and of Jeduthun, who should prophesy with lyres, harps, and cymbals").

This notion of prophesying is similar to that employed in characterizing Abraham as a prophet. In the Persian period, Yahwistic authors were at a remove from the classic examples of prophetic activity. As a result, characters as widely diverse as patriarchs and Levitical singers could be viewed as prophets, a situation unlikely in an earlier era. We would not expect to find prophetic literature, in the sense that we have been using that phrase, growing out of the activity of either Abraham or the Levitical singers. Hence, there is, as it were, an end to the creation of biblical prophetic literature, just as there is an end to prophecy as it was manifested in its several classical roles.

The end of the composition of prophetic literature and the end of Israelite prophecy are bound up together. There was, to be sure, a learned form of intermediation, namely, written prophecy, which we encounter in a number of the prophetic books.[28] However, the Persian period saw the end of Yahwistic prophecy as it had existed in previous centuries. The reasons are many: the absence of necessary social prerequisites, the difficulty of dealing with conflict between two prophets, the emerging primacy of Torah as the word of Yahweh. And it was this same period that saw the composition of the final portions of the prophetic literature in the Hebrew Bible.

Bibliography

Prophecy and the Pentateuch

Barstad, H. "The Understanding of Israel's Prophets in Deuteronomy." *SJOT* 8 (1994): 236–51.

Dion, P. "La *rwh* dans l'Heptateuque: la protestation pour la liberté du prophetisme en Nb 11:26–29." *Science et Esprit* 42 (1990): 167–91.

Gunneweg, A. "Das Gesetz und die Propheten: Eine Auslegung von Ex 33:7–11; Num 11:4–12:8; Dtn 31:14f; 34:10," *ZAW* 102 (1990): 168–80.

Hackett, J. *The Balaam Text from Deir 'Alla.* HSM 31. Chico, Calif.: Scholars Press, 1980.

Perlitt, L. "Mose als Prophet." *EvT* 31 (1971): 588–608.

Schmidt, W. H. "Pentateuch und Prophetie: Eine Skizze zu Verschiedenartigkeit und Einheit alttestamentlicher Theologie." In *Prophet und Prophetenbuch: Festschrift für Otto Kaiser zum 65. Geburtstag,* edited by V. Fritz, K. Pohlmann, and H.-C. Schmitt, 180–95. BZAW 185. Berlin: de Gruyter, 1989.

Schmitt, H.-C. "Redaktion des Pentateuch im Geist der Prophetie." *ZAW* 32 (1982): 170–89.

Zimmerli, W. "Der 'Prophet' im Pentateuch." *Studien zum Pentateuch: Walter Kornfeld zum 60. Geburtstag,* edited by G. Braulik, 197–211. Freiburg: Herder, 1977.

Zobel, K. *Prophetie und Deuteronomium: Die Rezeption prophetischer Theologie durch das Deuteronomium.* BZAW 199. Berlin: de Gruyter, 1992.

Prophecy and the Former Prophets

Campbell, A. *Of Prophets and Kings: A Late Ninth Century Document (1 Samuel 1–2 Kings 10).* CBQMS 17. Washington: Catholic Biblical Association, 1986.

Cross, F. "Yahweh and Ba'l." *Canaanite Myth and Hebrew Epic,* 147–94. Cambridge, Mass.: Harvard University Press, 1973.

Dietrich, W. *Prophetie und Geschichte: Eine redaktionsgeschichtliche Untersuchung zum deuteronomischen Geschichtswerk.* FRLANT 108. Göttingen: Vandenhoeck & Ruprecht, 1972.

O'Brien, M., and A. Campbell. *Unfolding the Deuteronomistic History: Origins, Upgrades, Present Text.* Minneapolis: Fortress, 2000.

Rofé, A. "The Classification of the Prophetical Stories." *JBL* 89 (1970): 427–40.

———. *The Prophetical Stories: The Narratives about the Prophets in the Hebrew Bible: Their Literary Types and History.* Jerusalem: Magnes, 1988.

Van Seters, J. *In Search of History: Historiography in the Ancient World and the Origins of Biblical History.* New Haven: Yale University Press, 1983.

Wilson, R. "The Former Prophets: Reading the Books of Kings." In *Old Testament Interpretation: Past, Present, and Future: Essays in Honor of Gene M. Tucker,* edited by J. Mays, K. Richards, and D. Petersen, 83–96. Nashville: Abingdon, 1995.

Prophecy and the Writings

Bellinger, W. *Psalmody and Prophecy.* JSOTSup 27. Sheffield: JSOT Press, 1984.

Mowinckel, S. "The Prophetic Word in the Psalms and the Prophetic Psalms." In *The Psalms in Israel's Worship,* 2:53–78. Nashville: Abingdon, 1962.

————. *Psalmenstudien. III. Kultprophetie und prophetischen Psalmen.* Kristiana: Dybwad, 1923.

Petersen, D. *Late Israelite Prophecy: Studies in Deutero-Prophetic and Literature and in Chronicles.* SBLMS 23. Missoula, Mont.: Scholars Press, 1977.

Tournay, R. *Seeing and Hearing God with the Psalms: The Prophetic Liturgy of the Second Temple in Jerusalem.* JSOTSup 118. Sheffield: JSOT Press, 1991.

Epilogue

This volume has been devoted to the study of prophetic literature, not to prophets per se or to the history of prophecy as that role existed in ancient Israel. We have come to understand prophetic literature as texts that derive from the activity of prophets. Of course, that literature encompasses individual prophetic books, but there is more. The legends about Elisha, which are embedded in the Deuteronomistic History, count as prophetic literature every bit as much as does the poetry in the book of Amos. Both 1 Kgs. 6:1–7, the legend about Elisha miraculously making an ax head float, and Amos 5:21–24, an oracle admonishing Israelites to live their religion, belong to the core of prophetic literature.

Prophets did not, necessarily, compose all the literature associated with them. Still, most exemplars of prophetic literature bear a hallmark. Each book, each collection of narratives, is distinctive. There are characteristic features of the poetry associated with Jeremiah—the prominence of the rhetoric of lament—that distinguish it from the discursive poetry of Ezekiel. Each intermediary enacted the role of prophet in particular ways, such that the literature attesting the prophetic behavior was itself unique.

There came a time after which such literature was no longer written and/or preserved. Those individuals in the Persian period whom some Yahwists would deem to be prophets, such as the Asaphites, no longer acted as holy men or uttered oracles to the king. Rather, the sons of Asaph were ensconced in the world of worship. Their literary productions, if there were any, would appear in the Psalter, not as separate prophetic books or even supplements to other prophets' books. Elements such as ethical admonitions that appear in the Psalter now have a different rhetorical force and form than they did as prophetic sayings or divine oracles. Such was one afterlife of prophetic poetry. As for the prose, hagiographic accounts continued to be written. One such example is the *Lives of the Prophets*, part of the Old Testament Pseudepigrapha. *Lives of the Prophets* continues a tradition attested in 1 Kgs. 13:31 and 2 Kgs. 13:21, in which the grave of a prophet has special significance. The author of *Lives of the Prophets* focuses attention on the burial sites of the prophets whom he attests. For example, he writes this about Amos: "Amos was from Tekoa. And when Amaziah had tortured him sorely, at last his son also killed him with a club by striking him on the temple. And while he was still breathing he went to his own district, and after some days he died and was buried there."[1] These legends supplement the canonical material, making Amos look more like a holy man and a martyr. Such is one type of literary legacy that stems from prophetic literature.

There are other forms of that legacy. One may point to apocalyptic eschatology and the expectation for the return of prophecy as examples. As for the former, embedded in prophetic books are elements that appear to be precursors of apocalyptic literature. Isaiah 24–27; Zechariah 9–14; Joel 2:28–3:21; and Ezekiel 38–39 offer intensely eschatological views of the future. For some in our own time, this is *the* hallmark of prophetic literature; it points to a cataclysmic endtime. To focus on these texts is, however, to ignore the vast majority of prophetic texts, which address the present or the immediate future. As for the latter, prophetic literature attests an expectation that prophets will return, a notion that presupposes prophecy has in some measure passed from the scene. Two texts are particularly important here. Joel 2:28 speaks of a time when "I [Yahweh] will pour out my spirit on all flesh; your sons and your daughters shall prophesy." In contrast, the epilogue to the book of Malachi anticipates a future point at which Yahweh "will send you the prophet Elijah before the great and terrible day of the LORD comes" (Mal. 4:5). Prophecy will return, whether in group form or only with an individual. These expectations obviously played a significant role in early Christianity as texts such as Matt. 17:9–13 and Acts 2:1–21 suggest.

Still, the most perduring legacy of prophetic literature is not its literary predecessors, not apocalyptic eschatology, not the expectation for the return of prophets. It is the literature itself, which, like a faceted gemstone, can appear so differently when it is turned in the light. In some texts, such as we find in the book of Sirach, Isaiah and the Twelve were remembered because they "comforted the mourners in Zion" (48:24) or "comforted the people of Jacob and delivered them with confident hope" (49:10), respectively. In other texts, the prophets offer a profound notion of lived religion. No text conceives it better than Mic. 6:8:

> He has told you, O mortal, what is good;
>   and what does the LORD require of you
> but to do justice, and to love kindness,
>   and to walk humbly with your God?

Notes

Chapter 1

1. The term *Hebrew Bible* is a more ecumenical way to refer to that body of literature otherwise known as the Old Testament.
2. On the use of the term *intermediary*, see Wilson, *Prophecy and Society*. Anthropologists use *intermediary* to characterize prophets and other individuals (e.g., shamans, priests, diviners) who enable communication between the deity and the world of human affairs.
3. See Overholt, *Channels of Prophecy*.
4. Other prophets would function in powerful ways with kings. For example, one of Elisha's band anointed Jehu as king (2 Kgs. 9:1–13), and Ahijah the Shilonite proclaimed to Jeroboam that he would become king of Israel (1 Kgs. 11:29–39).
5. Scholars differ in their judgments about the prominence of ecstatic behavior or trance possession among Israel's prophets. One might compare S. Parker, "Possession Trance and Prophecy in Pre-exilic Israel," *VT* 28 (1978): 271–85 to R. Wilson, "Prophecy and Ecstasy: A Reexamination," *JBL* 98 (1979): 321–37.
6. See Wilson, *Prophecy and Society*, and Petersen, *Roles of Israel's Prophets*.
7. See Lewis, *Ecstatic Religion*.
8. J. Hackett, *The Balaam Text from Deir 'Alla*, HSM 31 (Chico, Calif.: Scholars Press, 1980), 29.
9. Quoted in W. Moran, "New Evidence from Mari on the History of Prophecy," *Biblica* 50 (1969): 29–30.
10. Text 1.4 in Parpola, *Assyrian Prophecies*, 6.
11. Parpola, *Assyrian Prophecies*, xix.
12. Ibid., lxviii.
13. The classic study is N. Habel, "The Form and Significance of the Call Narratives," *ZAW* 77 (1965): 297–323.
14. See especially Rofé, *Prophetical Stories*, 75–105.
15. Adele Berlin's article "Introduction to Hebrew Poetry," *The New Interpreter's Bible*, Vol. IV (Nashville: Abingdon, 1996), 301–15, provides an excellent guide for readers of ancient Hebrew poetry. See also D. Petersen and K. Richards, *Interpreting Hebrew Poetry* (Minneapolis: Fortress, 1992).
16. J. Kugel, *The Idea of Biblical Poetry: Parallelism and Its History* (New Haven, Conn.: Yale University Press, 1981), 40–45.
17. R. Alter, *The Art of Biblical Poetry* (New York: Basic Books, 1985), 137–39.
18. R. Alter, *The Art of Biblical Narrative* (New York: Basic Books, 1981), 99.

243

19. G. Josipovici, *The Book of God: A Response to the Bible* (New Haven, Conn.: Yale University Press, 1988), 177.
20. E. Sternberg, *The Poetics of Biblical Narrative: Ideological Literature and the Drama of Reading* (Bloomington, Ind.: Indiana University Press, 1985), 483.
21. Ibid., 94–99.
22. Alter, *The Art of Biblical Poetry*, 139–41.
23. Ibid., 146.
24. MT refers to the (Hebrew) Masoretic text whereas LXX refers to the (Greek) Septuagint.
25. See Rad, *The Message of the Prophets.*
26. See Blenkinsopp, *A History of Prophecy in Israel.*
27. See D. McCarthy, *Old Testament Covenant: A Survey of Opinions* (Richmond: John Knox, 1972); R. Clements, *Prophecy and Covenant*, SBT 43 (Naperville, Ill.: Allenson, 1965).
28. See S. Paul, *Studies in the Book of the Covenant in the Light of Cuneiform and Biblical Law*, VTSup 18 (Leiden: Brill, 1970).
29. M. Sweeney, *Isaiah 1–39*, FOTL 16 (Grand Rapids: Eerdmans, 1996), 17.
30. *Torah* typically refers to the Pentateuch, and the *Writings* is the name given to the third part of the Hebrew canon (Torah, Prophets, Writings). Psalms is part of the Writings.

Chapter 2

1. See B. Duhm, *Das Buch Jesaja* (Göttingen: Vandenhoeck & Ruprecht, 1914).
2. Wildberger, *Isaiah 1–12*, 60.
3. Some scholars (e.g., O. Steck, *Der Abschluss der Prophetie im Alten Testament: Ein Versuch zur Frage der Vorgeschichte des Kanons*, BThSt 17 [Neukirchen-Vluyn: Neukirchener Verlag, 1991]) think that portions of the book were written as late as the Greco-Roman period.
4. It is interesting that there is only one brief oracle (Isa. 14:24–27) concerning Assyria in Isaiah's oracles against the nations. Such an omission may reflect the ambiguous role that Assyria played—the tool of God's punishment and then the object of God's punishment.
5. On the historical issues, see W. Gallagher, *Sennacherib's Campaign to Judah: New Studies*, SHCANE 18 (Leiden: Brill, 1999).
6. Clements, *Isaiah and the Deliverance*, 41–51, thinks most of these texts derive from redactors who worked during the reign of Josiah, a time when Judah anticipated the demise of the Neo-Assyrian Empire. Such a reading permits one to distinguish Isaiah ben Amoz's views on Assyria from those of the later writers who helped formulate the book.
7. One has the sense that poems composed for other purposes have been linked with Babylon at a later stage in the formation of the book.
8. See Clements, "Unity of the Book of Isaiah."
9. See Sweeney, *Isaiah 1–39*, 51–60, for an overview of this redaction-critical hypothesis.
10. See for a similar proposal, Blenkinsopp, *Isaiah 1–39*, 78–83.
11. Childs, *Isaiah*, 8.
12. Tucker, "The Book of Isaiah 1–39," 30.
13. I am indebted to Schoors, *I Am God Your Saviour*, for the notion of polemical genres.
14. The woe oracle can also be used beyond the borders of Israel. In at least two cases (10:5; 33:1) the woe is directed at Assyria. To be sure, Yahweh had intended Assyria

to act as "the rod of my anger" (10:5). However, Assyria had exceeded this mandate and become a violent international predator, thereby deserving the same sort of destruction it had been meting out to others.

15. G. von Rad, *Old Testament Theology* (New York: Harper & Row, 1965), 2:156.

16. P. Hanson, *The Dawn of Apocalyptic* (Philadelphia: Fortress, 1975), 119.

17. Sweeney, *Isaiah 1–39*, 54–57, thinks, based on the prominence of such discourse, that the book may have been used in a liturgical context, perhaps even formed for that purpose. K. Baltzer, *Deutero-Isaiah*, 7–14, has maintained that Isaiah 40–55 should be understood as "liturgical drama."

18. Childs terms it "a veritable catena of citations and allusions" (*Isaiah*, 108).

19. There are no "accounts" in Isaiah 40–66, though there are some sections that can be construed as prose (44:9–20 [the idol essay]; 59:21; 66:18–21).

20. Cf. Blenkinsopp, *Isaiah 1–39*, 321, who attributes this account to the Deuteronomists.

21. For a recent summary and critique of the *Denkschrift* hypothesis, see Childs, *Isaiah*, 42–44.

22. See N. Habel, "The Form and Significance of the Call Narratives," *ZAW*.

23. The ambiguity of *maśśā'* is the subject of an elaborate wordplay in Jer. 24:3–40.

24. Isaiah also labels the deity as "the LORD of hosts," but that phrase bears less overt theological significance in the book.

25. von Rad, *Old Testament Theology*, 2:155–70.

Chapter 3

1. Scholars debate vigorously the extent to which the character of Jeremiah as conveyed in the book reflects the historical Jeremiah. Robert Carroll contends that the book does not portray but creates the individual. William Holladay, in contrast, thinks the book portrays the historical Jeremiah.

2. The Greek translation of the Hebrew Bible was made during the Greco-Roman period.

3. The Qumran caves yielded fragments of four Hebrew manuscripts (2QJer, 4QJer[a,b,c]) of the book of Jeremiah (although Tov thinks there are six manuscripts [2QJer, 4QJer[a,b,c,d,e]]). The manuscripts reflect quite different forms of Jeremiah. For example, 4QJer[a] conforms generally to the Hebrew text type, whereas 4QJer[b,d] are similar to the LXX text type.

4. E. Tov, *Textual Criticism of the Hebrew Bible* (Minneapolis: Fortress, 1992), 321.

5. The verses that follow, 10:12–15, are duplicated by 51:15–19. It is difficult to know which location is the more original. However, given the composite character of 10:1–11, one suspects that verses 12–15 may be an addition to this collection of sayings about idols.

6. A. R. Pete Diamond, "Jeremiah's Confessions in the LXX and MT: A Witness to Developing Canonical Function?" *VT* 40 (1990): 37.

7. *Tanakh: The Holy Scriptures: The New JPS Translation according to the Traditional Hebrew Text* (Philadelphia: Jewish Publication Society, 1985).

8. E.g., L. Stulman, *The Other Jeremiah: A Reconstruction of the Hebrew Text underlying the Greek Version of the Prose Sections of Jeremiah* (Lanham, Md.: University Press of America, 1985).

9. See Stulman, *Order amid Chaos*, 23, 72.

10. See D. Bak, *Klagender Gott—Klagender Menschen: Studien zur Klage im Jeremiabuch*, BZAW 193 (Berlin: de Gruyter, 1990), who argues for a developing lament tradition in the book, of which the Jeremianic laments are themselves the final stage.

11. Cf. the judgment of Blenkinsopp in *A History of Prophecy in Israel:* that in the early poetry Jeremiah "has not yet found his own voice" (p. 140).

12. See H. G. Reventlow, *Liturgie und prophetisches Ich bei Jeremia* (Gütersloh: Gütersloher Verlag, 1963).

13. See W. Baumgartner, *Jeremiah's Poems of Lament* (Sheffield: Almond, 1988).

14. See S. Mowinckel, *Zur Komposition des Buches Jeremia* (Kristiania: Jacob Dybwad, 1914). Mowinckel thought the oracles against the nations were secondary to the collection/book of four sources and that there were even later, nonsystematic additions throughout the book.

15. See among others, Holladay, *Jeremiah*, 2:282.

16. A. Rofé, *The Prophetical Stories: The Narratives about the Prophets in the Hebrew Bible, Their Literary Types and History* (Jerusalem: Magnes, 1988), 109–10.

17. For a convenient list of these parallels, see J. Bright, "The Date of the Prose Sermons of Jeremiah," *JBL* 70 (1951): 15–29. The very notion of a Deuteronomistic style has been assessed recently by N. Lohfink, "Gab es eine deuteronomistische Bewegung?" in *Jeremia und die "deuteronomistische Bewegung,"* ed. W. Gross, BBB 98 (Weinheim: Beltz Athenänaum, 1995), 313–82.

18. See H. Weippert, *Die Prosareden des Jeremiabuches*, BZAW 132 (Berlin: de Gruyter, 1973).

19. McKane, *Critical and Exegetical Commentary on Jeremiah*, 1:lvi.

20. See Holladay, *Jeremiah*, 2:45. Holladay claims that most of the places where Jeremiah depends upon Hosea stem from early in Jeremiah's career.

21. This relationship may be similar to that of Jeremiah and Hosea, if, as some have suggested, Deuteronomy is of originally northern provenance.

22. Cf. C. Seitz, "The Prophet Moses and the Canonical Shape of Jeremiah," *ZAW* (1989): 3–27.

Chapter 4

1. In this regard, M. O'Dell has maintained that Ezekiel 1–5 is modeled on Leviticus 8–9, which depicts the service of priestly ordination ("You Are What You Eat: Ezekiel and the Scroll," *JBL* 117 [1998]:229–48). Her case is consistent with the position adumbrated here, namely, that things priestly influenced both Ezekiel's activity and the book but that Ezekiel did not function regularly as a priest at the temple. Marvin Sweeney, "Zadokite Priest and Visionary Prophet of the Exile" (unpublished paper), in contrast, argues that Ezekiel was a priest.

2. Pohlmann, *Buch des Propheten Hesekiel*, 1:19–20.

3. Zimmerli, following Gese among others, argued that much in these chapters stems from hands later than those of Ezekiel.

4. G. Fohrer thinks that there are twelve symbolic action reports in the book (*Die symbolischen Handlungen der Propheten*, ATANT 54 [Zurich: Zwingli, 1968]).

5. The word is at home in the world of ritual; see Zimmerli, *Ezekiel*, 1:190, who observes that Ezekiel uses the noun forty-three times.

6. Zimmerli, *Ezekiel*, 1:30.

7. Ibid., 1:50–52.

8. See J. Milgrom, *Leviticus 1–16*, AB 3 (New York: Doubleday, 1991).

9. Blenkinsopp, *Ezekiel*, 195.

10. Stevenson, *Vision of Transformation*.

11. See E. Tov, "Recensional Differences between the MT and LXX of Ezekiel," *ETL* 62 (1986): 89–101.

12. Greenberg, *Ezekiel 1–20*, 26.
13. Zimmerli, *Ezekiel*, 1:68–74; Pohlmann, *Buch des Propheten Hezekiel*, 1:22–38.
14. R. Clements, "The Ezekiel Tradition," in *Old Testament Prophecy: From Oracles to Canon* (Louisville, Ky.: Westminster John Knox, 1996), 145–58.

Chapter 5

1. See the essays in Nogalski and Sweeney, eds., *Reading and Hearing the Book of the Twelve*.
2. See Jones, *Formation of the Book of the Twelve*.
3. See Jeremias, *Hosea und Amos*.
4. See Nogalski, *Literary Precursors to the Book of the Twelve* and *Redactional Processes in the Book of the Twelve*. Cf. Schart, *Entstehung des Zwölfprophetenbuchs*.
5. At a minimum, the superscriptions to these books reflect issues of importance to the Deuteronomist; see, for example, the indictments in Zephaniah.
6. Steck, *Der Abschluss der Prophetie im Alten Testament*, has argued that latter portions of the Twelve reflect comparable literary processes and theological concerns, as do latter texts in Isaiah.
7. See N. Lohfink, "Die Gattung der 'Historischen Kurzgeschichte' in den letzten Jahren von Juda und in der Zeit des Babylonischen Exils," *ZAW* 90 (1978): 319–47.
8. There are a number of good studies on these books. This list reflects a concern for accessibility and relative currency.

Chapter 6

1. The only other possible instance of a prophet praying for someone is Elisha (see 2 Kgs. 4:33; 6:17, 18), though the term *ba'ad* is not used.
2. Numbers 12 also addresses the notion of prophecy. However, since it focuses on Moses, I discuss it below.
3. Cf. R. Wilson, *Prophecy and Society in Ancient Israel*, 151–54; G. Coats, *Rebellion in the Wilderness: The Murmuring Motif in the Wilderness Traditions of the Old Testament* (Nashville: Abingdon, 1968), 96–115.
4. S. Mowinckel, "'The Spirit' and 'The Word' in the Pre-Exilic Reforming Prophets," *JBL* 53 [1934]: 199–227, argued that there were two primary ways in which a prophet could be authorized—by spirit or by word. The author of Num. 11:10–25 seems to operate in a world in which prophecy is associated with spirit, not word. Further, though that author does not claim explicitly that Moses is a prophet, were he to have done so, Moses would have been enfranchised by dint of possessing the divine *ruah* or spirit.
5. Wilson, *Prophecy and Society*, 154.
6. See, similarly, Wilson, *Prophecy and Society*, 149–50.
7. On the former, see H.-J. Kraus, *Worship in Ancient Israel: A Cultic History of the Old Testament* (Richmond: John Knox, 1966), 102–12; on the latter, see Wilson, *Prophecy and Society*, 157–66.
8. R. Carroll, "The Elijah-Elisha Sagas: Some Remarks on Prophetic Succession in Ancient Israel," *VT* 19 (1969): 415. Some scholars have found traces of Mosaic influence in prophetic books. The following articles are representative: M. O'Kane, "Isaiah: A Prophet in the Footsteps of Moses," *JSOT* 69 (1996): 29–51; C. Patton, "'I Myself Gave Them Laws That Were Not Good': Ezekiel 20 and the Exodus Tradition," *JSOT* 69 (1996): 73–90; C. Seitz, "The Prophet Moses and the Canonical Shape of Jeremiah," *ZAW* 101 (1989): 3–27.

9. See Perlitt, "Mose als Prophet."

10. The Hebrew text reads "Moses his people," which makes little sense. The LXX does not contain these words. The translation, "Moses his servant" reflects readings extant in some Syriac manuscripts. Cf. G. Coats, *Moses: Heroic Man, Man of God*, JSOTSup 57 (Sheffield: JSOT Press, 1988), 182–85.

11. See, e.g., Carroll, "Elijah-Elisha Sagas," 401–2. However, H. Barstad, "The Understanding of Prophets in Deuteronomy," *JSOT* 8 (1994): 243, aptly notes that the text may well refer just to Joshua, as Moses' successor.

12. J. Blenkinsopp, *Prophecy and Canon: A Contribution to the Study of Jewish Origins* (Notre Dame, Ind.: University of Notre Dame Press, 1977), 44.

13. Perlitt, "Moses als Prophet," 593, maintains that Numbers 12 provides a corrective to Numbers 11.

14. I am reading *bemareh* with the LXX. The MT has suffered a haplography.

15. See also B. Levine, *Numbers 1–20*, AB 4 (New York: Doubleday, 1993), who understands the temple as the referent, though in a different sense.

16. Cf. Levine, *Numbers 1–20*, 343–44, who thinks royal imagery pervades this text.

17. See also Perlitt, "Mose als Prophet," 591–92; Blenkinsopp, *Prophecy and Canon*, 85–95; Wilson, *Prophecy and Society*, 162 n. 52.

18. See S. R. Driver, *A Critical and Exegetical Commentary on Deuteronomy*, ICC (Edinburgh: T. & T. Clark, 1895), 425, who points to Deut. 4:34; 6:22; 7:19; 11:3; 26:8; and 29:1–2.

19. See, similarly, Barstad, "Understanding of Israel's Prophets," 247: "The author of Deuteronomy is hostile to prophecy, as far as all present and future prophets are concerned. In earlier times, however, prophets were all right, but after Deuteronomy was given to Moses on Mt. Horeb there was no longer any need for further revelations."

20. M. Noth, *The Deuteronomistic History*, JSOTSup 15 (Sheffield: JSOT Press, 1981), 107–9.

21. See J. Van Seters, *In Search of History: Historiography in the Ancient World and the Origins of Biblical History* (New Haven, Conn.: Yale University Press, 1983), 306. See, similarly, W. Dietrich, *Prophetie und Geschichte: Eine redaktionsgeschichtliche Untersuchung zum deuteronomistischen Geschichtswerk*, FRLANT 108 (Göttingen: Vandenhoeck & Ruprecht, 1972).

22. M. O'Brien, *The Deuteronomistic History Hypothesis: A Reassessment*, OBO 92 (Freiburg: Universtitätsverlag Freiburg, 1989), 30–44.

23. See Campbell, *Of Prophets and Kings*; and O'Brien and Campbell, *Unfolding the Deuteronomistic History*, 24–33. Campbell maintains that the pattern by which Saul, David, and Jehu are anointed by prophets and in a fairly standard literary pattern attests to a source that links all three individuals. Moreover, Campbell observes that prophets spoke similar types of speeches to Jeroboam, Ahab, and Jehu about doom to the royal house. This prophetic record may have been rooted in the stories about Elisha but was probably composed after the reign of Jehu.

24. See Dietrich, *Prophetie und Geschichte*.

25. S. Mowinckel, *Psalmenstudien III. Kultprophetie und prophetische Psalmen*. A revised form of his argument may be found in English as "The Prophetic Word in the Psalms and the Prophetic Psalms," in *The Psalms in Israel's Worship* (Nashville: Abingdon, 1962), 53–84.

26. Bellinger, *Psalmody and Prophecy*, 91.

27. R. Tournay, *Seeing and Hearing God with the Psalms: The Prophetic Liturgy of the Second Temple in Jerusalem*, JSOTSup 118 (Sheffield: SOT Press, 1991).

28. See O. Steck, *The Prophetic Books and Their Theological Witness* (St. Louis: Chalice, 2000). Cf. R. Gray, *Prophetic Figures in Late Second Temple Jewish Palestine: The Evidence from Josephus* (New York: Oxford University Press, 1993).

Epilogue

1. *The Old Testament Pseudepigrapha*, ed. J. Charlesworth, ABRL (New York: Doubleday, 1985), 391.

Index of Scripture